| | |
|---|---|
| Course | **Introduction to Ethical Theory** |
| Course Number | **PHIL 2201** |
| Instructor | Rebecca Potts |
| | Minnesota West |
| | **Philosophy** |

http://create.mcgraw-hill.com

ISBN-10: 0390497835    ISBN-13: 9780390497833

# Contents

# Credits

# Crito

Plato

Plato was born in Athens in about 428 B.C.E. As a youth he associated with Socrates, a philosopher who constantly challenged fellow Athenians to think about virtue and to improve their souls. Plato's initial interest was in politics, but he soon became disillusioned, especially when, under the democracy that was restored after the rule of the "Thirty Tyrants," Socrates was arrested on false charges of impiety and the corruption of youth, convicted, and condemned to die. After the execution of Socrates, Plato moved to nearby Megara for a time and may have traveled to Egypt. In 388 he visited Italy and the city of Syracuse in Sicily. Returning to Athens, he founded the Academy, a school devoted both to philosophical inquiry and to the philosophically based education of politicians. Plato spent most of his life teaching at the Academy (Aristotle was his most famous student) and writing philosophical works. He made two more trips to Syracuse, in 368 and 361, apparently with the intention of turning the city's ruler, Dionysius the Younger, into a "philosopher-king." (If this was indeed his purpose, he failed.) Plato died in Athens in 347 at the age of eighty-one.

Most of Plato's works are written as conversations between Socrates and one or more interlocutors on some topic concerning morality. His best-known "dialogues" (the name by which his surviving works are known) are the *Euthyphro, Apology, Crito, Phaedo, Meno, Symposium,* and *Republic.*

Our reading is the *Crito,* a conversation between Socrates and his longtime friend Crito. The scene is Socrates's prison cell: He has been sentenced to death and will be executed as soon as the Athenian ship returns from its religious expedition to the island of Delos. Crito, who has regularly been visiting Socrates in prison, brings the news that the ship has been sighted and will soon arrive. Crito urges Socrates, one last time, to escape and save his life; all the arrangements have been made. Since Socrates seems unwilling to escape, despite his innocence of the charges for which he was condemned, Crito gives Socrates several reasons for escaping. Socrates replies that he will escape only if it would be moral to do so. He then states two moral principles that he and Crito have long agreed are valid: one should never intentionally wrong another, even if wronged; and one should keep one's just agreements.

To determine whether his escape would violate these moral principles, Socrates imagines the laws of Athens addressing him. Their speech convinces Socrates that to escape would be wrong because Socrates would be breaking both principles. First, Socrates would be harming another, namely the laws. The laws, moreover, had benefited Socrates and had never harmed him (in the case of his trial, it was the *jurors* who were unjust, not the laws). Second, Socrates would be breaking a just agreement—his agreement to abide by the laws of Athens. Socrates argues that when we live in a society and accept its benefits, we enter into a tacit agreement to obey its laws and are obligated to keep our agreement.

Socrates's conversation with Crito not only sets forth his theory of political obligation; it also illustrates his conviction that philosophy requires that one act in accordance with one's principles, no matter the cost. To violate a moral principle is to harm one's soul, and no bodily benefit gained by an unjust action can outweigh the damage that injustice does to one's soul.

▼

From *The Dialogues of Plato,* trans. Benjamin Jowett. 2nd ed., vol. 1. Oxford, England: Clarendon Press, 1875 (updated stylistically).

*Socrates:* Why have you come at this hour, Crito? It must be quite early.

*Crito:* Yes, certainly.

*Socrates:* What is the exact time?

*Crito:* The dawn is breaking.

*Socrates:* I am surprised that the keeper of the prison would let you in.

*Crito:* He knows me, because I often come, Socrates. Moreover, I have done him a kindness.

*Socrates:* And have you only just arrived?

*Crito:* I came some time ago.

*Socrates:* Then why did you sit and say nothing instead of at once awakening me?

*Crito:* I could never have done that, Socrates. I only wish I were not so sleepless and distressed myself. I have been looking at you, wondering how you can sleep so comfortably, and I didn't wake you on purpose, so that you could go on sleeping in perfect comfort. All through your life, I have often thought you were favored with a good disposition, but I have never been so impressed as in the present misfortune, seeing how easily and tranquilly you bear it.

*Socrates:* Why, Crito, when a man has reached my age he ought not to be distressed at the approach of death.

*Crito:* And yet other old men find themselves in similar misfortunes, and age does not prevent them from being distressed.

*Socrates:* That is true. But you have not told me why you come at this early hour.

*Crito:* I come with a message that is painful—not, I expect, to you, but painful and oppressive for me and all your friends, and I think it weighs most heavily of all on me.

*Socrates:* What? Has the ship come from Delos, on the arrival of which I am to die?[1]

*Crito:* No, the ship has not actually arrived, but it will probably be here today, as persons who have come from Sunium[2] tell me that they left the ship there. And therefore tomorrow, Socrates, will be the last day of your life.

*Socrates:* Very well, Crito; if such is the will of the gods, I am willing. But my belief is that there will be a day's delay.

*Crito:* Why do you think so?

*Socrates:* I will tell you. I am to die on the day after the arrival of this ship.

*Crito:* Yes; that is what the authorities say.

*Socrates:* But I do not think that the ship will be here until tomorrow. This I infer from a vision which I had last night, or rather only just now, when you fortunately allowed me to sleep.

*Crito:* And what was the nature of the vision?

*Socrates:* There appeared to me the likeness of a woman, fair and comely, clothed in bright raiment, who called to me and said: Socrates,

The third day hence to fertile Phthia shall you come.[3]

*Crito:* What a strange dream, Socrates!

*Socrates:* There can be no doubt about the meaning, Crito, I think.

*Crito:* Yes, the meaning is only too clear. But, my beloved Socrates, let me entreat you once more to take my advice and escape. For if you die, I will not only lose a friend who can never be replaced, but there is another evil: People who do not know you and me will believe that I might have saved you if I had been willing to give money, but that I did not care. Now, can there be a worse disgrace than this—that I should be thought to value money more than the life of a friend? For the many will not be persuaded that I wanted you to escape and that you refused.

*Socrates:* But why, my dear Crito, should we care about the opinion of the many? Good men—and they are the only persons who are worth considering—will think of these things truly as they occurred.

*Crito:* But you see, Socrates, that the opinion of the many must be regarded, for what is now happening shows that they can do the greatest evil to anyone who has lost their good opinion.

*Socrates:* I only wish it were so, Crito, and that the many could do the greatest evil; for then they would also be able to do the greatest good—and what a fine thing this would be! But in reality they can do neither; for they cannot make a man either wise or foolish, and whatever result they produce is the result of chance.

*Crito:* Well, I will not dispute with you. But please tell me, Socrates, whether you are acting out of worry about me and your other friends. Are you afraid that, if you escape from prison, we may get into trouble with the informers for having stolen you away and lose either the whole or a great part of our property—or that even a worse evil may happen to us? Now, if you fear on our account, be at ease; for in order to save you, we surely ought to run this or even a greater risk. Be persuaded, then, and do as I say.

*Socrates:* Yes, Crito, that is one fear which you mention, but by no means the only one.

*Crito:* Fear not. There are persons who are willing to get you out of prison at no great cost; and as for the informers, they are far from being exorbitant in their demands—a little money will satisfy them. My money, which is certainly sufficient, is at your service. And if, out of solicitude about me, you hesitate to use mine, there are non-Athenians here who will give you the use of theirs. One of them, Simmias the Theban, has brought a large sum of money for this very purpose; and Cebes and many others are prepared to spend their money in helping you to escape.

Therefore do not hesitate to save yourself because you are worried about this, and do not say, as you did in the court, that you will have difficulty in knowing what to do with yourself anywhere else. For men will love you in other places to which you may go, and not in Athens only. There are friends of mine in Thessaly, if you would like to go to them, who will value and protect you, and no Thessalian will give you any trouble. Nor can I think that you are at all justified, Socrates, in betraying your own life when you might be saved. You are only working to bring about what your enemies, who want to destroy you, would and did in fact work to accomplish. And further, I should say that you are deserting your own children; for you might bring them up and educate them, instead of which you go away and leave them, and they will have to take their chances. And if they do not meet with the usual fate of orphans, there will be small thanks to you. No man should bring children into the world who is unwilling to persevere to the end in their nurture and education. But you appear to be choosing the easier part, not the better and more courageous one, which would have been more becoming in one who has professed a life-long concern for virtue, like yourself. Indeed, I am ashamed not only of you but of us, who are your friends, when I reflect that the whole business will be attributed entirely to our lack of courage. The trial need never have come on or might have been managed differently. And now it may seem that we have made a ridiculous bungle of this last chance, thanks to our lack of toughness and courage, since we failed to save you and you failed to save yourself, even though it was possible and practicable if we were good for anything at all. So, Socrates, you must not let this turn into a disgrace as well as a tragedy for yourself and us. Make up your mind then, or rather have your mind already made up; for the time of deliberation is over, and there is only one thing to be done, which must be done this very night. And if we delay at all, it will be no longer practicable or possible. I implore you therefore, Socrates, be persuaded by me, and do not be contrary.

*Socrates:* My dear Crito, your solicitude is invaluable if it is rightly directed; but otherwise, the more intense, the more difficult it is to deal with. And so we should consider whether I ought to follow this course or not. You know it has always been true that I paid no heed to any consideration I was aware of except that argument which, on reflection, seemed best to me. I cannot abandon the arguments I used to make in times past just because this situation has arisen: They look the same to me as before, and I respect and honor them as much as ever. You must therefore understand that if, on the present occasion, we cannot make better arguments, I will not yield to you—not even if the power of the people conjures up the goblins of imprisonment and death and confiscation, as though we could be scared like little children. What will be the fairest way of considering the question? Shall I return to your old argument about the opinions of men? We were saying that some of them are to be regarded, and others not. Now were we right in maintaining this before I was condemned? And has the argument that was once good now proved to be talk for the sake of talking—mere childish nonsense? That is what I want to consider with your help, Crito: Whether, under my present circumstances, the argument will appear to be in any way different or not, and whether we shall subscribe to it or let it go. That argument, which, as I believe, is maintained by many persons of authority, was to the effect, as I was saying, that the opinions of some men are to be regarded, and of other men not to be regarded. Now you, Crito, are not going to die tomorrow—at least, there is no human probability of this—and therefore you are not liable to be deceived by the circumstances in which you are placed. Tell me, then, whether I am right in saying that some opinions, and the opinions of some men only, are to be valued, and that other opinions, and the opinions of other men, are not to be valued. I ask you whether I was right in maintaining this?

*Crito:* Certainly.

*Socrates:* The good opinions are to be regarded, and not the bad?

*Crito:* Yes.

*Socrates:* And the opinions of the wise are good, and the opinions of the unwise are bad?

*Crito:* Certainly.

*Socrates:* Now what was our argument about this? Does the serious athlete attend to the praise and blame and opinion of every man or of one man only—his physician or trainer, whoever he may be?

*Crito:* Of one man only.

*Socrates:* And he ought to fear the censure and welcome the praise of that one only, and not of the many?

*Crito:* Clearly so.

*Socrates:* And he ought to act and train and eat and drink in the way that seems good to his single master, who has understanding, rather than according to the opinion of all other men put together?

*Crito:* True.

*Socrates:* And if he disobeys and disregards the opinion and approval of the one, and regards the opinion of the many who have no understanding, will he not suffer harm?

*Crito:* Certainly he will.

*Socrates:* And what will the harm be? Where will it be localized, and what part of the disobedient person will it affect?

*Crito:* Clearly, it will affect the body; that is what is destroyed.

*Socrates:* Very good. And is not this true, Crito, of other things, which we need not separately enumerate? In questions of just and unjust, fair and foul, good and evil, which are the subjects of our present consultation, ought we to follow the opinion of the many, and to fear them, or the opinion of the one man who has understanding? Ought we not to fear and reverence him more than all the rest of the world, and, if we desert him, will we not ruin and mutilate that principle in us that is improved by justice and damaged by injustice? Is there such a principle?

*Crito:* Certainly there is, Socrates.

*Socrates:* Take a parallel instance. If, ignoring the advice of those who have understanding, we destroy that which is improved by health and is damaged by disease, would life be worth living? And that which has been destroyed is the body?

*Crito:* Yes.

*Socrates:* Would life be worth living with an evil and corrupted body?

*Crito:* Certainly not.

*Socrates:* And will life be worth living if that faculty that injustice damages and justice improves is ruined? Do we suppose that principle—whatever it may be in man which has to do with justice and injustice—to be inferior to the body?

*Crito:* Certainly not.

*Socrates:* More honorable than the body?

*Crito:* Far more.

*Socrates:* Then, my friend, we must not regard what the many say of us, but what he, the one man who has understanding of just and unjust, will say, and what the truth will say. And therefore you begin in error when you advise that we should regard the opinion of the many about just and unjust, good and evil, honorable and dishonorable. "Well," someone will say, "but the many can kill us."

*Crito:* That is plain, and a person might well say so. You are right, Socrates.

*Socrates:* But, dear Crito, the argument that we have gone over still seems as valid as before. And I would like to know whether I may say the same of another proposition—that not life, but a good life, is to be chiefly valued?

*Crito:* Yes, that also remains unshaken.

*Socrates:* And a good life is equivalent to an honorable and just one—that holds also?

*Crito:* Yes, it does.

*Socrates:* From these premises I proceed to argue the question whether I am justified in trying to escape without the consent of the Athenians. And if I am clearly right in escaping, then I will make the attempt; but if not, I will abstain. The other considerations that you mention—of money and loss of character and the duty of educating one's children—are, I fear, only the doctrines of the multitude, who, if they could, would restore people to life as readily as they put them to death—and with as little reason. But since we have been forced this far by the logic of our argument, the only question that remains to be considered is whether we shall do right in giving money and thanks to those who will rescue me, and in taking a direct role in the rescue ourselves, or whether in fact we will be doing wrong. And if it appears that we will be doing wrong, then neither death nor any other calamity that follows from staying and doing nothing must be judged more important than that.

*Crito:* I think that you are right, Socrates. How then shall we proceed?

*Socrates:* Let us consider the matter together, and you either refute me if you can, and I will be convinced, or else cease, my dear friend, from repeating to me that I ought to escape against the wishes of the Athenians. It is most important to me that I act with your assent and not against your will. And now please consider whether my starting point is adequately stated, and also try to answer my questions as you think best.

*Crito:* I will.

*Socrates:* Are we to say that we are never intentionally to do wrong, or that in one way we ought and in another way we ought not to do wrong? Or is doing wrong always evil and dishonorable, as we often concluded in times past? Or have all those past conclusions been thrown overboard during the last few days? And have we, at our age, been earnestly discoursing with one another all our life long only to discover that we are no better than children? Or, in spite of the opinion of the many, and in spite of consequences, whether better or worse, shall we insist on the truth of what was then said, that injustice is always an evil and a dishonor to him who acts unjustly? Shall we say so or not?

*Crito:* Yes.

*Socrates:* Then we must do no wrong.

*Crito:* Certainly not.

*Socrates:* Nor, when injured, injure in return, as the many imagine; for we must injure no one at all.

*Crito:* Clearly not.

*Socrates:* Again, Crito, may we do evil?

*Crito:* Surely not, Socrates.

*Socrates:* And what of doing evil in return for evil, which is the morality of the many—is that just or not?

*Crito:* Not just.

*Socrates:* For doing evil to another is the same as injuring him.

*Crito:* Very true.

*Socrates:* Then we ought not to retaliate or render evil for evil to anyone, whatever evil we may have suffered from him. But I would have you consider, Crito, whether you really mean what you are saying. For this opinion has never been held, and never will be held, by any considerable number of persons; and those who are agreed and those who are not agreed upon this point have no common ground and can only despise one another when they see how widely they differ. Tell me, then, whether you agree with and assent to my first principle, that neither injury nor retaliation nor warding off evil by evil is ever right. And shall that be the premise of our argument? Or do you decline and dissent from this? For so I have ever thought, and continue to think; but if you are of another opinion, let me hear what you have to say. If, however, you remain of the same mind as formerly, I will proceed to the next step.

*Crito:* You may proceed, for I have not changed my mind.

*Socrates:* The next thing I have to say, or, rather, my next question, is this: Ought a man to do what he has agreed to do, provided it is just, or ought he to violate his agreement?

*Crito:* He ought to do it.

*Socrates:* In light of that, tell me whether or not there is some victim—a particularly undeserving victim—who is hurt if I go away without persuading the city. And do we abide by what we agreed was just, or not?

*Crito:* I cannot answer your question, Socrates, because I do not see what you are getting at.

*Socrates:* Then consider the matter in this way. Imagine that I am about to run away (you may call the proceeding by any name you like), and the laws and the state come and interrogate me: "Tell us, Socrates," they say,"what are you up to? Are you not, by an act of yours, going to destroy us—the laws and the whole state—as far as in you lies? Do you imagine that a state can subsist and not be overthrown in which the decisions of law have no power but are set aside and trampled upon by individuals?" What will be our answer, Crito, to questions like these? Anyone, and especially a rhetorician, would have a good deal to say against abrogation of the law that requires a sentence to be carried out. He will argue that this law should not be set aside. Or shall we retort, "Yes, but the state has injured us and given an unjust sentence." Suppose I say that?

*Crito:* Very good, Socrates.

*Socrates:* "And was that our agreement with you?" the laws would answer; "or were you to abide by the sentence of the state?" And if I were to express my astonishment at their talking this way, they would probably add: "Take control of your astonishment and answer, Socrates—you are in the habit of asking and answering questions. Tell us: What complaint have you to make against us that justifies you in attempting to destroy us and the state? In the first place, did we not bring you into existence? Your father married your mother by our aid and brought you into the world. Say whether you have any objection to urge against those of us who regulate marriage." None, I should reply. "Or against those of us who after birth regulate the nurture and education of children, in which you also were trained? Were not the laws, which have the charge of education, right in commanding your father to train you in music and athletics?" Right, I should reply. "Well then, since you were brought into the world and nurtured and educated by us, can you deny in the first place that you are our child and slave, as your fathers were before you? And if this is true, do you really think you have the same rights as we do and that you are entitled to do to us whatever we do to you? Would you have any right to strike or revile or do any other evil to your father or your master, if you had one, because you had been struck or reviled by him or received some other evil at his hands? Would you say this? And because we think it right to destroy you, do you think that you have any right to destroy us in return, and your country, as far as in you lies? Will you, a professor of true virtue, pretend that you are justified in this? Has a philosopher like you failed to discover that our country is more to be valued and higher and holier than mother or father or any ancestor, and more to be regarded in the eyes of the gods and of men of understanding; also to be soothed and gently and reverently entreated when angry, even more than a father, and either to be persuaded or, if not persuaded, to be obeyed? And when you are punished by your country, whether with imprisonment or beatings, the punishment is to be endured in silence. And if your country leads you to wounds or death in battle, there you must follow, as is right. Neither may anyone yield or retreat or leave his rank, but whether in battle or in a court of law or in any other place, he must do what his city and his country order him, or he must change their view of what is just. And if he may do no violence to his father or mother, much less may he do violence to his country." What answer shall we make to this, Crito? Do the laws speak truly, or do they not?

*Crito:* I think that they do.

*Socrates:* Then the laws will say: "Consider, Socrates, if we are speaking truly that in your present attempt you are going to do us an injury. For, having brought you into the world, and nurtured and educated you, and given you and every other citizen a share in every good which we had to give, we further proclaim to any Athenian, by the liberty that we allow him, that if he does not like us when he has come of age and has seen the ways of the city and made our acquaintance, he may go where he pleases and take his goods with him. None of us laws will stand in the way if any of you who are dissatisfied with us and the city want to go to a colony or to move anywhere else. None of us forbids anyone to go where he likes, taking his property with him. But he who has experience of the manner in which we order justice and administer the state, and still remains, has entered into an implied contract that he will do as we command him. And he who disobeys us is, as we maintain, wrong in three ways: first, because in disobeying us he is disobeying his parents; second, because we are the authors of his education; third, because he has made an agreement with us that he will duly obey our commands, but he neither obeys them nor convinces us that our commands are unjust. We show flexibility; we do not brutally demand his compliance but offer him the choice of obeying or persuading us—yet he does neither.

"These are the sorts of accusations to which, as we were saying, you, Socrates, will be exposed if you accomplish your intentions; you, above all other Athenians." Suppose now I ask, why I rather than anybody else?

They might reasonably take me to task because I above all other men have acknowledged the agreement. "There is clear proof, Socrates," they will say, "that we and the city were not displeasing to you. Of all Athenians you have been the most constant resident in the city, which, since you never leave it, you may be supposed to love. For you never went out of the city either to see the games or to any other place, except when you were on military service; nor did you travel as other men do. Nor had you any curiosity to know other states or their laws; your affections did not go beyond us and our state. We were your special favorites, and you acquiesced in our government of you. And here in this city you had your children, which is a proof of your satisfaction. Moreover, you might in the course of the trial, if you had liked, have fixed the penalty at banishment, and then you could have done with the city's consent what you now attempt against its will. But you pretended that you preferred death to exile and that you were not unwilling to die. And now you do not blush at the thought of your old arguments and pay no respect to us, the laws, of whom you are the destroyer, and are doing what only a miserable slave would do, running away and turning your back on the compacts and agreements by which you agreed to act as a citizen. First of all, answer this question: Are we right in saying that by your actions, if not your words you agreed to our terms of citizenship? Is that true or not?" How shall we answer, Crito? Must we not assent?

*Crito:* We cannot help it, Socrates.

*Socrates:* Then will they not say: "You, Socrates, are breaking the compacts and agreements which you made with us. You were not compelled to agree, or tricked, or forced to make up your mind in a moment, but had a period of seventy years during which you were free to depart if you were dissatisfied with us and the agreements did not seem fair. You did not pick Sparta or Crete, whose fine government you take every opportunity to praise, or any other state of the Greek or non-Greek world. You spent less time out of Athens than men who are crippled or blind or otherwise handicapped. That shows how much more than other Athenians you valued the city and us too, its laws—for who would value a city without laws? And will you not now abide by your agreements? You will if you listen to us, Socrates, and you will not make yourself ridiculous by leaving the city.

"For just consider: If you transgress and err in this sort of way, what good will you do either to yourself or to your friends? That your friends will be driven into exile and deprived of citizenship or will lose their property is tolerably certain. And you yourself, if you go to one of the neighboring cities, like Thebes or Megara (both being well-ordered states, of course), will come as an enemy of their government, and all patriotic citizens will eye you suspiciously as a subverter of the laws, and you will confirm in the minds of the judges the justice of their own condemnation of you. For he who is a corrupter of the laws is more than likely to be a corrupter of the young and foolish portion of mankind. Will you then flee from well-ordered cities and law-abiding men? And will life be worth living if you do that? Or will you approach them and discourse unashamedly about—about what, Socrates? Will you discourse as you did here, about how virtue and justice and institutions and laws are the best things among men? Don't you think that such behavior coming from Socrates will seem disgusting? Surely one must think so. But if you go away from well-governed states to Crito's friends in Thessaly, where there is great disorder and license, they will be charmed to hear the tale of your escape from prison, set off with ludicrous particulars of the manner in which you were wrapped in a goatskin or some other disguise and metamorphosed in the usual manner of runaways. But will there be no one to comment that in your old age, when in all probability you had only a little time left to live, you were not ashamed to violate the most sacred laws from your greedy desire for a little more life? Perhaps not, if you keep them in good temper; but if they are out of temper, you will hear many degrading things. You will live as the flatterer and slave of all men, achieving nothing but the chance to feast in Thessaly, as though you had gone abroad in order to get a meal. And where will the old arguments be, about justice and virtue? But perhaps you wish to live for the sake of your children—to bring them up and educate them. Will you take them into Thessaly and deprive them of Athenian citizenship? Is this the benefit you will confer upon them? Or are you under the impression that they will be better cared for and educated here if you are still alive, although absent from them? Your friends will take care of them. Do you think that if you move to Thessaly they will take care of them, but that if you move into the other world they will not take care of them? No, if those who call themselves friends are good for anything, they will take care of them—to be sure, they will.

"Listen, then, Socrates, to us who have brought you up. Think not of life and children first and of justice afterwards, but of justice first—so that you may defend your conduct to the rulers of the world below. For neither will you nor any that belong to you be happier or holier or juster in this life, or happier in another, if you do as Crito bids. Now you depart in innocence, a sufferer and not a doer of evil—a victim not of the laws, but of men. But if you escape, returning evil for evil and injury for injury, breaking the compacts and agreements that you have made with us and wronging those you ought least of all to wrong—that is to say, yourself, your friends, your country, and us—we will be angry with you while you live, and our brothers, the laws in the world below, will receive you in no kindly spirit; for they will know that you have done your best to destroy us. Listen, then, to us and not to Crito."

This, dear Crito, is the voice I seem to hear murmuring in my ears, like the sound of the flute in the ears of the mystic—that voice, I say, is humming in my ears and prevents me from hearing any other. You must realize that you will be wasting your time if you speak against the convictions I hold at the moment. But if you think you will get anywhere, go ahead.

*Crito:* No, Socrates, I have nothing to say.

*Socrates:* Then be resigned, Crito, and let us follow this course, since this is the way the god points out.

---

▶ NOTES

1. Delos is an island in the Aegean Sea, about 85 miles from Athens. It was sacred to the god Apollo, and every year the Athenians sent a ship there in thanksgiving to him. Socrates's execution had been delayed because ritual purity required that no one be executed during the religious expedition. [D. C. ABEL, EDITOR]

2. Sunium is a promontory overlooking the Saronic Gulf of the Aegean Sea, about 30 miles from Athens. [D. C. ABEL]

3. This verse parallels the words of the Greek hero Achilles in Homer's *Iliad,* "On the third day I shall reach fertile Phthia" (Book III, line 363). Phthia is Achilles's homeland; hence Socrates interprets his dream to mean that he will die (his soul will arrive in the next world, its true home) in two days. ("The third day hence" means "in two days," since the Greeks, when counting a series, began with the present member of the series.) [D. C. ABEL]

**Chapter 3**

*Ethical Relativism*

When we study people around the world, we observe what appear to be different ethical guidelines and disparate solutions to ethical problems. In Ireland the prevailing view is that abortion is wrong, whereas in China women who already have one child are encouraged to have abortions. Some observers conclude that these differences are primarily related to the fact that people live in different societies. Each society seems to have some moral guidelines, and these guidelines often differ from society to society. Despite these differences, each society seems to have adequate guidelines to satisfy its ethical needs. This chapter explores whether this observation is correct. Are these social moral guidelines really adequate to allow us to solve moral problems and live together successfully?

The initial claims are that societies already have moral guidelines and that there are differences between the guidelines of different societies. Connected to these claims is an approach to ethics that discusses the status of a society's moral guidelines and their adequacy. *Ethical relativism* asserts that the only legitimate moral guidelines are those of actual societies or groups and that moral good and bad are connected to these actual ethical guidelines. Therefore, any moral guidelines created by ethical theories (such as those of utilitarianism) would be misguided and irrelevant. Because legitimate ethical guidelines are always associated with an actual society or group, and because these actual societies and groups do not endorse exactly the same moral guidelines, there is no legitimate universal set of moral guidelines. To many people, the idea that legitimate moral guidelines are always relative to an actual society seems intuitively correct. Ethical relativism is an approach to ethics connected to the ethical insight that *legitimate moral guidelines are necessarily related to an actual society*. Philosophers offer many different accounts of ethical relativism, but the discussion in this chapter builds directly on the ideas presented in this paragraph. In this chapter, I will also show how problems develop with ethical relativism when we try to move beyond these initial ideas to a better understanding of the view.

## One Version of Ethical Relativism

Ethical relativism relates moral good and bad to the ethical guidelines of actual societies or groups. It often starts from the observation that ethical beliefs and practices are not identical in all societies. This observation is consistent with cultural relativism. *Cultural relativism* is the view that different societies or cultures do things differently. For example, people wear different kinds of clothes, are governed by different kinds of political systems, and believe in different religions. Some societies also have different sets of ethical guidelines. If individuals from these different societies were to discuss their ethical principles and practices, they would probably disagree about what practices were right and wrong. These ethical disagreements would arise even though the individuals agreed on the description of the practices (e.g., they agreed on what constituted an abortion).[1] The progression from cultural relativism to ethical relativism occurs when the observation about ethical differences is followed by the claim that the only legitimate moral guidelines are those of actual societies. These actual moral guidelines create good and evil. If society's guidelines approve of something, it is ethical, and if these guidelines disapprove of something, it is unethical. *The ethical standard for ethical relativism is that a society's actual moral guidelines determine good and bad.*

If ethical relativism is to be effective, proponents of the theory must be able to identify the actual moral guidelines of a society. These guidelines create moral obligations for the members of the society. They determine what people ought to and ought not to do. If a woman's society has a moral guideline that asserts that abortion is evil, then she ought not to get an abortion. Her personal feelings about or attitudes toward abortion are irrelevant. Only the social moral guidelines of her society are legitimate for her.

Ethical relativists maintain that there is no universal or objective ethical standard that holds for all societies at all times.[2] This idea is an essential claim of ethical relativism. Legitimate notions of good and bad often vary from society to society and may change within a society over time. Therefore, ethical guidelines are relative to some society or group in a particular historical setting. Different ethical positions may be appropriate for different peoples. No single legitimate set of ethical guidelines is endorsed by every society; therefore, no legitimate universal or objective ethical guidelines can be identified.

## Ethical Relativism and Tolerance

Based on these ideas, many people believe ethical relativists ought to endorse tolerance for the different ethical guidelines and practices of other societies. They conclude that it is wrong for people in one society to condemn the moral guidelines or ethically significant practices of another. Without a legitimate set of universal ethical guidelines, condemnation by members of one society of the practices of another is unjustified. The ethical guidelines of one society would have no legitimate application to any other society.

This idea can be illustrated with an example about some ethically significant practice that is simultaneously endorsed by one society and condemned by another. For instance, modern-day Cuba presumably still condemns capitalism as exploitative and evil. In contrast, the ethical guidelines of the United States endorse capitalism. Here it seems that both of these societies would agree on a description of capitalism. The ethical relativist would suggest that the different moral guidelines produced different moral evaluations of capitalism. Capitalism is ethically right for citizens of the United States and ethically wrong for Cubans. Neither group is objectively right or wrong; therefore, each group should tolerate rather than condemn the other.

I believe it is a mistake to include in ethical relativism the idea of tolerance for the different ethical guidelines and ethically significant practices of other societies. This position supporting cross-cultural tolerance is a serious problem for ethical relativism, and the theory will operate without it. Bernard Williams, a contemporary British philosopher, explains that the assertion that we should not condemn the different beliefs and practices of other societies is a nonrelative or objective claim, and the ethical relativist has no grounding for such a claim.

> The central confusion of relativism is to try to conjure out of the fact that societies have differing attitudes and values an a priori nonrelative principle to determine the attitude of one society toward another; this is impossible.[3]

It is impossible because, according to ethical relativism, people have no basis for making ethical claims that are not related to the actual moral guidelines of their society. The most that ethical relativists are justified in claiming is that in our society we approve of tolerance or noninterference with other cultures and hence we should be tolerant. This, however, is not the position endorsed by the proponents of cross-cultural tolerance. They assert that everyone ought to tolerate the ethical differences of other societies regardless of their own moral guidelines. Williams's point is that there is no justification for this claim about what everyone should do. In the United States, our moral guidelines seem to approve of interference with other cultures and societies. We intervene regularly in the interest of promoting peace and preventing violations of human rights. Ethical relativists have no grounds for condemning our interference if such intervention is in accord with the moral guidelines of our society.

This idea, that we should leave cross-cultural tolerance out of ethical relativism, can be illustrated with an example. Assume that moral rights are part of the ethical guidelines endorsed by U.S. society. Rose is an ethical relativist and therefore believes that the legitimate moral guidelines are those endorsed by her society. She is especially insistent about the right to life. When she sees people in other countries being killed merely because of their political views or because they belong to certain ethnic groups, she claims the killing is evil and ought to be stopped. Rose's view of good and bad is based on the moral guidelines of her society—the only legitimate ethical standard available to her—and in her view other societies are acting unethically when they execute people for political reasons. Rose is not tolerant of these executions; she condemns them (and perhaps wants to eliminate them). She would not tolerate a society like Nazi Germany but rather would condemn it and want to see it destroyed.

To avoid Williams's problem, ethical relativism should endorse the idea that people will use the moral guidelines of their own society to evaluate everything. The key to ethical relativism is that good and bad are established by the actual moral guidelines of a society, and those actual guidelines may not include cross-cultural tolerance. Only if a society's actual moral guidelines include the principle of tolerance should citizens of that society tolerate the different ethical guidelines and practices of other societies. Although this version of ethical relativism avoids the serious problem with cross-cultural tolerance, it will have other problems. Before discussing them, however, I want to provide some support for the theory and discuss how it relates to the ethical assumptions and themes.

## Justification for the Ethical Standard and Strengths of the Theory

An earlier section identified the moral standard of ethical relativism, that a society's actual moral guidelines determine good and bad. The second thing an ethical theory is supposed to provide is a justification for the ethical standard. Why would someone endorse the ethical standard put forward by ethical relativism? What strengths does the theory have that would lead someone to endorse it? In this section, four possible justifications or arguments will be discussed; the first will be rejected and the other three left standing for the your consideration.

## Cultural Relativism

The first possible justification is based on cultural relativism and is actually a group of related arguments. A simple version of it goes like this. We observe that ethical guidelines vary from society to society (or are relative to a society). Therefore, ethical guidelines ought to vary from society to society. If ethical guidelines ought to vary from society to society, then no single set of guidelines is correct for all societies. If ethical guidelines ought to vary from society to society and there is no single legitimate set of them, then each society ought to consider its existing set of ethical guidelines to be legitimate. This argument is, of course, incorrect. First, even if ethical guidelines ought to vary, it does not follow that the existing guidelines are the appropriate ones. This would only legitimate their being different, not that the actual ones were somehow the best ones to have. More important, however, is the idea that just because things are a certain way does not allow us to conclude that they ought to be that way. The fact that many children are starving in the world today does not necessitate the conclusion that those children ought to be starving. If you think they ought to be starving, you need a separate argument to support that conclusion. From the observation that ethical guidelines vary from society to society, there can be no justified conclusion about what the legitimate ethical guidelines ought to be. Perhaps ethical guidelines ought to vary from society to society, and perhaps no one set of guidelines is correct for all societies. However, it is also possible that there is one correct set of ethical guidelines and that the people in many societies are simply wrong. Cultural relativism does not provide adequate support for ethical relativism.

## Moral Guidelines as a Social Institution

A second and more interesting reason for endorsing ethical relativism is related to morality. In this book, the term *morality* is used to refer to a specific set of moral guidelines. People might endorse ethical relativism because they view morality as a social institution. Societies create various institutions to help them function successfully. One such institution is morality. For example, relativists would claim that the United States has a morality, or a specific set of moral guidelines. Morality is necessary because the laws, by themselves, are not adequate to produce the kind of conduct that enables society to operate successfully. (This idea was discussed in Chapter 1.) People need to respect other people's lives, liberty, property, and privacy to produce a successfully functioning society. Without morality, people will only respect these things when they believe they might get caught and punished. Therefore, morality helps society function more successfully. If morality is a social institution, then the appropriate morality would be the actual moral guidelines of society. Presumably the society has the moral guidelines it does because these guidelines have proven to be effective in helping society function successfully. Because they have proven to be effective, they constitute the best morality. This reasoning acts as the justification for using the ethical standard of actual social moral guidelines as the basis for good and bad. Adopting this justification for ethical relativism supports the idea that each society has a legitimate set of moral guidelines and that good and evil are related to them. Therefore, one strength of the theory is that it is consistent with the way many people think about morality. People are more inclined to accept a theory that is consistent with an existing belief than one that is at odds with it.

## Cultural Relativism Once Again

Another justification for using the moral standard of ethical relativism and a related strength of the view is that it seems to fit with our observations about the world. Even though we cannot use cultural relativism to validate ethical relativism, at least ethical relativism does not contradict cultural relativism. The two positions are consistent. We observe that many societies seem to have different moral guidelines. This is consistent with cultural relativism, the idea that different societies do things differently. Cultural relativism is, of course, correct. Different societies eat different foods, have different political systems, and so on. Some societies also have different moral guidelines. Thus, ethical relativism is consistent with the facts of cultural diversity. This consistency with cultural relativism is another possible justification for using the ethical standard and a related strength of the theory.

## Ethnocentrism and Nationalism

A rough definition for *ethnocentrism* is the belief in the superiority of one's own ethnic group and its ways of doing things. A similarly imprecise definition for *nationalism* is the belief in the superiority of one's own nation and its ways of doing things. Social scientists often condemn both of these ways of thinking, but many people find them satisfying. It is agreeable to think that one's own group and nation are better than others. People can feel proud of their group and country and be happy to be associated with them. Certainly many Americans have no hesitation in declaring that the United States is the best country in the world. A third strength of this version of ethical relativism, at least for some people, is that it is consistent with ethnocentrism and nationalism. Ethical relativism asserts that the moral guidelines of a person's society are the appropriate ones for the person to endorse. In a sense, these guidelines are superior to all others. People can be confident in and proud of their moral judgments because they are based on guidelines that are superior to all others. Presumably this also could be a reason for using this ethical standard and a strength of the theory.

## Determining Morally Significant Actions

An ethical theory must distinguish between what are and are not morally significant actions. This is not an issue that ethical relativists frequently discuss; however, if a society's moral guidelines relate to an action, moral relativists believe it is morally significant. For instance, most societies have a guideline about keeping and breaking promises; therefore, keeping promises is morally significant in these societies. If a society does not have a guideline about something, then the action is not morally significant. For example, U.S. society has no opinion about whether you should dye your hair to change its color, therefore this action has no moral significance.

## Ethical Relativism and the Traditional Ethical Assumptions

It is difficult to decide whether or not ethical relativism accepts the traditional ethical assumptions. We might be inclined to say that ethical relativists would agree that ethics is rational. People can provide reasons related to actual social moral guidelines to support their ethical evaluations and their solutions to moral problems. However, ethical relativism and divine command theory have a similar limitation. The reasons a society has particular guidelines are irrelevant, just as the reasons God commands what he does are irrelevant. Thus, there are no ultimate reasons, based on reason, for the moral guidelines and judgments. The moral guidelines are arbitrary because the only reason for following them is that they are the actual guidelines of the society. People in different societies with different guidelines would have no way to discuss and debate the merits of their different ethical guidelines. Even ethical relativists within the same society could not legitimately debate the merits of their society's moral guidelines; they can only accept them. Therefore, in the sense of "rational" used in Chapter 1, ethical relativists cannot claim that ethics is rational.

Whether or not ethical relativism accepts moral equality is also an interesting question. In one sense it does; all members of a particular society are moral equals in that the moral guidelines of their society bind all of them. Also, all people are moral equals in that I judge all of them by the same set of moral guidelines, those of my society. In a wider sense, however, all human beings are not moral equals. Members of other societies are not treated impartially or in the same way as members of a person's own society. The actions of members of other societies are not judged by the moral guidelines of their own societies but by the moral guidelines of the society of the person doing the judging. For example, I judge myself and the members of my society by the moral guidelines of the United States, which are our guidelines, but I also judge members of other societies by the moral guidelines of the United States, which are foreign to them. Therefore, ethical relativists judge some people by ethical guidelines that those people accept and other people by ethical guidelines that are foreign to them and that they would probably not accept. On the whole, this version of ethical relativism does not consider people to be moral equals because it does not judge all people by their own society's ethical guidelines.

The issue of universalizability is also a contentious one. The version of ethical relativism I elaborated could accept the idea that people are capable of universalizing legitimate moral evaluations. If we simply apply the ethical guidelines of our own society to everyone, then we are universalizing our moral evaluations. The version of ethical relativism that includes cross-cultural tolerance would not universalize moral evaluations. Legitimate ethical evaluations made by members of other societies should be based on their own ethical guidelines. These guidelines might be the same as ours or different from ours. In either case, we cannot legitimately universalize our moral guidelines and evaluations. They are only appropriate for persons in our society. Any legitimate ethical conclusion should be grounded in the specific ethical guidelines of a particular society; it could not come about by universalizing our guidelines.

## Ethical Relativism and the Basic Ethical Themes

Ethical relativism takes a position on each of the ethical themes discussed in Chapter 1. The first theme was represented by this question: *What kind of moral guidelines makes something good or bad: subjective, relative, or objective ones?* Ethical relativists answer this question by claiming that the only legitimate ethical guidelines are relative ones. Legitimate ethical guidelines are those endorsed by an actual society. For an ethical relativist, personal moral guidelines and an individual's attitudes and emotions are irrelevant to ethical evaluation. Legitimate moral guidelines cannot be objective because they are not based on considerations of fact or reason that do not depend on the perceptions, emotions, or judgments of particular persons or the beliefs of a specific society. Ethical relativism is characterized by assertions that legitimate ethical guidelines are relative.

The second ethical theme was highlighted by this question: *What makes something good or bad; is it the consequences that are produced or the reasoning that leads up to it?* Ethical relativists seem to believe the reasoning that leads up to something is what makes it ethical. If an action is in accord with one or more of society's moral guidelines, then that action is ethical regardless of the consequences. If it violates one or more of society's moral guidelines, then it is unethical regardless of the consequences. The society's ethical guidelines create moral good and bad and are the only relevant ethical consideration.

A third ethical theme relates to this question: *Are good and bad related to following general rules without exceptions or connected to separately evaluating each action, belief, and so on?* The position of ethical relativism in relation to this theme is debatable, but I believe ethical relativists would be compelled to claim that we should faithfully follow the moral rules of our society. If society believes stealing other people's property is evil, then stealing is always evil, no matter what the benefit to the individual. Allowing exceptions to the basic moral rules of society would violate the idea that society needs morality to function smoothly. Of course, if the belief is that sometimes it is ethical to steal and other times it is not, then people would still be following a general rule even if they steal on some occasions and not on others.

The fourth important ethical theme relates to the proper focus of ethical attention: *Should the group, community, or majority of persons be the focus of ethics or should the focus be on the individual?* Ethical relativists focus on the group or society as the source of legitimate ethical guidelines. Individuals who disagree with the moral guidelines of their society and hold different ones will not be acting ethically if they act in accord with their personal moral principles and in opposition to the societal ethical principles. It is the actual ethical guidelines of the society or the group that are identified as the legitimate moral guidelines by ethical relativism.

## Contrasting Ethical Relativism with Divine Command Theory

Ethical relativism and divine command theory have many differences and only a few similarities (see Appendix 1). Ethical relativism relates moral guidelines to actual societies, whereas divine command theory connects moral guidelines to God. The ethical standard of ethical relativism is that a society's actual moral guidelines determine good and evil, whereas the ethical standard for divine command theory is that what God commands people to do is good and what God forbids people to do is bad. In regard to the traditional ethical assumptions, both ethical relativism and divine command theory assume that ethics is not rational and that some ethical evaluations can be universalized. They disagree on the assumption related to moral equality and impartiality. Proponents of ethical relativism do not treat people impartially, whereas advocates of divine command theory would claim that all people originally stand in the same relation to God. In relation to the themes about moral good and bad, both theories base good and bad on the reasoning that precedes an action and focus on general rules of conduct. Ethical relativism, of course, asserts that good and bad are relative to societies, whereas divine command theory argues that good and bad are objective. According to ethical relativism, good and bad relate to the group or society, whereas proponents of divine command theory state that good and bad are connected to the individual.

## Problems with Ethical Relativism

Until now I have presented and briefly elaborated on the ethical insight central to ethical relativism: that legitimate ethical guidelines are necessarily related to an actual society. In this section, you will see that problems develop with the theory as we try to fill out the basic ideas of ethical relativism and develop a better understanding of the theory. As I discuss the problems, I will relate them to the criteria for evaluating ethical theories presented in Chapter 1. In the final section of the chapter, I will present an overall evaluation.

### Actual Ethical Guidelines

The first step to a better understanding of ethical relativism is to try to locate the actual ethical guidelines of a society. This will help us to better understand what the ethical relativist means by the ethical guidelines of a society. Assume that I am an ethical relativist and a citizen of the United States; I must know the ethical guidelines of my country so that I can follow them. I am, of course, assuming that the society as a whole has a set of ethical guidelines.

Where do I find the actual ethical guidelines of my society? Laws are written down and can be discovered in law libraries, but ethical guidelines are not recorded in ethics libraries. There is no determinate set of ethical guidelines written down for the guidance of U.S. citizens. If there is an unwritten set, I am not aware of them. Therefore, I will have to look for them. There would seem to be four promising alternatives.

One way to find the actual ethical guidelines of a society is to examine the beliefs of the majority of the members of the society. To discover what guidelines are actually endorsed—for example, if I wanted to know whether my society approves of abortion—I might take a survey. In doing this, I would be assuming that other people are more knowledgeable than I am—even though I am a concerned citizen (and a teacher of ethics). I am hoping that they know the ethical guidelines of our society and will respond to my survey. They have to respond to the survey based on the ethical guidelines of our society and not on their personal preferences or feelings. If they did the latter, the results would reflect an ethical subjectivist approach (which will be discussed in Chapter 4). The ethical guidelines of a society are not simply the subjective guidelines of the majority of the citizens. This would result in the foundation of the social ethical guidelines (the citizens' subjective beliefs) being plagued with all the problems of ethical subjectivism, which are a very serious set of problems. Ethical guidelines are legitimate because society endorses them. However, if we do not already know what society endorses or what the ethical guidelines are, a survey of citizens' opinions will not be a successful way of discovering them. I do not believe citizens know what society approves and disapproves in all cases—especially with respect to issues like abortion where emotions run deep—therefore, this approach would be unsatisfactory. If we are unclear about the social ethical guidelines, we could not discover them by surveying citizens.

Another idea would be to look at the guidelines of the government or ruling group. Perhaps the government establishes the ethical guidelines for the society. In the United States the President and members of Congress try to reflect the opinions of their constituents, so this method would work no better in the United States than the first method, which I have argued is unsuccessful. In a dictatorship, we could discover the ethical guidelines if they were grounded in the feelings of the dictator and he or she imposed them on the whole society. We would need to know, for example, whether the dictator had a good feeling about abortion. The problem with this variation is that the ethical guidelines are founded on the dictator's feelings, and once again the foundation of the social moral guidelines would have the serious problems that affect ethical subjectivism. Therefore, this second approach to discovering the actual ethical guidelines is unsuccessful also.

A third possibility would be to examine the laws and then work backward. The assumption would be that ethical guidelines inspire laws. By looking at the laws, one might attempt to discover the society's moral guidelines. U.S. law allows abortion, so abortion must have been ethical when the law was made. This view implies that although we are unclear about the ethical guidelines of today, people in the past must have been better informed. They were clear enough about the ethical guidelines to make laws based on them. The problem is that the ethical guidelines are supposed to be based on the current moral guidelines of the society, but this "legal view" makes the dominant guidelines those of a past version of the society because the authority to establish ethical guidelines lies with the earlier version of society that created the laws. This seems illegitimate for ethical relativism. These moral guidelines are for an earlier version of society, and we would not know if they are still the ethical guidelines of the current society. Some laws are no longer endorsed by the majority of people. For example, the majority of people in the United States disapproved of Prohibition before ratification of the constitutional amendment that allowed people to once again produce and sell alcoholic beverages. A problem with this "legal view" is that existing laws may not all actually reflect the ethical guidelines held by the majority of people in the society.

A fourth possibility would be to look at the society's moral tradition. Presumably this moral tradition would be articulated in the society's fundamental documents. By consulting political documents, works of literature, art, and so on, we could discover whether the moral tradition of the United States approved of abortion. As ethical relativists, however, why should we be bound by moral tradition? The legitimate moral guidelines are those endorsed by society today, not those endorsed in the past. Like the "legal view," moral tradition makes the dominant guidelines those of a previous society and seems to deny the current society the authority to create its own moral guidelines. In addition, this seems incorrect because we would not know if these traditional guidelines are still the ethical guidelines of the current society.

All of these are possibilities for discovering the actual ethical beliefs of a society. One could also conceivably assert that the correct morality would be the intersection of all of them. In any case, the difficulty is obvious and twofold: (1) all of the ways of identifying the actual ethical guidelines are seriously problematic, and (2) we have no way to choose among them. In general, the problem for ethical relativism is that the theory does not seem to be able to identify the actual moral guidelines of a society. Therefore, ethical relativism cannot satisfy any of the criteria for evaluating ethical theories. The first criterion states that the ethical theory must be able to identify some ethical guidelines. If we cannot determine the actual moral guidelines of our society, then the idea proposed by ethical relativism about how to identify the ethical guidelines is incorrect. Ethical relativism will not be able to identify the necessary moral guidelines, nor can it satisfy any of the other criteria. It is not successful as an ethical theory.

## *Multiple Sets of Ethical Guidelines*

A better understanding of ethical relativism also requires us to determine whether the ethical guidelines of other groups, besides society as a whole, should count as legitimate moral guidelines. If the ethical guidelines endorsed by ethnic groups, local communities, special interest groups, and so on count, ethical relativism will have to deal with multiple sets of legitimate moral guidelines that may conflict. For the sake of this discussion, we shall assume that these groups have ethical guidelines that are written down. (If they do not, the first problem would apply to them as well as to society as a whole.) Imagine that Rose is a citizen of the United States, but she is also a member of other groups with their own particular ethical beliefs. She is a woman, a Latino, part of a family, and a resident of a local community. She also works for a large corporation. If all of these groups have ethical guidelines, would each set constitute legitimate guidelines? If they are all legitimate ethical guidelines, how should she resolve conflicts among them? Suppose the majority of women in the United States are "pro-choice," the majority of Latinos "pro-life," the majority of her family "pro-life," the majority of people in her local community "pro-choice," and the position of her corporation is "pro-choice." As an ethical relativist, Rose cannot determine which position to take on abortion. This situation would seem to imply that ethical relativism has additional problems with at least the second and fourth criteria for evaluating ethical theories. Ethical relativism would not be able to demonstrate that one set of moral guidelines is better than another (criterion two). Further, if Rose is faced with the problem of whether or not to get an abortion, ethical relativism would be unable to help her resolve the dilemma (criterion four).

Some form of ethical relativism (usually the kind involving cross-cultural tolerance) seems more plausible if we concentrate on tribes that are isolated in remote regions or on islands. It is relatively easy to regard a tribe on an isolated island as a distinct group or community. In the pluralistic contemporary world, however, it is much harder to find such distinctive societies. We tend to belong to a number of groups (an ethnic group, a socioeconomic class, a country, a company, a local community, a family, and so on). Given the existence of multiple groups with legitimate ethical guidelines, ethical relativism will not be a successful ethical theory because it will neither identify unambiguous ethical guidelines nor show why some moral guidelines are better than others.

This problem with multiple groups could be solved if we interpret the ethical relativist as saying that only the moral guidelines of the society as a whole count as legitimate ethical guidelines. This solution, however, makes resolving the first problem even more crucial, and we could not solve it.

### Moral Change and Dissent

An ethical theory must be able to identify some moral guidelines, but ethical relativism makes the production and identification of new ethical guidelines mysterious. Legitimate ethical guidelines are those that are endorsed by the society, and we know that sometimes these change (e.g., slavery is now unethical in the United States). The mystery is that guidelines change even though there is no apparent reason for change. Moral good and bad depend on the current ethical guidelines of a society, not on objective reasons the society has the guidelines it does, such as that people are being benefited or harmed. (If people grounded moral guidelines on objective reasons, they would be endorsing another ethical theory, perhaps rule utilitarianism.) If, however, the reasons why people create the guidelines they do are not important, then there is no motivation for change in the moral guidelines. Without any motivation for change, it is a mystery why a society would do so.

Another aspect of the mysterious nature of the production and identification of new ethical guidelines surfaces when we think about what ethical relativists must say about the relation between the moral guidelines of a society and the people who disagree with those guidelines. For them, there can be no legitimate ethical dissent within a society. If "good" equates to whatever is approved of by the moral guidelines of the society, then members of the society who dissent from the dominant ethical guidelines would always be wrong. In pre–Civil War Alabama, a member of the white community who believed slavery was evil would be wrong. According to an ethical relativist, good and evil for whites was determined by the white community at large or by the prevailing view in Southern society, not by dissenters. The slaves might agree with the dissenter, but because the dissenter is not a member of the slave community, the ethical position of that community cannot legitimate his or her dissent. The problem here is that dissent is always wrong, but dissent is a major factor in changing a society's ethical beliefs. Once again the production of new ethical guidelines seems mysterious.

As well as being mysterious, the production of new moral guidelines is arbitrary. If the only legitimate moral guidelines are those endorsed by an actual society, then any new moral guideline is unjustified. There could be no compelling ethical reason for the change. If there is no ethical justification or reason for a particular new guideline, then any added guideline is as good as any alternative addition. A society can add any moral guideline it wants to because as soon as it adds it the guideline will be legitimate. This makes the addition of new moral guidelines arbitrary.

46   *Chapter 3 / Ethical Relativism*

## Conclusion

Although grounded in an initially reasonable ethical insight, ethical relativism is not a successful ethical theory based on the criteria established in Chapter 1. Individual members of a society hold many personal moral beliefs, but we cannot identify the actual ethical guidelines of the society as a whole. We would also not know how to arbitrate between the differing moral guidelines of the different groups to which a person belonged. Therefore, ethical relativism does not meet any of the criteria for a successful ethical theory. We need to reject the "ethical insight" that legitimate moral guidelines are necessarily related to an actual society. Although we cannot, with any certainty, find the moral guidelines of a society, there would seem to be no such problem identifying those of specific individuals. Certainly we could, with some work, identify an individual's personal moral guidelines. In the next chapter we will look at two theories based on specific individuals. These theories will not have the problems that plague ethical relativism, although they may have problems of their own.

### QUESTIONS FOR REVIEW

*Here are some questions to help you review the main concepts in this chapter.*

1. What ethical insight is related to ethical relativism?
2. What is cultural relativism? What is ethical relativism? Explain the difference between the two.
3. What ethical standard do ethical relativists use to determine good and bad?
4. Why do some philosophers claim that ethical relativism leads to tolerance of other societies' different moral guidelines and judgments? Why does the author reject that position?
5. In your opinion, what is the best justification for the moral standard and the related strength of ethical relativism?
6. How do ethical relativists differentiate between what is and what is not a morally significant action?
7. Would ethical relativists accept any or all of the traditional ethical assumptions? Support your answer.
8. What position does ethical relativism take on each of the four ethical themes?
9. Discuss one similarity and one difference between ethical relativism and divine command theory.

10. In your opinion, which problem with ethical relativism is the most serious? Explain why.

11. Is ethical relativism a successful ethical theory? Support your answer.

## NOTES

1. This assumes that people from different societies could agree on the descriptions of the practices (e.g., what counts as a lie, a bribe, a theft, or self-defense). A more radical version of ethical relativism claims that people from different societies could not even agree on the descriptions of the practices.

2. There could be a legitimate universal moral code if by coincidence all societies developed the same set of moral guidelines. This, of course, has not happened so far.

3. Bernard Williams, *Morality: An Introduction to Ethics* (New York: Harper & Row, 1972), p. 23.

# The Elements of Moral Philosophy

James Rachels

James Rachels was born in Columbus, Georgia, in 1941. He attended Mercer University in Macon and received his bachelor's degree in 1962. He then began doctoral studies in philosophy at the University of North Carolina at Chapel Hill, completing his Ph.D. in 1967. Rachels has held appointments at the University of Richmond (1966–1968), New York University (1968–1972), and the University of Miami (1972–1977). Since 1977 he has been at the University of Alabama at Birmingham, where he is currently University Professor of Philosophy.

Rachels's publications include *Moral Problems: A Collection of Philosophical Essays* (editor, 1971; 3d ed., 1979), *Understanding Moral Philosophy* (1976), *The End of Life: Euthanasia and Morality* (1986), *The Elements of Moral Philosophy* (1986; 2d ed., 1993), *The Right Thing to Do: Basic Readings in Moral Philosophy* (editor, 1989), and *Created from Animals: The Moral Implications of Darwinism* (1990).

Our reading is Chapter 2 of *The Elements of Moral Philosophy*, "The Challenge of Cultural Relativism." Cultural relativism is the doctrine that moral values are determined by culture and that there is no independent basis, outside of cultural norms, for determining whether something is morally right or wrong. In other words, there are no *absolute* values because they are all *relative* to culture. Rachels explains that many thinkers conclude that because different cultures have different moral codes, cultural relativism must be true. He points out, however, that the existence of cultural differences of opinion does not prove that there are no objectively correct answers about what is right and wrong.

Rachels shows that if we accept cultural relativism, we are committed to several implausible consequences. He then argues that differences in cultural values are less drastic than they at first appear to be, and that certain basic values are common to all cultures.

▼

▶ CHAPTER 2. THE CHALLENGE OF CULTURAL
RELATIVISM

### How Different Cultures Have Different Moral Codes

Darius, a king of ancient Persia, was intrigued by the variety of cultures he encountered in his travels. He had found, for example, that the Callatians (a tribe of Indians) customarily ate the bodies of their dead fathers. The Greeks, of course, did not do that—the Greeks practiced cremation and regarded the funeral pyre as the natural and fitting way to dispose of the dead. Darius thought that a sophisticated understanding of the world must include an appreciation of such differences between cultures. One day, to teach this lesson, he summoned some Greeks who happened to be present at his court and asked them what they would take to eat the bodies of their dead fathers. They were shocked, as Darius knew they would be, and replied that no amount of money could persuade them to do such a thing. Then

Darius called in some Callatians, and while the Greeks listened asked them what they would take to burn their dead fathers' bodies. The Callatians were horrified and told Darius not even to mention such a dreadful thing.

This story, recounted by Herodotus in his *Histories*,[1] illustrates a recurring theme in the literature of social science: different cultures have different moral codes. What is thought right within one group may be utterly abhorrent to the members of another group, and vice versa. Should we eat the bodies of the dead or burn them? If you were a Greek, one answer would seem obviously correct; but if you were a Callatian, the opposite would seem equally certain.

It is easy to give additional examples of the same kind. Consider the Eskimos. They are a remote and inaccessible people. Numbering only about 25,000, they live in small, isolated settlements scattered mostly along the northern fringes of North America and Greenland. Until the beginning of this century, the outside world knew little about them. Then explorers began to bring back strange tales.

Eskimo customs turned out to be very different from our own. The men often had more than one wife, and they would share their wives with guests, lending them for the night as a sign of hospitality. Moreover, within a community, a dominant male might demand—and get—regular sexual access to other men's wives. The women, however, were free to break these arrangements simply by leaving their husbands and taking up with new partners—free, that is, so long as their former husbands chose not to make trouble. All in all, the Eskimo practice was a volatile scheme that bore little resemblance to what we call marriage.

But it was not only their marriage and sexual practices that were different. The Eskimos also seemed to have less regard for human life. Infanticide, for example, was common. Knud Rasmussen, one of the most famous early explorers, reported that he met one woman who had borne twenty children but had killed ten of them at birth. Female babies, he found, were especially liable to be destroyed, and this was permitted simply at the parents' discretion, with no social stigma attached to it. Old people also, when they became too feeble to contribute to the family, were left out in the snow to die. So there seemed to be, in this society, remarkably little respect for life.

To the general public, these were disturbing revelations. Our own way of living seems so natural and right that for many of us it is hard to conceive of others living so differently. And when we do hear of such things, we tend immediately to categorize those other peoples as "backward" or "primitive." But to anthropologists and sociologists, there was nothing particularly surprising about the Eskimos. Since the time of Herodotus, enlightened observers have been accustomed to the idea that conceptions of right and wrong differ from culture to culture. If we assume that *our* ideas of right and wrong will be shared by all peoples at all times, we are merely naive.

**Cultural Relativism**

To many thinkers, this observation—"Different cultures have different moral codes"—has seemed to be the key to understanding morality. The idea of universal truth in ethics, they say, is a myth. The customs of different societies are all that exist. These customs cannot be said to be "correct" or "incorrect," for that implies we have an independent standard of right and wrong by which they may be judged. But there is no such independent standard; every standard is culture-bound. The great pioneering sociologist William Graham Sumner, writing in 1906, put the point like this:

> The "right" way is the way which the ancestors used and which has been handed down. The tradition is its own warrant. It is not held subject to verification by experience. The notion of right is in the folkways. It is not outside of them, of independent origin, and brought to test them. In the folkways, whatever is, is right. This is because they are traditional, and therefore contain in themselves the authority of the ancestral ghosts. When we come to the folkways we are at the end of our analysis.[2]

This line of thought has probably persuaded more people to be skeptical about ethics than any other single thing. *Cultural relativism,* as it has been called, challenges our ordinary belief in the objectivity and universality of moral truth. It says, in effect, that there is no such thing as universal truth in ethics; there are only the various cultural codes, and nothing more. Moreover, our own code has no special status; it is merely one among many.

As we shall see, this basic idea is really a compound of several different thoughts. It is important to separate the various elements of the theory because, on analysis, some parts of the theory turn out to be correct, whereas others seem to be mistaken. As a beginning, we may distinguish the following claims, all of which have been made by cultural relativists:

1. Different societies have different moral codes.
2. There is no objective standard that can be used to judge one societal code better than another.
3. The moral code of our own society has no special status; it is merely one among many.
4. There is no "universal truth" in ethics—that is, there are no moral truths that hold for all peoples at all times.
5. The moral code of a society determines what is right within that society; that is, if the moral code of a society says that a certain action is right, then that action *is* right, at least within that society.
6. It is mere arrogance for us to try to judge the conduct of other peoples. We should adopt an attitude of tolerance toward the practices of other cultures.

Although it may seem that these six propositions go naturally together, they are independent of one another, in the sense that some of them might be true even if others are false. In what follows, we will try to identify what is correct in cultural relativism, but we will also be concerned to expose what is mistaken about it.

### The Cultural Differences Argument

Cultural relativism is a theory about the nature of morality. At first blush it seems quite plausible. However, like all such theories, it may be evaluated by subjecting it to rational analysis; and when we analyze cultural relativism we find that it is not so plausible as it first appears to be.

The first thing we need to notice is that at the heart of cultural relativism there is a certain *form of argument*. The strategy used by cultural relativists is to argue from facts about the differences between cultural outlooks to a conclusion about the status of morality. Thus we are invited to accept this reasoning:

1. The Greeks believed it was wrong to eat the dead, whereas the Callatians believed it was right to eat the dead.
2. Therefore, eating the dead is neither objectively right nor objectively wrong. It is merely a matter of opinion, which varies from culture to culture.

Or, alternatively:

1. The Eskimos see nothing wrong with infanticide, whereas Americans believe infanticide is immoral.
2. Therefore, infanticide is neither objectively right nor objectively wrong. It is merely a matter of opinion, which varies from culture to culture.

Clearly, these arguments are variations of one fundamental idea. They are both special cases of a more general argument, which says:

1. Different cultures have different moral codes.
2. Therefore, there is no objective "truth" in morality. Right and wrong are only matters of opinion, and opinions vary from culture to culture.

We may call this the *Cultural Differences Argument*. To many people, it is very persuasive. But from a logical point of view, is it a *sound* argument?

It is not sound. The trouble is that the conclusion does not really follow from the premise—that is, even if the premise is true, the conclusion still might be false. The premise concerns what people *believe:* in some societies, people believe one thing; in other societies, people believe differently. The conclusion, however, concerns *what really is the case.* The trouble is that this sort of conclusion does not follow logically from this sort of premise.

Consider again the example of the Greeks and Callatians. The Greeks believed it was wrong to eat the dead; the Callatians believed it was right. Does it follow, *from the mere fact that they disagreed,* that there is no objective truth in the matter? No, it does not follow; for it *could* be that the practice was objectively right (or wrong) and that one or the other of them was simply mistaken.

To make the point clearer, consider a very different matter. In some societies, people believe the earth is flat. In other societies, such as our own, people believe the earth is (roughly) spherical. Does it follow, *from the mere fact that they disagree,* that there is no "objective truth" in geography? Of course not; we would never draw such a conclusion because we realize that, in their beliefs about the world, the members of some societies might simply be wrong. There is no reason to think that if the world is round everyone must know it. Similarly, there is no reason to think that if there is moral truth everyone must know it. The fundamental mistake in the Cultural Differences Argument is that it attempts to derive a substantive conclusion about a subject (morality) from the mere fact that people disagree about it.

It is important to understand the nature of the point that is being made here. We are *not* saying (not yet, anyway) that the conclusion of the argument is false. Insofar as anything being said here is concerned, it is still an open question whether the conclusion is true. We *are* making a purely logical point and saying that the conclusion does not *follow from* the premise. This is important, because in order to determine whether the conclusion is true, we need arguments in its support. Cultural relativism proposes this argument, but unfortunately the argument turns out to be fallacious. So it proves nothing.

### The Consequences of Taking Cultural Relativism Seriously

Even if the Cultural Differences Argument is invalid, cultural relavism might still be true. What would it be like if it were true?

In the passage quoted above, William Graham Sumner summarizes the essence of cultural relativism. He says that there is no measure of right and wrong other than the standards of one's society: "The notion of right is in the folkways. It is not outside of them, of independent origin, and brought to test them. In the folkways, whatever is, is right."

Suppose we took this seriously. What would be some of the consequences?

**1.** *We could no longer say that the customs of other societies are morally inferior to our own.* This, of course, is one of the main points stressed by cultural relativism. We would have to stop condemning other societies merely because they are "different." So long as we concentrate on certain examples, such as the funerary practices of the Greeks and Callatians, this may seem to be a sophisticated, enlightened attitude.

However, we would also be stopped from criticizing other, less benign practices. Suppose a society waged war on its neighbors for the purpose of taking slaves. Or suppose a society was violently anti-Semitic and its leaders set out to destroy the Jews. Cultural relativism would preclude us from saying that either of these practices was wrong. We would not even be able to say that a society tolerant of Jews is *better* than the anti-Semitic society, for that would imply some sort of transcultural standard of comparison. The failure to condemn *these* practices does not seem "enlightened"; on the contrary, slavery and anti-Semitism seem wrong *wherever* they occur. Nevertheless, if we took cultural relativism seriously, we would have to admit that these social practices also are immune from criticism.

**2.** *We could decide whether actions are right or wrong just by consulting the standards of our society.* Cultural relativism suggests a simple test for determining what is right and what is wrong: all one has to do is ask whether the action is in accordance with the code of one's society. Suppose a resident of South Africa is wondering whether his country's policy of *apartheid*—rigid racial segregation—is morally correct. All he has to do is ask whether this policy conforms to his society's moral code. If it does, there is nothing to worry about, at least from a moral point of view.

This implication of cultural relativism is disturbing because few of us think that our society's code is perfect—we can think of ways it might be improved. Yet cultural relativism would not only forbid us from criticizing the codes of *other* societies; it would stop us from criticizing our *own*. After all, if right and wrong are relative to culture, this must be true for our own culture just as much as for others.

**3.** *The idea of moral progress is called into doubt.* Usually, we think that at least some changes in our society have been for the better. (Some, of course, may have been changes for the worse.) Consider this example: Throughout most of Western history the place of women in society was very narrowly circumscribed. They could not own property; they could not vote or hold political office; with a few exceptions, they were not permitted to have paying jobs; and generally they were under the almost absolute control of their husbands. Recently much of this has changed, and most people think of it as progress.

If cultural relativism is correct, can we legitimately think of this as progress? Progress means replacing a way of doing things with a *better* way. But by what standard do we judge the new ways as better? If the old ways were in accordance with the social standards of their time, then cultural relativism would say it is a mistake to judge them by the standards of a different time. Eighteenth-century society was, in effect, a different society from the one we have now. To say that we have made progress implies a judgment that present-day society is better, and that is just the sort of transcultural judgment that, according to cultural relativism, is impermissible.

Our idea of social *reform* will also have to be reconsidered. A reformer such as Martin Luther King, Jr., seeks to change his society for the better. Within the constraints imposed by cultural relativism, there is one way this might be done. If a society is not living up to its own ideals, the reformer may be regarded as acting for the best: the ideals of the society are the standard by which we judge his or her proposals as worthwhile. But the "reformer" may not challenge the ideals themselves, for those ideals are by definition correct. According to cultural relativism, then, the idea of social reform makes sense only in this very limited way.

These three consequences of cultural relativism have led many thinkers to reject it as implausible on its face. It does make sense, they say, to condemn some practices, such as slavery and anti-Semitism, wherever they occur. It makes sense to think that our own society has made some moral progress, while admitting that it is still imperfect and in need of reform. Because cultural relativism says that these judgments make no sense, the argument goes, it cannot be right.

### Why There Is Less Disagreement Than It Seems

The original impetus for cultural relativism comes from the observation that cultures differ dramatically in their views of right and wrong. But just how much do they differ? It is true that there are differences. However, it is easy to overestimate the extent of those differences. Often, when we examine what *seems* to be a dramatic difference, we find that the cultures do not differ nearly as much as it appears.

Consider a culture in which people believe it is wrong to eat cows. This may even be a poor culture, in which there is not enough food; still, the cows are not to be touched. Such a society would *appear* to have values very different from our own. But does it? We have not yet asked why these people will not eat cows. Suppose it is because they believe that after death the souls of humans inhabit the bodies of animals, especially cows, so that a cow may be someone's grandmother. Now do we want to say that their values are different from ours? No; the difference lies elsewhere. The difference is in our belief systems, not in our values. We agree that we shouldn't eat Grandma; we simply disagree about whether the cow *is* (or could be) Grandma.

The general point is this. Many factors work together to produce the customs of a society. The society's values are only one of them. Other matters, such as the religious and factual beliefs held by its members and the physical circumstances in which they must live, are also important. We cannot conclude, then, merely because customs differ, that there is a disagreement about *values*. The difference in customs may be attributable to some other aspect of social life. Thus there may be less disagreement about values than there appears to be.

Consider the Eskimos again. They often kill perfectly normal infants, especially girls. We do not approve of this at all; a parent who did this in our society would be locked up. Thus there appears to be a great difference in the values of our two cultures. But suppose we ask *why* the Eskimos do this. The explanation is not that they have less affection for their children or less respect for human life. An Eskimo family will always protect its babies if conditions permit. But they live in a harsh environment, where food is often in short supply. A fundamental postulate of Eskimo thought is: "Life is hard, and the margin of safety small." A family may want to nourish its babies but be unable to do so.

As in many "primitive" societies, Eskimo mothers will nurse their infants over a much longer period of time than mothers in our culture. The child will take nourishment from its mother's breast for four years, perhaps even longer. So even in the best of times there are limits to the number of infants that one mother can sustain. Moreover, the Eskimos are a nomadic people—unable to farm, they must move about in search of food. Infants must be carried, and a mother can carry only one baby in her parka as she travels and goes about her outdoor work. Other family members can help, but this is not always possible.

Infant girls are more readily disposed of because, first, in this society the males are the primary food providers—they are the hunters, according to the traditional division of labor—and it is obviously important to maintain a sufficient number of food gatherers. But there is an important second reason as well. Because the hunters suffer a high casualty rate, the adult men who die prematurely far outnumber the women who die early. Thus if male and female infants survived in equal numbers, the female adult population would greatly outnumber the male adult population. Examining the available statistics, one writer concluded that "were it not for female infanticide . . .there would be approximately one-and-a-half times as many females in the average Eskimo local group as there are food-producing males."[3]

So among the Eskimos, infanticide does not signal a fundamentally different attitude toward children. Instead, it is a recognition that drastic measures are sometimes needed to ensure the family's survival. Even then, however, killing the baby is not the first option considered. Adoption is common; childless couples are especially happy to take a more fertile couple's "surplus." Killing is only the last resort. I emphasize this in order to show that the raw data of the anthropologists can be misleading; it can make the differences in values between cultures appear greater than they are. The Eskimos' values are not all that different from our values. It is only that life forces upon them choices that we do not have to make.

### How All Cultures Have Some Values in Common

It should not be surprising that, despite appearances, the Eskimos are protective of their children. How could it be otherwise? How could a group survive that did *not* value its young? This suggests a certain argument, one which shows that all cultural groups must be protective of their infants:

1. Human infants are helpless and cannot survive if they are not given extensive care for a period of years.
2. Therefore, if a group did not care for its young, the young would not survive, and the older members of the group would not be replaced. After a while the group would die out.
3. Therefore, any cultural group that continues to exist must care for its young. Infants that are *not* cared for must be the exception rather than the rule.

Similar reasoning shows that other values must be more or less universal. Imagine what it would be like for a society to place no value at all on truth telling. When one person spoke to another, there would be no presumption at all that he was telling the truth—for he could just as easily be speaking falsely. Within that society, there would be no reason to pay attention to what anyone says. (I ask you what time it is, and you say

"Four o'clock." But there is no presumption that you are speaking truly; you could just as easily have said the first thing that came into your head. So I have no reason to pay attention to your answer—in fact, there was no point in my asking you in the first place!) Communication would then be extremely difficult, if not impossible. And because complex societies cannot exist without regular communication among their members, society would become impossible. It follows that in any complex society there *must* be a presumption in favor of truthfulness. There may of course be exceptions to this rule: there may be situations in which it is thought to be permissible to lie. Nevertheless, these will be exceptions to a rule that *is* in force in the society.

Let me give one further example of the same type. Could a society exist in which there was no prohibition on murder? What would this be like? Suppose people were free to kill other people at will, and no one thought there was anything wrong with it. In such a "society," no one could feel secure. Everyone would have to be constantly on guard. People who wanted to survive would have to avoid other people as much as possible. This would inevitably result in individuals trying to become as self-sufficient as possible—after all, associating with others would be dangerous. Society on any large scale would collapse. Of course, people might band together in smaller groups with others that they *could* trust not to harm them. But notice what this means: they would be forming smaller societies that *did* acknowledge a rule against murder. The prohibition of murder, then, is a necessary feature of all societies.

There is a general theoretical point here, namely, that *there are some moral rules that all societies will have in common, because those rules are necessary for society to exist.* The rules against lying and murder are two examples. And in fact, we do find these rules in force in all viable cultures. Cultures may differ in what they regard as legitimate exceptions to the rules, but this disagreement exists against a background of agreement on the larger issues. Therefore, it is a mistake to overestimate the amount of difference between cultures. Not *every* moral rule can vary from society to society.

### What Can Be Learned from Cultural Relativism

At the outset, I said that we were going to identify both what is right and what is wrong in cultural relativism. Thus far I have mentioned only its mistakes: I have said that it rests on an invalid argument, that it has consequences that make it implausible on its face, and that the extent of cultural disagreement is far less than it implies. This all adds up to a pretty thorough repudiation of the theory. Nevertheless, it is still a very appealing idea, and the reader may have the feeling that all this is a little unfair. The theory *must* have something going for it, or else why has it been so influential? In fact, I think there *is* something right about cultural relativism, and now I want to say what that is. There are two lessons we should learn from the theory, even if we ultimately reject it.

**1.** Cultural relativism warns us, quite rightly, about the danger of assuming that all our preferences are based on some absolute rational standard. They are not. Many (but not all) of our practices are merely peculiar to our society, and it is easy to lose sight of that fact. In reminding us of it, the theory does a service.

Funerary practices are one example. The Callatians, according to Herodotus, were "men who eat their fathers"—a shocking idea, to us at least. But eating the flesh of the dead could be understood as a sign of respect. It could be taken as a symbolic act that says: We wish this person's spirit to dwell within us. Perhaps this was the understanding of the Callatians. On such a way of thinking, burying the dead could be seen as an act of rejection, and burning the corpse as positively scornful. If this is hard to imagine, then we may need to have our imaginations stretched. Of course we may feel a visceral repugnance at the idea of eating human flesh in any circumstances. But what of it? This repugnance may be, as the relativists say, only a matter of what is customary in our particular society.

There are many other matters that we tend to think of in terms of objective right and wrong, but that are really nothing more than social conventions. Should women cover their breasts? A publicly exposed breast is scandalous in our society, whereas in other cultures it is unremarkable. Objectively speaking, it is neither right nor wrong—there is no objective reason why either custom is better. Cultural relativism begins with the valuable insight that many of our practices are like this—they are only cultural products. Then it goes wrong by concluding that, because *some* practices are like this, *all* must be.

**2.** The second lesson has to do with keeping an open mind. In the course of growing up, each of us has acquired some strong feelings: we have learned to think of some types of conduct as acceptable, and others we have learned to regard as simply unacceptable. Occasionally, we may find those feelings challenged. We may encounter someone who claims that our feelings are mistaken. For example, we may have been taught that homosexuality is immoral, and we may feel quite uncomfortable around gay people and see them as alien and "different." Now someone suggests that this may be a mere prejudice; that there is nothing evil about homosexuality; that gay people are just people, like anyone else, who happen, through no choice of their own, to be attracted to others of the same sex. But because we feel so strongly about the matter, we may find it hard to take this seriously. Even after we listen to the arguments, we may still have the unshakable feeling that homosexuals *must*, somehow, be an unsavory lot.

Cultural relativism, by stressing that our moral views can reflect the prejudices of our society, provides an antidote for this kind of dogmatism. When he tells the story of the Greeks and Callatians, Herodotus adds:

> For if anyone, no matter who, were given the opportunity of choosing from amongst all the nations of the world the set of beliefs which he thought best, he would inevitably, after careful consideration of their relative merits, choose that of his own country. Everyone without exception believes his own native customs, and the religion he was brought up in, to be the best.[4]

Realizing this can result in our having more open minds. We can come to understand that our feelings are not necessarily perceptions of the truth—they may be nothing more than the result of cultural conditioning. Thus when we hear it suggested that some element of our social code is *not* really the best and we find ourselves instinctively resisting the suggestion, we might stop and remember this. Then we may be more open to discovering the truth, whatever that might be.

We can understand the appeal of cultural relativism, then, even though the theory has serious shortcomings. It is an attractive theory because it is based on a genuine insight—that many of the practices and attitudes we think so natural are really only cultural products. Moreover, keeping this insight firmly in view is important if we want to avoid arrogance and have open minds. These are important points, not to be taken lightly. But we can accept these points without going on to accept the whole theory.

---

▶ NOTES

1. Herodotus, *The Histories,* trans. Aubrey de Sélincourt, rev. A. R. Burn (Harmondsworth, England: Penguin, 1972), pp. 219–220. [J.R.] Herodotus (about 484–425 B.C.E.) was a Greek historian. [D.C.A., ed.]

2. William Graham Sumner, *Folkways* (Boston: Ginn & Co., 1906), p. 28. [J. R.]

3. E. Adamson Hoebel, *The Law of Primitive Man: A Study in Comparative Legal Dynamics* (Cambridge, Mass.: Harvard University Press, 1954), p. 76. [J.R.]

4. Herodotus, *Histories,* p. 219. [J.R.]

**Chapter 6**

# *Act and Rule Utilitarianism*

In most cases, human beings seem to have no trouble making moral evaluations or judgments. Every day people do things we easily classify as morally good or bad. When I read in the newspaper that a woman has been violently raped and murdered, I do not have to consult the moral law to conclude that the act is evil. The woman has been harmed and killed, and that is sufficient for me. The ease with which we make most moral judgments seems to conflict with the abstract, complicated, and problematic nature of Kantian ethics. The approach to ethics considered in this chapter, utilitarianism, can perhaps better explain the ease with which most moral judgments are made. Utilitarianism may also be more effective at providing guidance on the difficult moral issues where Kantian ethics suffers from the problems of accurate descriptions for actions and conflicting moral laws.

Utilitarianism can explain how people reach their everyday moral conclusions because it is an ethical theory that focuses on harm and benefit or happiness and unhappiness to morally significant beings. The theory is related to the ethical insight that *an action is morally bad if it harms someone, whereas it is morally good if it helps or benefits someone.* Many people think about good and bad in this way. When you consider whether or not to do something that will affect others, do you think about whether anyone will be harmed or helped by your action? If you do, then utilitarianism may appeal to you.

When we focus on the harm and benefit or happiness and unhappiness produced by our actions, we are looking at the results or consequences of those actions. Ethical theories that claim that good and evil are related to consequences or results are called *consequentialist theories.* Utilitarianism is a consequentialist ethical theory that provides a means to evaluate actions.

## Act Utilitarianism and Ethical Egoism

Ethical egoism, another consequentialist ethical theory, was discussed in Chapter 4. Both ethical egoism and utilitarianism are consequentialist theories and both could relate to the previous insight, but it is important to clearly differentiate between them. The crucial differences concern the objective the theory assigns to the moral agent and their respective views of good and bad. Ethical egoism states that moral agents should act in their own self-interest and maximize net benefit for themselves. What is good is what produces a net benefit for a particular individual; what is bad is what produces a net harm to the individual. In contrast, utilitarianism claims that moral agents should maximize net benefit for the greatest number of morally significant beings affected by a certain action. As a utilitarian, I cannot merely act in my own self-interest; I must consider everyone who will be benefited or harmed. What is good is what promotes more benefit than harm for the morally significant beings affected; what is bad is what promotes more harm than benefit for the morally significant beings affected. The utilitarian position, and the difference between it and ethical egoism, will become even clearer in the remainder of this chapter.

## Utilitarianism

Utilitarianism was popularized by two British thinkers, Jeremy Bentham (1748–1832) and John Stuart Mill (1806–1873).[1] They centered their ideas on a common principle: *What is good is what tends to produce a net utility for the persons affected.* The word "utilitarianism" comes from the idea of "utility," which roughly means usefulness. Bentham defines it more precisely:

> By utility is meant the property in any object, whereby it tends to produce benefit, advantage, pleasure, good, or happiness (all this in the present case comes to the same thing) or (what comes again to the same thing) to prevent the happening of mischief, pain, evil, or unhappiness to the party whose interest is considered.[2]

In place of "utility," Bentham primarily uses the term "pleasure," whereas Mill mostly employs the term "happiness," but the two formulations are similar in that both Bentham and Mill thought that pleasure was the essential component of happiness. Both philosophers would have accepted the idea that good was what promoted more pleasure or happiness than pain or unhappiness for the persons affected.

This chapter will discuss both versions of utilitarianism. Bentham's view illustrates a theory called act utilitarianism. Mill's view adapts Bentham's ideas in two primary ways. Although Mill joins Bentham in being concerned with the quantity of pleasure, Mill adds the idea of the quality of pleasure to his utilitarian view. The other main difference is that Mill is more concerned than Bentham with moral rules. Recently some moral philosophers have argued that Mill was a rule utilitarian, whereas Bentham was an act utilitarian. Although there is agreement on the claim about Bentham, the assertion about Mill remains controversial. The subtleties of interpreting the ideas of these famous philosophers is beyond the scope of this book. Thus, this chapter will be limited to a discussion of some of Mill's statements about moral rules, and I will use these statements as a stepping stone to a description of the rule utilitarian position.

## Jeremy Bentham and Act Utilitarianism

Jeremy Bentham begins *An Introduction to the Principles of Morals and Legislation* by declaring that people are governed by two masters, pleasure and pain. In general, human beings are subject to pleasure and pain and desire pleasure while avoiding pain. In addition to observing this fact, Bentham goes on to assert that pleasure and pain or happiness and unhappiness are the only concepts that can give meaning to moral good and bad. His ethical standard could be phrased as follows: *Actions are good and bad according to the tendency they have to augment or diminish the pleasure or happiness of the parties whose interests are in question.* The only actions that one ought to perform are those that are in accord with this principle. According to Bentham, connecting "ought" to pleasure or happiness is the only way that "ought" can gain a legitimate moral meaning. Bentham did not claim that he could definitively prove that pleasure and happiness were the source of moral goodness and obligation; he merely insisted that this standard was better than any alternative one.

Bentham claimed that it could not be conclusively proven that happiness was the source of moral goodness. One explanation, however, for Bentham's identification of happiness as the source of goodness is as follows. We might assert that happiness is the ultimate end of all our activities and that we should use whatever is the ultimate end of all our activities as our standard of ethical evaluation. Some of our goals have *instrumental value;* that is, they are a means to achieve other goals. I may want to do well on a test so I can earn a good grade in a course. The good grade on the test is a *means* to achieve the *end* of the good grade in the course. The good grade in the course is a means to a further end— graduating from college with a superior grade point average. Graduating from college with a superior grade point average may be a means to the end of getting a well-paying job, and getting a well-paying job may be the means to obtain money. The money allows me to buy a house, a car, and other possessions. It allows me to take vacations and so on. Why do I want these possessions and vacations? They are the means to happiness—but why do I want to be happy? I believe I am better off when I am happy than when I am unhappy. The whole chain ultimately ends with happiness and the idea that happiness is best for us. Philosophers would say that whatever lies at the end of the chain possesses *intrinsic value*. Bentham's idea could be interpreted as claiming that happiness has intrinsic value and that we should use whatever has intrinsic value to ethically evaluate our actions and beliefs.

Bentham uses the term "happiness" at times and "pleasure" at others. In his definition of "utility," he also mentions "benefit." There are advantages and disadvantages to all of these terms. Utilitarianism needs a concept that will accomplish three main things. First, it must provide a content for "good" and "bad" that will be open to observation and calculation. Second, the concept must provide a common denominator for different moral matters. There will be no Kantian problem with conflicting moral laws because all competing moral claims will be able to be translated into the common denominator of happiness, pleasure, or benefit. Finally, the theory requires a concept that includes everything of intrinsic value. "Pleasure" seems to be the most narrow and definite term, and this has the advantage of making it seem the easiest to observe and calculate. The fact that it is narrow, however, suggests that it leaves out a lot of what is really valuable. "Happiness" appears broader, so it probably leaves out less of intrinsic value but will be harder to observe and calculate. "Benefit" may be the widest term and would seem to contain everything of ultimate value, yet it may be the hardest to observe and calculate.[3] In this chapter, "happiness" will be used most often, but "pleasure" and "benefit" will be used at times. Remember that all of these terms refer to the same basic concept: whatever is of ultimate or intrinsic value for persons.

Bentham focuses on individual actions. An action is good if it produces more happiness or pleasure than unhappiness or pain for everyone affected by it. He is primarily interested in the quantitative aspects of pleasure and pain. It does not matter if the action involves reading poetry, playing chess, eating chocolate ice cream, or watching game shows on television. All that matters is the amount of pleasure and pain produced by the action. The moral agent should sum up the value of all the pleasures to all the people involved and then add all the pains to everyone affected. If there is a greater amount of pleasure, then the act is good; if the pain is greater, it is bad. Thus, the essential elements for Bentham are the focus on specific actions and the contrasting quantities of pleasure and pain to those affected.

The assumption made by Bentham is that all people calculate pleasure and pain or happiness and unhappiness. Some do it consciously, others unconsciously. Some calculate carefully, others carelessly. Obviously, Bentham felt that conscious and careful calculation were superior. He also rejected ethical egoism wherein people calculate only the effects on themselves. He argued that an action was only ethical if there was more pleasure than pain after everyone affected had been considered.

Whose pleasure and pain must be taken into account when we are trying to act ethically? In Chapter 1, the term "morally significant beings" was used to identify those beings who ought to be given ethical consideration. Bentham observed that traditionally only human beings, and at one time only adult male human beings, were regarded to be full-status morally significant beings. In contrast to this view, he thought that any being who could experience pain and pleasure must be considered. This would presumably include, at least, all mammals because they have nervous systems like ours and experience pain and pleasure. Peter Singer, a contemporary act utilitarian, claims that the capacity to have interests is the crucial criterion, although he adds that "The capacity for suffering and enjoying things is a prerequisite for having interests at all, a condition that must be satisfied before we can speak of interests in any meaningful way."[4] Singer adds that sentience is enough to make a being worthy of equal consideration of interests, so his position may not be very different from Bentham's.[5] Singer would also presumably include all mammals as morally significant beings, although he argues that a stronger case can be made for some of them such as chimpanzees, gorillas, and orangutans.

## Act Utilitarian Calculations

Bentham assumed that happiness or what benefits people is a good thing and that unhappiness or what harms people is bad. On that basis, he claimed that people ought to maximize pleasure, happiness, and benefit and minimize pain, unhappiness, and harm for as many morally significant beings as possible. To discover actions that produce a net pleasure, happiness, or benefit, this ethical theory utilizes calculations of benefits against harms, benefits against alternative benefits, and harms against alternative harms.

Here is a simplified example of act utilitarian ethical evaluation, although it will make more sense if the term "benefit" is substituted for "pleasure" or "happiness" and "harm" replaces "pain" or "unhappiness." Benefit and harm are superior because they are more general words and can cover a wider variety of things.

Suppose that a management team decides not to upgrade the safety of a new model of automobile by adding a certain part that would provide greater protection for the fuel tank. If they do not add the part, they believe they will save money. Because they want to make as much money as possible, they decide not to add the part. As time goes by, people are killed in low-speed accidents who would not have been killed if the part had been added.

Years later we might look back on that decision and its consequences to determine if the decision was ethical. First, we would identify the significant consequences and divide them into harms and benefits. The significant benefits were that the company saved about eighteen million dollars during the six years that the car remained unaltered. The company also was able to save the one million dollars it would have cost to alter the assembly lines so that the part could have been added. A final benefit is that each car was finished two minutes faster than if the part had been included, which meant that over the years more cars were built. Assume that this produced another two million dollars in profits. The significant harms were that, during the six years, thirty people were killed in low-speed crashes who would have survived if the part had been added. Another sixty people were seriously injured or burned. The relatives and friends of the victims suffered because of the deaths and injuries. Fifty vehicles were destroyed by fire. The company spent fifty million dollars to settle lawsuits connected to the deaths and injuries. The company's reputation was temporarily damaged, and it lost five million dollars in profits because of the lower sales associated with their poor reputation.

After identifying the consequences, we would try to decide whether the benefits outweigh the harms or vice versa. In this case, it is easy to see that the harms outweigh the benefits: The company lost more money than it saved, people were killed and injured, their friends and families suffered, vehicles were destroyed, and the company's reputation was damaged. There is nothing on the benefit side to outweigh these consequences. Therefore, a utilitarian would conclude that it was unethical for the managers to decide not to upgrade the safety of the fuel system.

This sample of a utilitarian analysis is incomplete and simplistic, but a more complete treatment would reach the same conclusion. According to Bentham, a complete utilitarian analysis would have to look beyond the obvious harms and benefits. Bentham discusses seven aspects of a utilitarian evaluation: intensity, duration, certainty, propinquity, fecundity, purity, and extent. This procedure is sometimes called the "utilitarian calculus" or "hedonistic calculus."

First, the agent must consider the intensity or significance of the harms and benefits, which I did to some extent in the example. The deaths were a very significant occurrence, and it would require a lot of benefit to outweigh them. Mill suggests that the more significant aspect when we weigh the significance of competing benefits or harms is the one that a competent agent would prefer. Contrary to Mill, one might also argue that the significance is inherent in the benefits and harms. This controversy did not arise in the automobile example because it was clear that the harms outweighed the benefits.

Second, the duration of each harm and benefit must be considered. A minor pain that lasts for years is more of a harm than a serious pain that is over in a couple of seconds. In my example, the deaths had the consequences of greatest duration because these people were deprived of lives that might have lasted many years. None of the other factors were that far-reaching.

A third factor mentioned by Bentham is certainty: the certainty that the consequences we anticipate will follow from the action actually do so. In the automobile example, I was looking back on this action with something approaching total knowledge. Certainty was not an important factor because I was certain about all the occurrences. I did not have to predict the consequences; I knew what they were.

A fourth consideration is what Bentham called propinquity. How remote is the harm or benefit? How soon will we experience the consequences? Bentham thought that an immediate harm was worse than one that would not happen for a long time. Once again, because I was looking back at the management decision, this aspect is not vital.

A fifth factor is the fecundity of the consequences; that is, how likely is it that the action will produce future benefits? An action that will promote future benefits is better than one that will not do so. Because the decision about the automobiles took place in the past and no further consequences would result from it, there are no future benefits.

A sixth factor is the purity of the consequences. How likely is it that the action will produce future harm? In my example, future harm was not relevant because I had already identified all the harms that had occurred over time.

The last factor is the extent or number of people affected by the harms and benefits. In the management case, I tried to identify the extent of the consequences by considering all the people who were affected.

Although act utilitarianism grows out of a relatively simple insight about benefit and harm, it becomes complicated when we try to identify all of the consequences connected to an action and all of the morally significant beings affected by it. Utilitarian calculations are often difficult to carry out. In some cases, they can be performed completely. In other cases, such as the automobile example, we can produce a reasonable conclusion with which most people would agree. In still other cases, we will probably not be able to determine the consequences and affected persons with sufficient accuracy.

# Justification for the Ethical Standard and Strengths of the Theory

Bentham's version of utilitarianism has a number of strengths. This section discusses those strengths and related justifications for using his ethical standard. A later section investigates problems with act utilitarianism.

## A Clear Content for Ethics

Bentham thought that act utilitarianism would make ethics more scientific. It would provide a clear content—pain and pleasure—for good and bad. This content would enable the determination of good and bad in a straightforward way using the utilitarian calculus. This clear content also provides a common denominator for different moral matters. There will be no Kantian problem with conflicting moral laws because all competing moral claims will be able to be translated into the common denominator of happiness, pleasure, or benefit. This clear content is one of the justifications for using this ethical standard and a related strength of the act utilitarian theory. Act utilitarianism's clear content makes it seem simpler to understand, to use, and at least in one way less problematic than Kantian ethical theory.

## Responding to the Situation of the Agent

A second justification for the standard and a related strength of the theory is that the ethical theory responds to the particular situation faced by the moral agent. Ethics is not a matter of following abstract and general rules without exceptions, but instead investigates the actual situation in which the moral agent finds himself or herself. Many people seem more comfortable with an ethical theory that allows them to evaluate each action separately. They do not want to be compelled to follow general moral rules without exceptions. Thus, this is a strength of the theory and a reason for using Bentham's ethical standard.

## Consistency with the Basic Objective of Human Beings

A third justification for the standard and related strength of the theory is that the theory appears to be consistent with the basic objective of human beings. As a general observation, it does seem accurate that persons seek pleasure, happiness, and whatever benefits them. People differ in many ways, but they have this in common: They all want to be happy. It is reasonable to connect moral good and bad to what is sought by everyone. The controversial step is the one from the individual's happiness being the source of moral good to the greatest happiness of the greatest number of people being the source of moral good. If people want to live together successfully, however, they should take this step.

There are some significant strengths to Bentham's act utilitarian position but also some problems connected to it that will be discussed in a later section. Some contemporary philosophers have endorsed the act utilitarian position, but as will be discussed later, it competes for adherents with another version of utilitarianism called rule utilitarianism.

## Determining Morally Significant Actions

The third thing we have been looking for in an ethical theory is a means of separating morally significant actions from those that are not morally significant. Whatever produces significant pleasure or pain, happiness or unhappiness, or benefit or harm for a morally significant being and is brought about by a moral agent is morally significant. Matters that have no significant pleasure or pain, happiness or unhappiness, or benefit or harm are not morally significant. In an effort to better understand act utilitarianism, the next two sections relate it to the traditional ethical assumptions and the themes related to good and bad.

## Act Utilitarianism and the Traditional Ethical Assumptions

Act utilitarianism accepts the traditional ethical assumptions. First, ethics is rational; we can use reason to reach theoretical and practical conclusions about ethics. We can provide reasons related to pleasure and pain, happiness and unhappiness, and benefit and harm to support our ethical evaluations and our solutions to moral problems, and these reasons and solutions can be evaluated. Some reasons and solutions will be better than others. Moral agents can use their rational considerations about pleasure and pain, happiness and unhappiness, and benefit and harm to guide their actions. Finally, act utilitarians believe people who share an ethical framework can discuss moral problems and arrive at mutually acceptable solutions.

Second, act utilitarians endorse the view that all persons (full-status morally significant beings) are moral equals and should be treated impartially. They treat persons impartially because identical benefits count the same no matter who is the beneficiary: a benefit to a stranger counts as much as a benefit to a family member, or even to you. Act utilitarians must maximize benefit for the greatest number of morally significant beings. When they are doing this, all people are moral equals.

This means that there may be times when to be ethical you must act contrary to your own self-interest. Think about the CD example from Chapter 1. I wanted to buy a few new CDs for my collection, but I already have a couple hundred of them. Instead of buying the CDs, I could donate the money to a legitimate charity that would use it to cure some people from potentially fatal diseases. I may want to buy the CDs, but the ethical thing to do is to donate the money to the charity. The benefit of saving the lives will outweigh the pleasure I get from listening to the CDs. I must remember that even though the sick people are strangers they are my moral equals. Therefore, if I want to be moral, I should help them.

Finally, act utilitarianism accepts the idea of universalizing ethical judgments. As in the CD example, if it is ethical for me to donate the money to a legitimate charity, then it is the ethical thing for anyone to do in a sufficiently similar situation. A "sufficiently similar situation" is sufficiently similar with respect to net harm and benefit. Assuming that we can identify sufficiently similar situations, we can universalize our ethical judgments.

## Act Utilitarianism and the Basic Ethical Themes

Act utilitarianism has a position on each of the four basic ethical themes discussed in Chapter 1. The first theme is represented by this question: *What kind of moral guidelines makes something good or bad: subjective, relative, or objective ones?* Act utilitarians believe the source of legitimate moral guidelines is objective considerations of fact; that is, facts about pleasure and pain, happiness and unhappiness, or benefit and harm. Thus, act utilitarians endorse objective guidelines. Individual actions or groups of related actions that cause more net harm than benefit are objectively evil. For example, the murder of millions of Jews and other people by the Nazis during the thirties and forties was objectively evil because the harm of murdering these innocent people far outweighed any benefits for the Nazis.

Another significant theme in ethics is indicated by this question: *What makes something good or evil; is it the consequences that are produced or the reasoning that led up to it?* Utilitarians are ethical consequentialists who believe the goodness or badness of something is a result of the consequences that are brought about by it. The reasoning is secondary for a utilitarian; our reasons are good if we intend to bring about beneficial consequences. However, an action that was meant to benefit someone might turn out to be bad if it actually causes harm.

The third theme relates to this question: *Should we faithfully follow general rules of behavior, or should we separately evaluate each action and belief?* In theory, act utilitarians evaluate each action separately, but they point out that there are classes of actions wherein the harm or benefit might always outweigh any other factor. For example, rape would always seem to cause more harm than benefit. We do not have to recalculate every case of rape. Sometimes the verdict of human experience is so clear that we know the answer without actually doing the calculation. In relation to such classes of actions, utilitarians could save time by making use of ethical rules. Of course, act utilitarians should always be open to the possibility of an exception to the rule if in a particular case disregarding the rule maximized net benefit. There might be cases where it is ethical to kill, steal, lie, cheat, or break promises (for example, if keeping a promise to someone would cause that person great harm). The ultimate focus for act utilitarians is on specific actions, but they can use rules as timesaving devices.

The fourth theme is connected to the proper focus of ethical attention: *Should the group, community, or majority of persons be the focus of ethics or should the focus be on the individual?* Utilitarians believe the focus of ethics should be the greatest good for the greatest number of people. In some cases, utilitarians would sacrifice the individual for the greater good of the group because the good of the larger number of persons outweighs the good of the individual. We believe automobiles are an ethical product for a business to produce even though thousands of individuals are killed in automobile accidents each year. The enormous benefit of automobiles outweighs the deaths of these people. Act utilitarianism focuses on the group, not the individual, and promotes the greatest good or benefit for the greatest number of people.

## Contrasting Act Utilitarianism with Kantian Ethical Theory

Act utilitarianism has some similarities to and some differences from Kantian ethical theory (see Appendix 1). The basic ethical guideline identified by act utilitarianism is the utilitarian principle that actions are good and bad according to the tendency they have to augment or diminish the happiness of the parties whose interests are in question. Kantian theory uses the two forms of the Categorical Imperative and concentrates on acting from respect for the moral law. Act utilitarianism and Kantian ethical theory both accept all of the traditional ethical assumptions: rationality, impartiality, and universalizability. The two theories also agree on the first ethical theme. They both claim that legitimate moral guidelines are based on objective considerations. Act utilitarianism, however, bases moral guidelines on objective considerations of fact (pleasure, pain, happiness, and so forth), whereas Kantian ethical theory bases moral guidelines on objective considerations of reason. The theories diverge on the other ethical themes. Act utilitarianism focuses on consequences, whereas Kantian ethical theory concentrates on the reasoning that precedes the action. Act utilitarianism relates good and bad to specific actions, whereas Kantian ethical theory connects good and bad to following general rules without exceptions. Finally, act utilitarianism relates good and bad to the group, whereas Kantian ethical theory centers on the individual. Act utilitarianism does not have the problems Kantian ethical theory does, but as will be discussed in the next section, it has its own set of problems.

## Problems with Act Utilitarianism

Act utilitarianism does a reasonable job of satisfying the first three criteria for a successful ethical theory. It identifies the utilitarian principle as the basic ethical guideline and asserts that this guideline is better than others. This ethical guideline would prohibit the unlimited pursuit of self-interest. Although act utilitarianism satisfies the first three criteria for a successful ethical theory, it has difficulty with criterion four: the theory must produce effective solutions to ethical problems. I will discuss several of the problems connected to act utilitarianism and relate them to criterion four. The focus will then shift to John Stuart Mill's version of utilitarianism.

### Doing the Calculations

The first problem with act utilitarianism is the difficulty connected to doing the utilitarian calculations. If we cannot successfully complete the calculations, the theory cannot help us to effectively solve ethical problems. This problem with the calculations has three main aspects.

First, it is difficult to identify all the consequences of an action. An accurate utilitarian analysis must go beyond the immediate consequences and find all the results. This is a difficult undertaking. Short-range consequences can be difficult to identify, and long-range consequences are even harder to identify, especially when you are trying to predict them before the action has occurred. In the automobile example described earlier, we were looking back over time and therefore could identify the results with some accuracy. If we had to try to judge in advance whether the act was ethical, it would be much harder because we would have to predict future consequences. With accurate and extensive information, we can make reasonable predictions about the future, but such predictions are never guaranteed to be correct. In addition, how can we be sure we have extended our search for consequences far enough into the future? Assume that there is a great public outcry after the deaths and injuries related to not improving the safety of the automobile. The public begins to put pressure on legislators to improve automobile safety, and legislators apply pressure on the National Highway and Traffic Safety Administration (NHTSA). After a year of study, the NHTSA issues a regulation to prevent this kind of safety problem in the future. Is this a consequence of the decision of the managers not to improve the safety of their automobiles? If so, does it change our ethical evaluation of that case? This question would be difficult to answer in a satisfactory way. An ethical theory should help us to solve moral problems, but sometimes difficulties with doing the calculations will interfere with act utilitarianism accomplishing this objective.

The second aspect of the problem is that it is difficult to weigh pleasures and pains, happiness and unhappiness, or harms and benefits when they are very different kinds of things. Imagine that a NHTSA mandated safety feature for automobiles will save twenty lives a year but cost U.S. car buyers one hundred million dollars. How do we weigh twenty lives against one hundred million dollars? We place a high value on human life, but is it worth five million dollars to save a life? Perhaps we really cannot even make a reasonable judgment about this matter unless we know what would be done with the one hundred million dollars. If people will spend it to improve their lives, will they improve them sufficiently to balance the loss of twenty lives? Utilitarians depend on calculations, but the elements that must be weighed are sometimes impossible to compare. Once again, this factor will make it hard to solve some ethical problems.

The final aspect of the problem is less serious than the others and would not even occur if the act utilitarian primarily relied on the time-saving rules mentioned earlier. Without these rules, act utilitarians would have to spend a lot of their time identifying and weighing pleasures, pains, harms, and benefits. The utilitarian calculations might take up an enormous amount of our time, making solving ethical problems very time-consuming. This difficulty, coupled with the previous two aspects of the problem, suggests that act utilitarian theory will only be partially successful at meeting criterion four. In relatively simple and clear-cut cases, we will be able to do the calculations, but in other cases, we will encounter trouble.

### Results Contrary to Moral Intuitions

Another serious problem, also relating to criterion four, is that act utilitarianism produces a variety of results that are contrary to many people's moral intuitions. People normally think that stealing, cheating, breaking promises, and killing innocent people are all wrong. Act utilitarianism, however, would justify these actions in certain situations where performing them would produce more benefit than harm. This seems misguided to many people because they think these actions should always be unethical. An even more serious problem for many thinkers is that act utilitarianism focuses on the majority or group and is willing to sacrifice a minority if it would bring about the greatest good of the greatest number of people. This seems intuitively wrong to many people. Why should it be ethical to allow some people to be harmed or killed to benefit a greater number of other people? This practice would be particularly disturbing should you be a member of the minority that is being sacrificed. It might balance out if sometimes you were part of the majority and were benefited and at other times were part of the minority and were harmed. However, it is also possible that you might always end up in the minority; thus, you would always suffer harm to benefit the majority. It seems intuitively wrong that some minority should always be sacrificed for the good of the majority. To cite a complicated and controversial example, many people think the U.S. government was wrong to kill and seriously injure about two hundred thousand civilians at Hiroshima and Nagasaki to hasten the end of World War II and make an Allied invasion of Japan unnecessary. Most people would agree that it is ethical to kill combatants in a war (and it may even be fair or just to kill noncombatants, such as munitions factory workers, who are directly supporting the war effort), but it is unethical to kill noncombatants or civilians (who are not directly supporting the war effort). Many Japanese civilians in these cities, especially children and elderly people, had no role in supporting the war effort, and it was wrong to kill them. The critics of the U.S. action would argue that the bombs should have been dropped elsewhere or not at all. Thus, some thinkers believe utilitarianism is a poor moral theory, charging that it does not really treat persons as moral equals because it is willing to sacrifice some of them for the benefit of others. Because of these various results inconsistent with people's moral intuitions, some philosophers claim that act utilitarianism is not really helping us to solve ethical problems in an effective manner.

### Moral Luck

The final problem undercuts the ability of act utilitarianism to help us solve ethical problems. If good and evil depend on the consequences of an action, then the ability to perform good actions is not totally in the control of the moral agent. An element of luck enters the moral realm.[6] Imagine that I send a check to a charity but that the check is permanently lost in the mail. No beneficial consequences resulted from my action, and therefore the action was not good. In a sense, my bad luck prevented me from performing a good action. When I realize that the check has never been cashed, I can cancel it and send another one—but that is a different check and a different action. Many philosophers believe the ability to perform good actions should be completely in the control of the moral agent; they reject consequentialist theories for this reason. This problem relates to the fourth criterion for evaluating ethical theories. When I mailed my check, I thought I had solved my ethical problem. I had given money to charity and had done the ethical thing. It turns out that I had not really solved the problem in the way that I thought; I had not done anything ethical. Because consequences can never be guaranteed beforehand, utilitarian theory does not always help us to effectively solve ethical problems.

These problems with act utilitarianism have led many moral philosophers to reject this theory. However, many of them are not satisfied with Kantian ethics either. Some of these thinkers have turned to rule utilitarianism as a way to get the best of both act utilitarianism and Kantian ethics. Before rule utilitarianism is discussed, however, it is important to understand John Stuart Mill's version of utilitarianism and his ideas on the quality of pleasures and moral rules.

## Mill's Utilitarianism

John Stuart Mill starts off his moral theory in a way that is very similar to Bentham by claiming that an ultimate ethical principle could act as the foundation for moral guidelines. According to Mill:

> The creed which accepts as the foundation of morals "utility" or the "greatest happiness principle" holds that actions are right in proportion as they tend to promote happiness; wrong as they tend to produce the reverse of happiness. By happiness is intended pleasure and the absence of pain; by unhappiness, pain and the privation of pleasure.[7]

Thus, Mill's formulation of the utilitarian ethical standard is that *actions are good in proportion to which they tend to promote happiness and bad as they tend to produce unhappiness.* He has arrived at this position in the same basic way that it was speculated Bentham did. Mill argues that all action is undertaken for the sake of some end. Although there may be many intermediate ends for our actions, ultimately all action is designed to produce happiness or avoid unhappiness. Happiness is the only ultimate end and should be the foundation of moral goodness. For Mill, the source of moral goodness is not connected to what people ought to desire but simply to what they do desire. His justification comes from looking at what people do, and he claims that no other justification would be more convincing.

Mill claims that actions are right in proportion as they tend to promote happiness. Part of what he means is that the more happiness or the more unhappiness prevention associated with an action, the better it is. This idea of quantity of desirable ends was the only important one for Bentham. Mill, however, is equally concerned with the quality of the pleasure. He uses "pleasure" because he associates pleasure and the absence of pain with happiness. He says,

> If I am asked what I mean by difference of quality in pleasures, or what makes one pleasure more valuable than another, merely as a pleasure, except its being greater in amount, there is but one possible answer. Of two pleasures, if there be one to which all or almost all who have experience of both give a decided preference, irrespective of any feeling of moral obligation to prefer it, that is the more desirable pleasure. If one of the two is, by those who are competently acquainted with both, placed so far above the other that they prefer it, even though knowing it to be attended with a greater amount of discontent, and would not resign it for any quantity of the other pleasure which their nature is capable of, we are justified in ascribing to the preferred enjoyment a superiority in quality so far outweighing quantity as to render it, in comparison, of small account.[8]

Mill thinks we can use human preferences to distinguish the quality of pleasures.[9] Those that are preferred are higher in quality than those that are not, and presumably the quality increases with the intensity of the preference. He also seems to claim that the quality of a pleasure is more important than its quantity. Thus, actions are good in proportion as they tend to promote pleasures of greater quantity and especially greater quality. If quantity and quality were to come in conflict, we should presumably choose quality.

Mill used this notion of quality to refute critics of Bentham's utilitarianism who had called it a philosophy suitable for pigs. Bentham's idea was that whatever produced pleasure was good. Thus, if eating chocolate or watching situation comedies on television gave more pleasure than reading Shakespeare or listening to Mozart, then it is better for you to eat chocolate or watch television. Mill thought this was mistaken. Those who had the experience of both under the right conditions would prefer the higher pleasure. He concludes, "Now it is an unquestionable fact that those who are equally acquainted with and equally capable of appreciating and enjoying both do give a marked preference to the manner of existence that employs their higher faculties."[10] Mill understands that there will be objections to this. What about people who prefer lower pleasures? Mill responds that we all have a capacity to enjoy higher things but that this capacity is easily destroyed by hostile influences, or by lack of time and opportunity. Simply because some people prefer lower pleasures does not prove that higher and lower pleasures have equal value.

Like Bentham, Mill argues that his position is not a form of egoism. The utilitarian standard seeks to promote the greatest net happiness for the greatest number of people, or as he remarks about the utilitarian ethical standard, "for that standard is not the agent's own happiness, but the greatest happiness altogether."[11] The ethical goal, therefore, is a life rich in pleasure or happiness both in point of quantity and quality for the greatest number of people. This view requires the agent to count his or her happiness no more than any other person's. Mill comments, "As between his own happiness and that of others, utilitarianism requires him to be as strictly impartial as a disinterested and benevolent spectator."[12] An ethical person should strive to maximize the happiness of the greatest number of persons, not simply his or her personal happiness.

In summary, Mill's view is that actions are good in proportion to the extent to which they tend to produce more happiness than unhappiness for the persons affected. Actions are bad in proportion to which they tend to produce more unhappiness than happiness for the persons affected. We should evaluate our conduct using considerations of the quality and the quantity of happiness/pleasure and unhappiness/pain produced. The test of quality and the way to measure it will be the preferences of those who have experienced the actions in question and are best able to make an informed comparison.

## Mill and Moral Rules

Moral rules play a much larger role in Mill's moral theory than in Bentham's. One of the contexts in which he discusses rules is in his response to the objection that utilitarianism will be too time-consuming because it will force us to evaluate every individual action. Mill points out that the history of the human species has provided us with a great deal of information about actions. People have learned about the tendencies of actions to produce happiness and unhappiness, and morality is based on this knowledge. Thus, human experience has produced moral rules that correspond to the tendencies of actions to promote happiness or unhappiness. For example, persons have realized that killing innocent people produces more unhappiness than happiness and that keeping promises is more beneficial than breaking them. Thus, we conclude that "killing innocent people is wrong" and "keeping promises is good." Mill refers to these as secondary principles or secondary moral rules. The primary moral rule is, of course, the utilitarian ethical standard. He adds, "Whatever we adopt as the fundamental principle of morality, we require subordinate principles to apply it by."[13] In his opinion, it is impossible to do without these secondary principles. He comments, "There is no case of moral obligation in which some secondary principle is not involved."[14] In light of these comments, Mill's view of moral life seems different from Bentham's. Bentham is more focused on evaluating individual actions, whereas Mill endorses following these secondary principles.

Mill realizes that secondary principles can conflict. For example, we usually agree that lying is wrong and that hurting people's feelings is wrong also. There may be times, however, when telling someone the truth might hurt the person's feelings. How do we resolve these conflicts? Mill answers that we can resolve them using the utilitarian ethical standard: "If utility is the ultimate source of moral obligations, utility may be invoked to decide between them when their demands are incompatible."[15] In fact, in the same paragraph Mill adds that it is only in cases of conflict between secondary principles that the primary moral rule needs to be invoked. Therefore, Mill believes he has avoided the Kantian problem with conflicting moral rules.

The vital issue is whether people are morally justified in making exceptions to these secondary principles. Kant's position was that no exceptions could be made to moral laws. Mill clearly appears to favor exceptions to moral rules when he states, "It is not the fault of any creed, but of the complicated nature of human affairs, that rules of conduct cannot be so framed as to require no exceptions, and that hardly any kind of action can safely be laid down as either always obligatory or always condemnable."[16] Thus, Mill seems to believe exceptions to these secondary principles are justified in some cases. A particular lie or breaking a promise might be morally justified if it maximized happiness in a significant way. Thus, exceptions to the secondary moral principles would be allowed if the exceptions are in accord with the basic utilitarian standard or principle. Of course, no exceptions to the basic utilitarian principle would be allowed. Although Mill's theory is more focused on rules than Bentham's, Mill seems willing to allow legitimate exceptions to those rules.

## Mill's Idea of Justice

Mill's discussion of justice in the last chapter of *Utilitarianism* contains a number of important additional considerations about moral rules. Here Mill introduces the idea of rights, which will be vital in Chapter 7 for the discussion of moral rights theory. Mill states:

> Justice is the name for certain classes of moral rules which concern the essentials of human well-being more nearly, and are therefore of more absolute obligation, than any other rules for the guidance of life; and the notion which we have found to be of the essence of the idea of justice—that of a right residing in an individual—implies and testifies to this more binding obligation.[17]

Thus, one kind or class of moral rules is designated by the term "justice." These moral rules take the form of rights. Rights reside in persons and can be violated by the actions of others. Mill explains rights as follows, "When we call anything a person's right, we mean that he has a valid claim on society to protect him in possession of it, either by force of law or by that of education and opinion. If he has what we consider a sufficient claim, on whatever account, to have something guaranteed to him by society, we say that he has a right to it."[18] To have a right is to have something that society ought to defend.

Mill tries to differentiate the moral rules related to justice from moral rules or secondary principles in general. Both kinds of rules relate to duty, but philosophers speak of two kinds of duties. *Duties of imperfect obligation* are those in which, although the actions are obligatory, the particular occasions on which we perform them are left up to us. These are general moral rules, not examples of justice as Mill is using the term. For example, Mill thinks charity is obligatory but that we are not obligated to be charitable to any particular person at any particular time. The charitable actions we perform and when we perform them are up to us. *Duties of perfect obligation* are duties related to the rights of others and are examples of justice. If a person has a certain right, then I have a duty to respect that right. This is not a duty that allows me to choose the person, time, and place to fulfill it. I must always respect the rights of this particular person. This strong position on respecting the rights of others makes Mill look less like an act utilitarian. He is not clear, however, about whether there can be legitimate exceptions to respecting the rights of others.

Mill believes moral rights or the rules of justice are common to all human beings or moral agents; they are universal. Why should a society acknowledge and defend these supposed universal rights? Mill answers that it should do so because they promote general utility. People should realize that our security and happiness are linked to the security and happiness of other members of our society. Only a system of rights can maximize overall happiness.

At this point, it is clear that Mill thought that moral rules played a crucial role in ethics. Some philosophers believe Mill should be designated a "rule utilitarian." In a subsequent section, the rule utilitarian moral theory will be discussed. Mill, of course, did not use the phrase "rule utilitarianism" and for the purpose of this text, it is not important whether he should or should not be included under this heading. The important point is that rule utilitarianism provides an interesting alternative to act utilitarianism and Kantian ethics. Before looking at this theory, however, two problems with Mill's view ought to be mentioned.

## Two Problems with Mill's Version of Utilitarianism

There are a number of problems with Mill's version of utilitarianism. I will discuss two of them here because they were not included in the earlier section on act utilitarian problems. The first problem involves the procedure for determining good and evil in relation to the quality of pleasures. Mill thinks we can use human preferences to determine quality and, hence, good and evil. He thinks these preferences are consistent and reliable, but in some areas that view is mistaken. Human preferences are notoriously changeable. Sometimes a person prefers watching game shows on television, at other times reading a good book. People sometimes prefer the feeling of satisfaction and the knowledge that they have helped people that comes from giving to charity, and at other times they prefer the satisfaction and pleasure derived from buying luxuries for themselves or their families. Mill thinks people who have had the experience of both higher and lower pleasures will prefer the higher ones, but a more accurate appraisal is that they will sometimes prefer higher ones and at other times lower ones. People are not always constant in their preferences.

The second aspect of the first problem connected to preferences is also related to the idea that people who have been exposed to both higher and lower pleasures will prefer the higher ones. Again, this is simply not true. As evidenced by how they spend their evenings, most Americans seem to prefer television game shows or situation comedies to reading Shakespeare or listening to Mozart. Mill tries to explain this by saying that we all have a capacity to enjoy higher things but that this capacity is easily destroyed by hostile influences or by lack of time and opportunity. This is an inadequate explanation. There is no great hostility directed toward Shakespeare or Mozart, and if people have the time for television game shows or situation comedies, they have the time for higher entertainment. When the movie *Amadeus* became a hit, there was increased interest in Mozart, but this interest waned as people returned to other entertainment. A number of years ago, another popular movie, *Shakespeare in Love,* generated a lot of good publicity for the famous playwright, but the sympathetic atmosphere does not seem to have produced a greater interest in reading his plays instead of watching television. Many people who have been exposed to both simply prefer the "lower pleasures."

The third aspect of the first problem related to preferences is that it is difficult to weigh competing preferences, especially when they are very different kinds of things. This makes it difficult to know what actions are most ethical. Presumably, Mill expects us to choose between actions that satisfy competing preferences by picking the one that informed people would most prefer. How does this work in a real moral dilemma? How do you make decisions about issues like euthanasia, abortion, and gun control, or about less dramatic ones such as lying, breaking promises, and giving to charity? These things involve a wide variety of competing preferences that are sometimes very different. With regard to gun control, how do we weigh the preferences of gun owners to own guns for protection and recreation against the preferences of other people who would feel safer in a society with fewer guns? Mill gives no practical advice about how to weigh them. The general problem is that it is not clear that preferences can be used to create an effective ethical theory along the lines that Mill suggests.

The second problem is that Mill (and Bentham) cannot provide a convincing justification for why rational, self-interested persons will be motivated to substitute the greatest happiness of the majority for their own greatest happiness as their primary motivation. In other words, why will they choose to be utilitarians instead of ethical egoists? People are not merely factors in utilitarian calculations; they are autonomous, rational, self-interested beings. They usually act in their own self-interest. They may at times make sacrifices for those with whom they have close relationships, such as family members and friends. Why, however, would they sacrifice for the general well-being? We might argue that increasing the general well-being will ultimately increase personal well-being, but this is not Mill's program. Moral agents are to be motivated by the general welfare, not their personal welfare. As a practical matter, it is also probable that the best way for me to increase my personal well-being is to act so as to benefit myself directly, not to act to increase the general well-being and hope that some benefit will eventually trickle down to me. Therefore, Mill has a serious problem related to whether or not people will be motivated to act as utilitarians would have them act.

## Rule Utilitarianism

When moral philosophers understand the problems associated with act utilitarianism, some of them turn to a different form of utilitarianism, called rule utilitarianism. Rule utilitarianism does not solve all the problems with act utilitarianism, but it does seem to solve the problems of results contrary to moral intuitions and moral luck. Rule utilitarianism is also a consequentialist ethical theory, but it examines the consequences of generally following moral rules rather than focusing on the consequences of specific actions. The ethical standard for rule utilitarianism might be phrased: *It is good for persons to act from those moral rules, the general following of which would promote the greatest net benefit for the morally significant beings affected; it is bad for persons to act from rules, the general following of which would promote the greatest net harm for the morally significant beings affected.* Based on this standard, an action will be good if it follows from a legitimate moral rule that meets this standard.

Like Kantians, rule utilitarians claim that we can identify a rule to guide any morally significant action. Suppose I send some money to a charity because I believe everyone ought to help those who are less fortunate. The complete description of the action ought to include identification of the rule that guided it. For example, I performed the action—giving this money to this charity—because I thought I should act in accord with my rule: Everyone ought to help those who are less fortunate. The action will be ethical if it follows from the right kind of rule, one whose general following would maximize net benefit for those affected by the persons following it. If the general following of the rule "Everyone ought to help those who are less fortunate" would produce more net benefit than harm for those affected by persons following it, then it is a legitimate moral rule, and we should follow it if we want to be ethical. Thus, rule utilitarianism has two aspects: (1) we should determine the legitimate moral rules that maximize net benefit for those affected by the general following of them and follow these moral rules without exceptions, and (2) if contemplating whether or not to perform an action, we should do so only if it would follow from a legitimate moral rule.

Rule utilitarians must follow legitimate moral rules without exceptions or they would become act utilitarians. An exception would be a particular case where breaking the rule would maximize net benefit in that specific case. Rule utilitarians would not do this because they do not examine the consequences in particular cases. If they examined particular cases and broke their rules in every case where violating the rule would maximize net benefit, they would be no different from act utilitarians and would not be able to avoid the problems specific to act utilitarianism. Rule utilitarians do acknowledge that situations may change. When they do, new rules may be needed because following them will produce more net human benefit than following the old rules. For example, perhaps at one time the general following of the rule "It is unethical to get a divorce" maximized human benefit. If conditions become easier for divorced people (especially single parents), then a new moral rule may be necessary. The inability to make exceptions to moral rules is an essential difference between rule and act utilitarianism. As was mentioned earlier, act utilitarians can use moral rules as timesaving devices, but they must always consider the possibility that an exception will maximize net benefit.

Rule utilitarianism solves the problem with results contrary to moral intuitions because it makes cheating, stealing, and possibly even killing civilians unethical. For example, the general following of the rule "It is unethical to cheat on tests" would produce more net benefit than harm for those affected. If everyone cheats on tests, there will be an enormous amount of harm. Tests will become meaningless, and educators will lose this valuable tool for assessing students. Therefore, the rule is a legitimate moral rule, and we should follow it without exceptions. Cheating is always unethical to a rule utilitarian. Rule utilitarians do not seem to get results contrary to people's moral intuitions.

Rule utilitarianism also greatly diminishes the problem with moral luck. Luck is less of a factor in the consequences of the general following of moral rules than in specific cases. Even though my check to a charity may not get there, and hence sending the check does not produce any beneficial consequences, in general checks usually get to charities. Even with occasional bad luck, the moral rule that "It is ethical for affluent people to help those in need" would maximize net benefit and should always be followed.

Rule utilitarianism will not alleviate the first two aspects of the problem connected to difficulties with doing the calculations. In general, it will be just as difficult to identify and weigh all the consequences connected to the general following of a moral rule as it is to distinguish those resulting from a specific action. Sometimes, determining the consequences for rules may be easier than doing so for specific actions and sometimes harder. For example, it is impossible to know all the consequences of the general following of the rule "It is unethical to ever kill civilians in wartime"; we could only guess whether or not this would produce a net benefit. If it is impossible to calculate all of the consequences of some potential moral rules, then rule utilitarianism can have only limited success in helping us solve moral problems. We would not be able to determine the complete set of legitimate moral rules, but we would be able to sufficiently identify the consequences of some moral rules and evaluate them. Thus, there will be some moral rules for rule utilitarianism to use. Rule utilitarianism also does not alleviate the problem of weighing very different kinds of consequences, such as large sums of money against lives. On this issue, both versions of utilitarianism are equally problematic.

Neither will rule utilitarianism solve the two problems discussed in connection with Mill's ideas. It will not make the attempt to evaluate the quality of pleasures using human preferences any easier. It will also not make it more likely that people will be motivated by the happiness of the greatest number of persons instead of their own personal happiness. Act and rule utilitarianism face these problems equally.

Rule utilitarianism is an improvement over act utilitarianism in a couple of areas, but it is no more successful than act utilitarianism in regard to the other problems. Before we conclude that rule utilitarianism is the best version of utilitarianism, however, we must address a serious criticism act utilitarians bring against rule utilitarianism. If we are really interested in maximizing net happiness or benefit, act utilitarians claim that we would be foolish not to make an exception to a rule when that exception would maximize benefit in a specific case and have no wider implications. They consider rule utilitarians unwise for blindly following moral rules and for never being willing to consider even the most beneficial exceptions. To balance out the problems with injustice and moral luck, act utilitarians contend that their version of utilitarianism will actually produce more net benefit and less net harm.

## Conclusion

In regard to the criteria for evaluating ethical theories, act and rule utilitarianism are only partially successful ethical theories. Both theories do produce a basic ethical guideline and secondary moral guidelines. Both argue that these ethical guidelines are better than others, and both produce ethical guidelines that would prohibit the unlimited pursuit of self-interest. However, both theories encounter problems related to criterion four—that the theory must assist us in solving moral problems successfully. Act utilitarianism is faced with the problems related to results contrary to moral intuitions and moral luck. Rule utilitarianism will be charged with not really maximizing overall benefit. Both theories have problems actually doing the calculations necessary to determine good and bad. Therefore, both ethical theories will only have limited success in helping us solve ethical problems effectively. Both will probably only help us solve ethical problems in relatively simple cases.

Is either act or rule utilitarianism an improvement over Kantian ethics and the four earlier approaches to ethics? These theories do seem better than the first four approaches, but it is not clear that they are superior to Kantian ethics. Both utilitarianism and Kantian ethics satisfied the first three criteria but were unable to completely satisfy the fourth one. Therefore, we should lay them aside for the time being and turn elsewhere to see what other approaches to ethics are available.

In this chapter I briefly discussed the idea of moral rights. Some philosophers believe we can create an ethical theory based on moral rights that would do what rule utilitarianism failed to do—successfully combine the best features of Kantian ethics and act utilitarianism. In Chapter 7 I discuss moral rights theory, which some philosophers think is an improvement over both Kantian ethical theory and utilitarianism.

## QUESTIONS FOR REVIEW

*Here are some questions to help you review the main concepts in this chapter.*

1. What is the ethical insight related to utilitarianism?

2. What is a crucial difference between act utilitarianism and ethical egoism?

3. What is Bentham's version of the essential principle or standard of act utilitarianism?

4. According to Bentham, what criterion should we use to determine morally significant beings?

5. What were the six most significant benefits and harms in the automobile safety case? If these were the only consequences, what ethical conclusion would you reach about the decision not to upgrade the safety of the fuel tank?

6. Discuss one justification for the utilitarian ethical standard and the related strength of the act utilitarian theory.

7. How do act utilitarians divide morally significant actions from ones that are not morally significant?

8. What position does act utilitarianism take on each of the three traditional ethical assumptions?

9. What views does act utilitarianism endorse on each of the four ethical themes?

10. Identify one similarity and two differences between act utilitarianism and Kantian ethical theory.

11. What do you think is the most significant problem with act utilitarianism? Why is act utilitarianism only a partially successful ethical theory?

12. Identify two differences between Mill's and Bentham's versions of utilitarianism. Which do you prefer? Explain why.

13. Discuss one of the additional problems with utilitarianism identified in relation to Mill's version of utilitarianism.

14. What is the ethical standard for rule utilitarianism?

15. What problems do act and rule utilitarianism share? Why does rule utilitarianism not suffer from the problems of results contrary to moral intuitions and moral luck?

16. In your opinion, which form of utilitarianism is more effective at helping us solve moral problems? Support your answer.

## NOTES

1. The most common source for Bentham's ideas about ethics is *An Introduction to the Principles of Morals and Legislation* (New York: Hafner Publishing Company, 1948). For Mill, the usual source is John Stuart Mill, *Utilitarianism* (Indianapolis, IN: Hackett Publishing Company, 1979).

2. Jeremy Bentham, *An Introduction to the Principles of Morals and Legislation*, p. 2.

3. I favor formulation of the utilitarian rule in terms of "benefit" rather than "pleasure" or "happiness" because these latter terms can lead people astray. In the ordinary sense of "pleasure" and "happiness," some things may not be pleasant or make us happy, but they may still be good. For example, learning is not always pleasant, nor does it always produce happiness, especially when we have to work very hard to acquire the knowledge. Learning, however, is often beneficial or good even if it is not pleasant. Another consideration is that some people reject the idea that pleasure is good. People sometimes pursue pleasure early in life, but then tire of it. They may then seek success, fame, or power. They may choose to serve others or to serve God in a life of self-sacrifice. They may seek knowledge or enlightenment. Ultimately, they follow the path that seems most beneficial. A key idea for act utilitarianism is that it is good to do things that make morally significant beings better off and bad to do things that make them worse off. In my opinion, "benefit" and "harm" articulate this utilitarian idea better than "pleasure" and "happiness." My version of the utilitarian principle is: What is good is what produces more benefit than harm for the morally significant beings affected; what is bad is what produces more harm than benefit for the morally significant beings affected.

4. Peter Singer, *Practical Ethics* (Cambridge, MA: Cambridge University Press, 1993), p. 57.

5. Ibid., p. 131.

6. See Bernard Williams, "Moral Luck," in *Moral Luck: Philosophical Papers, 1973–1980* (Cambridge, MA: Cambridge University Press, 1981).

7. Mill, *Utilitarianism*, p. 7.

8. Ibid., p. 8.

9. This idea of preferences has been used by some contemporary philosophers as a substitute for pleasure, happiness, or benefit. They claim that good actions provide the greatest net satisfaction of the rational preferences of persons. Sometimes the term "interests" is substituted for "preferences." Most philosophers believe this substitution is not an overall improvement. It improves some aspects while making others worse.

10. Mill, *Utilitarianism,* p. 9.
11. Ibid., p. 11.
12. Ibid., p. 16.
13. Ibid., p. 24.
14. Ibid., p. 25.
15. Ibid.
16. Ibid.
17. Ibid., p. 58.
18. Ibid., p. 52.

# Utilitarianism

John Stuart Mill

John Stuart Mill was born in London in 1806. He was educated personally by his father, the Scottish economist and philosopher James Mill, who put him through a rigorous program of study from his earliest years. Mill was reading Greek at age three and Latin at age eight. As a boy he read works of many classical authors in the original language, including works by Plato and Aristotle. When he was thirteen, he began studying the economic theories of Adam Smith and David Ricardo. The following year he traveled to France and spent a year with the family of Samuel Bentham (brother of the English jurist and philosopher Jeremy Bentham). After returning to England, he began to study Roman law, with a view to possibly becoming a lawyer. But in 1823, when he was seventeen, he took a job at the British East India Company, where he was employed for the next thirty-five years. Mill was elected to Parliament in 1865, but failed to gain reelection in 1868. After his defeat he retired to Avignon, France, where he died in 1873.

Mill's major writings include *A System of Logic* (1843), *Principles of Political Economy* (1848), *On Liberty* (1859), *Utilitarianism* (published serially in *Fraser's Magazine* in 1861, separately in 1863), and *The Subjection of Women* (written in 1861, published in 1869).

Our reading is from *Utilitarianism,* the work that has become the most popular and influential treatment of utilitarianism. Utilitarianism is the moral theory that was first set forth by Jeremy Bentham. It claims that the morality of an action is determined by how well it promotes "utility," which is defined as the greatest good for the greatest number. Utilitarians differ, however, on how to define "good" and whom to include in the "greatest number."

According to Mill, "good" means happiness, and happiness means pleasure and the absence of pain; the "greatest number" includes not only human beings but all creatures capable of feeling pleasure and pain. Mill's version of utilitarianism, therefore, claims that the moral thing to do in any situation is the action that causes the greatest sum total of pleasure for all the sentient beings involved. Mill typically says that utility is to be determined wholly on the basis of the *individual action,* but at times he seems to endorse the view that one should always follow the *rule* (for example, "Don't kill innocent people") that, when universally followed, would promote the greatest utility—even if, in a particular situation, following the rule would not do so. Philosophers have come to call these two versions of utilitarianism, respectively, *act utilitarianism* and *rule utilitarianism.*

In our selection from Chapter II, "What Utilitarianism Is," Mill briefly describes his theory and then defends it against several objections. In the selection from Chapter IV, "Of What Sort of Proof the Principle of Utility Is Susceptible," he explains in what sense one can prove that the happiness (pleasure) of the individual and the group are desirable and are the only things desirable.

### Chapter II: What Utilitarianism Is

. . . The creed which accepts as the foundation of morals, utility, or the greatest happiness principle, holds that actions are right in proportion as they tend to promote happiness, wrong as they tend to produce the reverse of happiness. By happiness is intended pleasure and the absence of pain; by unhappiness, pain and the privation of pleasure. To give a clear view of the moral standard set up by the theory, much more requires to be said; in particular, what things it includes in the ideas of pain and pleasure; and to what extent this is left an open question. But these supplementary explanations do not affect the theory of life on which this theory of morality is grounded—namely, that pleasure and freedom from pain are the only things desirable as ends; and that all desirable things (which are as numerous in the utilitarian as in any other scheme) are desirable either for the pleasure inherent in themselves, or as means to the promotion of pleasure and the prevention of pain.

Now such a theory of life excites in many minds, and among them in some of the most estimable in feeling and purpose, inveterate dislike. To suppose that life has (as they express it) no higher end than pleasure—no better and nobler object of desire and pursuit—they designate as utterly mean and grovelling; as a doctrine worthy only of swine, to whom the followers of Epicurus[1] were, at a very early period, contemptuously likened; and modern holders of the doctrine are occasionally made the subject of equally polite comparisons by its German, French, and English assailants.

When thus attacked, the Epicureans have always answered that it is not they, but their accusers, who represent human nature in a degrading light; since the accusation supposes human beings to be capable of no pleasures except those of which swine are capable. If this supposition were true, the charge could not be gainsaid, but would then be no longer an imputation; for if the sources of pleasure were precisely the same to human beings and to swine, the rule of life which is good enough for the one would be good enough for the other. The comparison of the Epicurean life to that of beasts is felt as degrading, precisely because a beast's pleasures do not satisfy a human being's conceptions of happiness. Human beings have faculties more elevated than the animal appetites, and when once made conscious of them, do not regard anything as happiness which does not include their gratification. I do not, indeed, consider the Epicureans to have been by any means faultless in drawing out their scheme of consequences from the utilitarian principle. To do this in any sufficient manner, many Stoic,[2] as well as Christian elements require to be included. But there is no known Epicurean theory of life which does not assign to the pleasures of the intellect, of the feelings and imagination, and of the moral sentiments, a much higher value as pleasures than to those of mere sensation. It must be admitted, however, that utilitarian writers in general have placed the superiority of mental over bodily pleasures chiefly in the greater permanency, safety, uncostliness, etc., of the former—that is, in their circumstantial advantages rather than in their intrinsic nature.[3] And on all these points utilitarians have fully proved their case; but they might have taken the other, and, as it may be called, higher ground, with entire consistency. It is quite compatible with the principle of utility to recognise the fact, that some *kinds* of pleasure are more desirable and more valuable than others. It would be absurd that while, in estimating all other things, quality is considered as well as quantity, the estimation of pleasures should be supposed to depend on quantity alone.

If I am asked what I mean by difference of quality in pleasures, or what makes one pleasure more valuable than another, merely as a pleasure, except its being greater in amount, there is but one possible answer. Of two pleasures, if there be one to which all or almost all who have experience of both give a decided preference, irrespective of any feeling of moral obligation to prefer it, that is the more desirable pleasure. If one of the two is, by those who are competently acquainted with both, placed so far above the other that they prefer it, even though knowing it to be attended with a greater amount of discontent, and would not resign it for any quantity of the other pleasure which their nature is capable of, we are justified in ascribing to the preferred enjoyment a superiority in quality, so far outweighing quantity as to render it, in comparison, of small account.

Now it is an unquestionable fact that those who are equally acquainted with, and equally capable of appreciating and enjoying, both, do give a most marked preference to the manner of existence which employs their higher faculties. Few human creatures would consent to be changed into any of the lower animals, for a promise of the fullest allowance of a beast's pleasures; no intelligent human being would consent to be a fool, no instructed person would be an ignoramus, no person of feeling and conscience would be selfish and base, even though they should be persuaded that the fool, the dunce, or the rascal is better satisfied with his lot than they are with theirs. They would not resign what they possess more than he for the most complete satisfaction of all the desires which they have in common with him. If they ever fancy they would, it is only in cases of unhappiness so extreme that to escape from it they would exchange their lot for almost any other, however undesirable in their own eyes. A being of higher faculties requires more to make him happy, is capable probably of more acute suffering, and is certainly accessible to it at more points, than one of an inferior type; but in spite of these liabilities, he can never really wish to sink into what he feels to be a lower grade of existence. We may give what explanation we please of this unwillingness; we may attribute it to pride, a name which is given indiscriminately to some of the most and to some of the least estimable feelings of which mankind are capable; we may refer it to the love of liberty and personal independence, an appeal to which was with the Stoics one of the most effective means for the inculcation of it; to the love of power, or to the love of excitement, both of which do really enter into and contribute to it. But its most appropriate appellation is a sense of dignity, which all human beings possess in one form or other and in some, though by no means in exact, proportion to their higher faculties; and which is so essential a part of the happiness of those in whom it is strong, that nothing which conflicts with it could be, otherwise than momentarily, an object of desire to them. Whoever supposes that this preference takes place at a sacrifice of happiness—that the superior being, in anything like equal circumstances, is not happier than the inferior—confounds the two very different ideas of happiness and content. It is indisputable that the being whose capacities of enjoyment are low has the greatest chance of having them fully satisfied; and a highly-endowed being will always feel that any happiness which he can look for, as the world is constituted, is imperfect. But he can learn to bear its imperfections, if they are at all bearable; and they will not make him envy the being who is indeed unconscious of the imperfections, but only because he feels not at all the good which those imperfections qualify. It is better to be a human being dissatisfied than a pig satisfied; better to be Socrates dissatisfied than a fool satisfied. And if the fool or the pig is of a different opinion, it is because they only know their own side of the question. The other party to the comparison knows both sides. . . .

I have dwelt on this point, as being a necessary part of a perfectly just conception of utility or happiness, considered as the directive rule of human conduct. But it is by no means an indispensable condition to the acceptance of the utilitarian standard; for that standard is not the agent's own greatest happiness, but the greatest amount of happiness altogether; and if it may possibly be doubted whether a noble character is always the happier for its nobleness, there can be no doubt that it makes other people happier and that the world in general is immensely a gainer by it. Utilitarianism, therefore, could only attain its end by the general cultivation of nobleness of character, even if each individual were only benefited by the nobleness of others, and his own, so far as happiness is concerned, were a sheer deduction from the benefit. But the bare enunciation of such an absurdity as this last, renders refutation superfluous.

According to the greatest happiness principle, as above explained, the ultimate end, with reference to and for the sake of which all other things are desirable (whether we are considering our own good or that of other people), is an existence exempt as far as possible from pain, and as rich as possible in enjoyments, both in point of quantity and quality; the test of quality, and the rule for measuring it against quantity, being the preference felt by those who, in their opportunities of experience, to which must be added their habits of self-consciousness and self-observation, are best furnished with the means of comparison. This, being according to the utilitarian opinion the end of human action, is necessarily also the standard of morality; which may accordingly be defined [as] the rules and precepts for human conduct, by the observance of which an existence such as has been described might be, to the greatest extent possible, secured to all mankind; and not to them only, but, so far as the nature of things admits, to the whole sentient creation. . . .

I must again repeat what the assailants of utilitarianism seldom have the justice to acknowledge, that the happiness which forms the utilitarian standard of what is right in conduct, is not the agent's own happiness, but that of all concerned. As between his own happiness and that of others, utilitarianism requires him to be as strictly impartial as a disinterested and benevolent spectator. In the golden rule of Jesus of Nazareth, we read the complete spirit of the ethics of utility. To do as one would be done by,[4] and to love one's neighbour as oneself,[5] constitute the ideal perfection of utilitarian morality. As the means of making the nearest approach to this ideal, utility would enjoin, first, that laws and social arrangements should place the happiness, or (as speaking practically it may be called) the interest, of every individual, as nearly as possible in harmony with the interest of the whole; and secondly, that education and opinion, which have so vast a power over human character, should so use that power as to establish in the mind of every individual an indissoluble association between his own happiness and the good of the whole; especially between his own happiness and the practice of such modes of conduct, negative and positive, as regard for the universal happiness prescribes: so that not only he may be unable to conceive the possibility of happiness to himself consistently with conduct opposed to the general good, but also that a direct impulse to promote the general good may be in every individual one of the habitual motives of action, and the sentiments connected therewith may fill a large and prominent place in every human being's sentient existence. If the impugners of the utilitarian morality represented it to their own minds in this its true character, I know not what recommendation possessed by any other morality they could possibly affirm to be wanting to it; what more beautiful or more exalted developments of human nature any other ethical system can be supposed to foster, or what springs of action, not accessible to the utilitarian, such systems rely on for giving effect to their mandates.

The objectors to utilitarianism cannot always be charged with representing it in a discreditable light. On the contrary, those among them who entertain anything like a just idea of its disinterested character sometimes find fault with its standard as being too high for humanity. They say it is exacting too much to require that people shall always act from the inducement of promoting the general interests of society. But this is to mistake the very meaning of a standard of morals and to confound the rule of action with the motive of it. It is the business of ethics to tell us what are our duties, or by what test we may know them; but no system of ethics requires that the sole motive of all we do shall be a feeling of duty; on the contrary, ninety-nine hundredths of all our actions are done from other motives, and rightly so done, if the rule of duty does not condemn them. It is the more unjust to utilitarianism that this particular misapprehension should be made a ground of objection to it, inasmuch as utilitarian moralists have gone beyond almost all others in affirming that the motive has nothing to do with the morality of the action, though much with the worth of the agent. He who saves a fellow creature from drowning does what is morally right, whether his motive be duty, or the hope of being paid for his trouble; he who betrays the friend that trusts him, is guilty of a crime, even if his object be to serve another friend to whom he is under greater obligations.

But to speak only of actions done from the motive of duty and in direct obedience to principle: it is a misapprehension of the utilitarian mode of thought, to conceive it as implying that people should fix their minds upon so wide a generality as the world, or society at large. The great majority of good actions are intended, not for the benefit of the world, but for that of individuals, of which the good of the world is made up; and the thoughts of the most virtuous man need not on these occasions travel beyond the particular persons concerned, except so far as is necessary to assure himself that in benefiting them he is not violating the rights—that is, the legitimate and authorized expectations—of anyone else. The multiplication of happiness is, according to the utilitarian ethics, the object of virtue: the occasions on which any person (except one in a thousand) has it in his power to do this on an extended scale, in other words, to be a public benefactor, are but exceptional; and on these occasions alone is he called on to consider public utility; in every other case, private utility, the interest or happiness of some few persons, is all he has to attend to. Those alone the influence of whose actions extends to society in general, need concern themselves habitually about so large an object. In the case of abstinences indeed—of things which people forbear to do, from moral considerations, though the consequences in the particular case might be beneficial—it would be unworthy of an intelligent agent not to be consciously aware that the action is of a class which, if practised generally, would be generally injurious, and that this is the ground of the obligation to abstain from it. The amount of regard for the public interest implied in this recognition is no greater than is demanded by every system of morals, for they all enjoin to abstain from whatever is manifestly pernicious to society. . . .

We not uncommonly hear the doctrine of utility inveighed against as a *godless* doctrine. If it be necessary to say anything at all against so mere an assumption, we may say that the question depends upon what idea we have formed of the moral character of the Deity. If it be a true belief that God desires, above all things, the happiness of his creatures, and that this was his purpose in their creation, utility is not only not a godless doctrine, but more profoundly religious than any other. If it be meant that utilitarianism does not recognise the revealed will of God as the supreme law of morals, I answer that a utilitarian who believes in the perfect goodness and wisdom of God necessarily believes that whatever God has thought fit to reveal on the subject of morals, must fulfil the requirements of utility in a supreme degree. . . .

Again, defenders of utility often find themselves called upon to reply to such objections as this—that there is not time, previous to action, for calculating and weighing the effects of any line of conduct on the general happiness. This is exactly as if anyone were to say that it is impossible to guide our conduct by Christianity because there is not time, on every occasion on which anything has to be done, to read through the Old and New Testaments. The answer to the objection is that there has been ample time, namely, the whole past duration of the human species. During all that time mankind have been learning by experience the tendencies of actions, on which experience all the prudence, as well as all the morality of life, is dependent. People talk as if the commencement of this course of experience had hitherto been put off, and as if, at the moment when some man feels tempted to meddle with the property or life of another, he had to begin considering for the first time whether murder and theft are injurious to human happiness. Even then I do not think that he would find the question very puzzling; but, at all events, the matter is now done to his hand. It is truly a whimsical supposition that if mankind were agreed to considering utility to be the test of morality, they would remain without any agreement as to what is useful, and would take no measures for having their notions on the subject taught to the young and enforced by law and opinion. There is no difficulty in proving any ethical standard whatever to work ill, if we suppose universal idiocy to be conjoined with it; but on any hypothesis short of that, mankind must by this time have acquired positive beliefs as to the effects of some actions on their happiness; and [the] beliefs which have thus come down are the rules of morality for the multitude, and for the philosopher until he has succeeded in finding better. . . .

**Chapter IV: Of What Sort of Proof the Principle of Utility Is Susceptible**

. . . Questions of ultimate ends do not admit of proof, in the ordinary acceptation of the term. To be incapable of proof by reasoning is common to all first principles; to the first premises of our knowledge, as well as to those of our conduct. But the former, being matters of fact, may be the subject of a direct appeal to the faculties which judge of fact—namely, our senses and our internal consciousness. Can an appeal be made to the same faculties on questions of practical ends? Or by what other faculty is cognizance taken of them?

Questions about ends are, in other words, questions what things are desirable. The utilitarian doctrine is that happiness is desirable, and the only thing desirable, as an end; all other things being only desirable as means to that end. What ought to be required of this doctrine—what conditions is it requisite that the doctrine should fulfil—to make good its claim to be believed?

The only proof capable of being given that an object is visible, is that people actually see it. The only proof that a sound is audible, is that people hear it: and so of the other sources of our experience. In like manner, I apprehend, the sole evidence it is possible to produce that anything is desirable, is that people do actually desire it. If the end which the utilitarian doctrine proposes to itself were not, in theory and in practice, acknowledged to be an end, nothing could ever convince any person that it was so. No reason can be given why the general happiness is desirable, except that each person, so far as he believes it to be attainable, desires his own happiness. This, however, being a fact, we have not only all the proof which the case admits of, but all which it is possible to require, that happiness is a good: that each person's happiness is a good to that person, and the general happiness, therefore, a good to the aggregate of all persons. Happiness has made out its title as *one* of the ends of conduct, and consequently one of the criteria of morality.

But it has not, by this alone, proved itself to be the sole criterion. To do that, it would seem, by the same rule, necessary to show not only that people desire happiness, but that they never desire anything else. Now it is palpable that they do desire things which, in common language, are decidedly distinguished from happiness. They desire, for example, virtue and the absence of vice, no less really than pleasure and the absence of pain. The desire of virtue is not as universal, but it is as authentic a fact, as the desire of happiness. And hence the opponents of the utilitarian standard deem that they have a right to infer that there are other ends of human action besides happiness, and that happiness is not the standard of approbation and disapprobation.

But does the utilitarian doctrine deny that people desire virtue, or maintain that virtue is not a thing to be desired? The very reverse. It maintains not only that virtue is to be desired, but that it is to be desired disinterestedly, for itself. Whatever may be the opinion of utilitarian moralists as to the original conditions by which virtue is made virtue; however they may believe (as they do) that actions and dispositions are only virtuous because they promote another end than virtue; yet this being granted, and it having been decided, from considerations of this description, what *is* virtuous, they not only place virtue at the very head of the things which are good as means to the ultimate end, but they also recognise as a psychological fact the possibility of its being, to the individual, a good in itself, without looking to any end beyond it; and hold that the mind is not in a right state, not in a state conformable to utility, not in the state most conducive to the general happiness, unless it does love virtue in this manner—as a thing desirable in itself, even although, in the individual instance, it should not produce those other desirable consequences which it tends to produce, and on account of which it is held to be virtue. This opinion is not, in the smallest degree, a departure from the happiness principle. The ingredients of happiness are very various and each of them is desirable in itself, and not merely when considered as swelling an aggregate. The principle of utility does not mean that any given pleasure, as music, for instance, or any given exemption from pain, as for example health, are to be looked upon as means to a collective something termed happiness, and to be desired on that account. They are desired and desirable in and for themselves; besides being means, they are a part of the end. Virtue, according to the utilitarian doctrine, is not naturally and originally part of the end, but it is capable of becoming so; and in those who love it disinterestedly it has become so, and is desired and cherished, not as a means to happiness, but as a part of their happiness. . . .

We have now, then, an answer to the question, of what sort of proof the principle of utility is susceptible. If the opinion which I have now stated is psychologically true—if human nature is so constituted as to desire nothing which is not either a part of happiness or a means of happiness, we can have no other proof, and we require no other, that these are the only things desirable. If so, happiness is the sole end of human action, and the promotion of it the test by which to judge of all human conduct; from whence it necessarily follows that it must be the criterion of morality, since a part is included in the whole.

And now to decide whether this is really so; whether mankind do desire nothing for itself but that which is a pleasure to them, or of which the absence is a pain; we have evidently arrived at a question of fact and experience, dependent, like all similar questions, upon evidence. It can only be determined by practised self-consciousness and self-observation, assisted by observation of others. I believe that these sources of evidence, impartially consulted, will declare that desiring a thing and finding it pleasant, aversion to it and thinking of it as painful, are phenomena entirely inseparable, or rather two parts of the same phenomenon; in strictness of language, two different modes of naming the same psychological fact: that to think of an object as desirable (unless for the sake of its consequences), and to think of it as pleasant, are one and the same thing; and that to desire anything, except in proportion as the idea of it is pleasant, is a physical and metaphysical impossibility.

---

▶ NOTES

1. Epicurus (341–270 B.C.E.) was a Greek philosopher. [D.C.A., ed.]
2. Stoicism is the school of philosophy founded by the Greek philosopher Zeno of Citium (about 335–263 B.C.E). [D.C.A.]
3. Mill refers here primarily to Jeremy Bentham (1748–1832), the English jurist and philosopher who first proposed the theory of utilitarianism. [D.C.A.]
4. Matthew 7:21; Luke 6:31 [D.C.A.]
5. Matthew 22:39 [D.C.A.]

## CHAPTER 8

# The Debate over Utilitarianism

The utilitarian doctrine is that happiness is desirable, and the only thing desirable, as an end; all other things being desirable as means to that end.

JOHN STUART MILL, *UTILITARIANISM* (1861)

Man does not strive after happiness; only the Englishman does that.
FRIEDRICH NIETZSCHE, *TWILIGHT OF THE IDOLS* (1889)

## 8.1. The Classical Version of the Theory

Classical Utilitarianism, the theory of Bentham and Mill, can be summarized in three propositions: First, actions are to be judged right or wrong solely by virtue of their consequences. Nothing else matters. Second, in assessing consequences, the only thing that matters is the amount of happiness or unhappiness that is created. Everything else is irrelevant. Third, each person's happiness counts the same. As Mill put it,

> the happiness which forms the utilitarian standard of what is right in conduct, is not the agent's own happiness, but that of all concerned. As between his own happiness and that of others, utilitarianism requires him to be as strictly impartial as a disinterested and benevolent spectator.

Thus, right actions are those that produce the greatest possible balance of happiness over unhappiness, with each person's happiness counted as equally important.

The appeal of this theory to philosophers, economists, and others who theorize about human decision making has been enormous. The theory continues to be widely accepted, even though it has been challenged by a number of apparently devastating arguments. These antiutilitarian arguments are so numerous, and so persuasive, that many have concluded the theory must be abandoned. But the remarkable thing is that so many have not abandoned it. Despite the arguments, a great many thinkers refuse to let the theory go. According to these contemporary utilitarians, the antiutilitarian arguments only show that the classical theory needs to be improved; they say the basic idea is sound and should be preserved, but recast into a more satisfactory form.

In what follows, we will examine some of these arguments against Utilitarianism and consider whether the classical version of the theory may be revised satisfactorily to meet them. These arguments are of interest not only for the assessment of Utilitarianism but for their own sakes, as they raise some fundamental issues of moral philosophy.

## 8.2. Is Happiness the Only Thing That Matters?

The question *What things are good?* is different from the question *What actions are right?* and Utilitarianism answers the second question by referring back to the first one. Right actions, it says, are the ones that produce the most good. But what is good? The classical utilitarian reply is: one thing, and one thing only, namely happiness. As Mill put it, "The utilitarian doctrine is that happiness is desirable, and the only thing desirable, as an end; all other things being desirable as means to that end."

The idea that happiness is the one ultimate good (and unhappiness the one ultimate evil) is known as Hedonism. Hedonism is a perennially popular theory that goes back at least as far as the ancient Greeks. It has always been attractive because of its beautiful simplicity and because it expresses the intuitively plausible notion that things are good or bad on account of the way they make us *feel.* Yet a little reflection reveals serious flaws in this theory. The flaws stand out when we consider examples like these:

*A promising young pianist's hands are injured in an automobile accident so that she can no longer play.* Why is this bad for her? Hedonism would say it is bad because it causes her unhappiness. She will feel frustrated and upset whenever she thinks of what might have been, and *that* is her misfortune. But this way of explaining the misfortune seems to get things the wrong way around. It is not as though, by feeling unhappy, she has made an otherwise neutral situation into a bad one. On the contrary, her unhappiness is a rational response to a situation that *is* unfortunate. She could have had a career as a concert pianist, and now she cannot. That is the tragedy. We could not eliminate the tragedy just by getting her to cheer up.

*You think someone is your friend, but he ridicules you behind your back.* No one tells you, so you never know. Is this unfortunate for you? Hedonism would have to say no, because you are never caused any unhappiness. Yet we feel there is something bad going on. You think he is your friend, and you are "being made a fool," even though you are unaware of it and you suffer no unhappiness.

Both these examples make the same basic point. We value all sorts of things, such as artistic creativity and friendship, for their own sakes. It makes us happy to have them, but only because we already think them good. (We do not think them good because they make us happy—this is how Hedonism "gets things the wrong way around.") Therefore, it is a misfortune to lose them, independently of whether or not the loss is accompanied by unhappiness,

In this way, Hedonism misunderstands the nature of happiness. Happiness is not something that is recognized as good and sought for its own sake, with other things desired only as a means of bringing it about. Instead, happiness is a response we have to the attainment of things that we recognize *as* good, independently and in their own right. We think that friendship is a good thing, and so having friends makes us happy. That is very different from first setting out after happiness, then deciding that having friends might make us happy, and then seeking friends as a means to this end.

For this reason, there are not many hedonists among contemporary philosophers. Those sympathetic to Utilitarianism have therefore sought a way to formulate their view without assuming a hedonistic account of good and evil. Some, such as the English philosopher G. E. Moore (1873–1958), have tried to compile short lists of things to be regarded as good in themselves. Moore suggested that there are three obvious intrinsic goods—pleasure, friendship, and aesthetic enjoyment—and that right actions are those that increase the world's supply of these things. Other utilitarians have bypassed the question of how many things are good in themselves, leaving it an open question and saying only that right actions are the ones that have the best results, however that is measured. Still others bypass the question in another way, holding only that we should act so as to maximize the satisfaction of people's *preferences*. It is beyond the scope of this book to discuss the merits or demerits of these varieties of Utilitarianism. I mention them only in order to note that, although the hedonistic assumption of the classical utilitarians has largely been rejected, contemporary utilitarians have not found it difficult to carry on. They do so by urging that Hedonism was never a necessary part of the theory in the first place.

## 8.3. Are Consequences All That Matter?

The idea that only consequences matter is, however, a necessary part of Utilitarianism. The theory's most fundamental idea is that in order to determine whether an action would be right, we should look at *what will happen as a result of doing it*. If it were to turn out that some other matter is also important in determining rightness, then Utilitarianism would be undermined at its very foundation.

Some of the most serious antiutilitarian arguments attack the theory at just this point: They urge that various other considerations, in addition to utility, are important in determining right and wrong. Here are three such arguments.

**Justice.** Writing in the academic journal *Inquiry* in 1965, H. J. McCloskey asks us to consider the following case:

> Suppose a utilitarian were visiting an area in which there was racial strife, and that, during his visit, a Negro rapes a white woman, and that race riots occur as a result of the crime, white mobs, with the connivance of the police, bashing and killing Negroes, etc. Suppose too that our utilitarian is in the area of the crime when it is committed such that his testimony would bring about the conviction of a particular Negro. If he knows that a quick arrest will stop the riots and lynchings, surely, as a Utilitarian, he must conclude that he has a duty to bear false witness in order to bring about the punishment of an innocent person.

This is a fictitious example, of course, although it was obviously inspired by the lynch-law that prevailed at one time in some parts of the United States. In any case, the argument is that if someone were in this position, then on utilitarian grounds he should bear false witness against the innocent person. This might have some bad consequences—the innocent man might be executed—but there would be enough good consequences to outweigh them: The riots and lynchings would be stopped. The best outcome would be achieved by lying; therefore, according to Utilitarianism, lying is the thing to do. But, the argument continues, it would be wrong to bring about the execution of an innocent person. Therefore, Utilitarianism, which implies it would be right, must be incorrect.

According to the critics of Utilitarianism, this argument illustrates one of the theory's most serious shortcomings: namely, that it is incompatible with the ideal of justice. Justice requires that we treat people fairly, according to their individual needs and merits. McCloskey's example illustrates how the demands of justice and the demands of utility can come into conflict. Thus, an ethical theory that says utility is the whole story cannot be right.

**Rights.**  Here is a case that is not fictitious; it is from the records of the U.S. Court of Appeals, Ninth Circuit (Southern District of California), 1963, in the case of *York* v. *Story:*

> In October, 1958, appellant [Ms. Angelynn York] went to the police department of Chino for the purpose of filing charges in connection with an assault upon her. Appellee Ron Story, an officer of that police department, then acting under color of his authority as such, advised appellant that it was necessary to take photographs of her. Story then took appellant to a room in the police station, locked the door, and directed her to undress, which she did. Story then directed appellant to assume various indecent positions, and photographed her in those positions. These photographs were not made for any lawful purpose.
>
> Appellant objected to undressing. She stated to Story that there was no need to take photographs of her in the nude, or in the positions she was directed to take, because the bruises would not show in any photograph.
>
> Later that month, Story advised appellant that the pictures did not come out and that he had destroyed them. Instead, Story circulated these photographs among the personnel of the Chino police department. In April, 1960,

two other officers of that police department, appellee Louis Moreno and defendant Henry Grote, acting under color of their authority as such, and using police photographic equipment located at the police station made additional prints of the photographs taken by Story. Moreno and Grote then circulated these prints among the personnel of the Chino police department.

Ms. York brought suit against these officers and won. Her legal rights had clearly been violated. But what of the *morality* of the officers' behavior? Utilitarianism says that actions are defensible if they produce a favorable balance of happiness over unhappiness. This suggests that we consider the amount of unhappiness caused to Ms. York and compare it with the amount of pleasure taken in the photographs by Officer Story and his cohorts. It is at least possible that more happiness than unhappiness was caused. In that case, the utilitarian conclusion apparently would be that their actions were morally all right. But this seems to be a perverse way of thinking. Why should the pleasure afforded Story and his cohorts matter at all? Why should it even count? They had no right to treat Ms. York in this way, and the fact that they enjoyed doing so hardly seems a relevant defense.

Here is an (imaginary) related case. Suppose a Peeping Tom spied on Ms. York by peering through her bedroom window, and secretly took pictures of her undressed. Further suppose that he did this without ever being detected and that he used the photographs entirely for his own amusement, without showing them to anyone. Now under these circumstances, it seems clear that the only consequence of his action is an increase in his own happiness. No one else, including Ms. York, is caused any unhappiness at all. How, then, could Utilitarianism deny that the Peeping Tom's actions are right? But it is evident to moral common sense that they are not right. Thus, Utilitarianism appears to be unacceptable.

The moral to be drawn from this argument is that Utilitarianism is at odds with the idea that people have *rights* that may not be trampled on merely because one anticipates good results. In these cases, it is Ms. York's right to privacy that is violated; but it would not be difficult to think of similar cases in which other rights are at issue—the right to freedom of religion, to free speech, or even the right to life itself. It may happen that good purposes are served, from time to time, by violating these rights. But we do not think that our rights should be set aside so easily. The notion of a personal right is not a utilitarian notion. Quite the opposite: It is a notion that places limits on how an individual may be treated, regardless of the good purposes that might be accomplished.

**Backward-Looking Reasons.** Suppose you have promised someone you will do something—say, you promised to meet her downtown this afternoon. But when the time comes to go, you don't want to do it; you need to do some work and you would rather stay home. What should you do? Suppose you judge that the utility of getting your work accomplished slightly outweighs the inconvenience your friend would be caused. Appealing to the utilitarian standard, you might then conclude that it is right to stay home. However, this does not seem correct. The fact that you promised imposes an obligation on you that you cannot escape so easily. Of course, if a great deal was at stake—if, for example, your mother had just been stricken with a heart attack and you had to rush her to the hospital—you would be justified in breaking the promise. But a *small* gain in utility cannot overcome the obligation imposed by the fact that you promised. Thus Utilitarianism, which says that consequences are the only things that matter, once again seems to be mistaken.

There is an important general lesson to be learned from this argument. Why is Utilitarianism vulnerable to this sort of criticism? It is because the only kinds of considerations that the theory holds relevant to determining the rightness of actions are considerations having to do with the future. Because of its exclusive concern with consequences, Utilitarianism has us confine our attention to what *will happen* as a result of our actions. However, we normally think that considerations about the past are also important. (The fact that you promised your friend to meet her is a fact about the past.) Therefore, Utilitarianism seems to be faulty because it excludes backward-looking considerations.

Once we understand this point, other examples of backward-looking considerations come easily to mind. The fact that someone did not commit a crime is a good reason why he should not be punished. The fact that someone once did you a favor may be a good reason why you should now do him a favor. The fact that you did something to hurt someone may be a reason why you should now make it up to her. These are all facts about the past that are relevant to determining our obligations. But Utilitarianism makes the past irrelevant, and so it seems deficient for just that reason.

## 8.4. Should We Be Equally Concerned for Everyone?

The final component of utilitarian morality is the idea that we must treat each person's welfare as equally important—as Mill put it, that we must be "as strictly impartial as a disinterested and benevolent spectator." This sounds plausible when it is stated abstractly, but it has troublesome implications. One problem is that the requirement of "equal concern" places too great a demand on us; another problem is that it disrupts our personal relationships.

**The Charge That Utilitarianism Is Too Demanding.** Suppose you are on your way to the theater when someone points out that the money you are about to spend could be used to provide food for starving people or inoculations for third-world children. Surely, those people need food and medicine more than you need to see a play. So you forgo your entertainment and give the money to a charitable agency. But that is not the end of it. By the same reasoning, you cannot buy new clothes, a car, a computer, or a camera. Probably you should move into a cheaper apartment. After all, what is more important—your having these luxuries or children having food?

In fact, faithful adherence to the utilitarian standard would require you to give away your resources until you have lowered your own standard of living to the level of the neediest people you could help. We might admire people who do this, but we do not regard them as simply doing their duty. Instead, we regard them as saintly people whose generosity goes *beyond* what duty requires. We distinguish actions that are morally required from actions that are praiseworthy but not strictly required. (Philosophers call the latter *supererogatory* actions.) Utilitarianism seems to eliminate this distinction.

But the problem is not merely that Utilitarianism would require us to give up most of our material resources. Equally important, abiding by Utilitarianism's mandates would make it impossible for us to carry on our individual lives. Each of our lives includes projects and activities that give it character and meaning; these are what make our lives worth living. But an ethic that requires the subordination of everything to the impartial promotion of the general welfare would require us to abandon those projects and activities. Suppose you are a cabinet-maker, not getting rich but making a comfortable living; you have two children that you love; and on weekends you like to perform with an amateur theater group. In addition you are interested in history and you read a lot. How could there be anything wrong with this? But judged by the utilitarian standard, you are leading a morally unacceptable life. After all, you could be doing a lot more good if you spent your time in other ways.

**Personal Relationships.** In practice, none of us is willing to treat all people as equals, for it would require that we abandon our special relationships with friends and family. We are all deeply partial where our friends and family are concerned. We love them and we go to great lengths to help them. To us, they are not just members of the great crowd of humanity—they are special.  But all this is inconsistent with impartiality. When you are impartial, intimacy, love, affection, and friendship fly out the window.

The fact that Utilitarianism undermines our personal relationships seems to many critics to be its single greatest fault. Indeed, at this point Utilitarianism seems to have lost all touch with reality. What would it be like to be no more concerned for one's husband or wife than for strangers whom one has never met? The very idea is absurd; not only is it profoundly contrary to normal human emotions, but the institution of marriage could not even exist apart from understandings about special responsibilities and obligations. Again, what would it be like to treat one's children with no greater love than one has for strangers? As John Cottingham puts it, "A parent who leaves his child to burn, on the ground that the building contains someone else whose future contribution to the general welfare promises to be greater, is not a hero; he is (rightly) an object of moral contempt, a moral leper."

## 8.5.  The Defense of Utilitarianism

These arguments add up to an overwhelming indictment of Utilitarianism. The theory, which at first seemed so progressive and commonsensical, now seems indefensible: It is at odds with such fundamental moral notions as justice and individual rights, and it seems unable to account for the place of backward-looking reasons in justifying conduct. It would have us abandon our ordinary lives and spoil the personal relationships that mean everything to us. Not surprisingly, the combined weight of these arguments has prompted many philosophers to abandon the theory altogether.

Many thinkers, however, continue to believe that Utilitarianism, in some form, is true. In reply to the above arguments, three general defenses have been offered.

**The First Line of Defense: Fanciful Examples Don't Matter.** The first line of defense is to argue that the antiutilitarian arguments make unrealistic assumptions about how the world works. The arguments about rights, justice, and backward-looking reasons share a common strategy. A case is described, and then it is said that from a utilitarian point of view a certain action is required—bearing false witness, violating someone's rights, or breaking a promise. It is then said that these things are not right. Therefore, it is concluded, the utilitarian conception of rightness cannot be correct.

But this strategy succeeds only if we agree that the actions described really would have the best consequences. But why should we agree with that? In the real world, bearing false witness does *not* have good consequences. Suppose, in the case described by McCloskey, the "utilitarian" tried to incriminate the innocent man in order to stop the riots. He probably would not succeed; his lie might be found out, and then the situation would be even worse than before. Even if the lie did succeed, the real culprit would remain at large, to commit additional crimes. Moreover, if the guilty party were caught later on, which is always a possibility, the liar would be in deep trouble, and confidence in the criminal justice system would be undermined. The moral is that although one might *think* that one can bring about the best consequences by such behavior, one can by no means be certain of it. In fact, experience teaches the contrary: Utility is not served by framing innocent people.

112    THE ELEMENTS OF MORAL PHILOSOPHY

The same goes for the other cases cited in the antiutilitarian arguments. Violating people's rights, breaking one's promises, and lying all have bad consequences. Only in philosophers' imaginations is it otherwise. In the real world, Peeping Toms are caught, just as Officer Story and his cohorts were caught; and their victims suffer. In the real world, when people lie, others are hurt and their own reputations are damaged; and when people break their promises, and fail to return favors, they lose their friends.

Therefore, far from being incompatible with the idea that we should not violate people's rights, or lie, or break our promises, Utilitarianism explains why we should not do those things. Moreover, apart from the utilitarian explanation, these duties would remain mysterious and unintelligible. What could be more mysterious than the notion that some actions are right "in themselves," severed from any notion of a good to be produced by them? Or what could be more unintelligible than the idea that people have "rights" unconnected with any benefits derived from the acknowledgment of those rights? Utilitarianism is not incompatible with common sense; on the contrary, Utilitarianism is commonsensical.

So that is the first line of defense. How effective is it? Unfortunately, it contains more bluster than substance. While it can plausibly be maintained that *most* acts of false witness and the like have bad consequences in the real world, it cannot reasonably be asserted that *all* such acts have bad consequences. Surely, at least once in a while, one can bring about a good result by doing something that moral common sense condemns. Therefore, in at least some real-life cases Utilitarianism will come into conflict with common sense. Moreover, even if the antiutilitarian arguments had to rely exclusively on fictitious examples, those arguments would nevertheless retain their power; for showing that Utilitarianism has unacceptable consequences in hypothetical cases is a valid way of pointing up its theoretical defects. The first line of defense, then, is weak.

**The Second Line of Defense: The Principle of Utility Is a Guide for Choosing Rules, Not Individual Acts.** The second line of defense admits that the classical version of Utilitarianism is inconsistent with moral common sense and proposes to save the theory by giving it a new formulation which *will* be in line with our commonsense evaluations. In revising a theory, the trick is to identify precisely which of its features is causing the trouble and to change that, leaving the rest of the theory undisturbed. What is it about the classical version that generates all the unwelcome results?

The troublesome aspect of classical Utilitarianism, it was said, is its assumption that *each individual action* is to be evaluated by reference to the Principle of Utility. If on a certain occasion you are tempted to bear false witness, the classical version of the theory says that whether it would be wrong is determined by the consequences of *that particular lie;* similarly, whether you should keep a promise depends on the consequences of *that particular promise;* and so on for each of the examples we have considered. This is the assumption that caused all the trouble; it is what leads to the conclusion that you can do any sort of questionable thing if it has the best consequences.

Therefore, the new version of Utilitarianism modifies the theory so that individual actions will no longer be judged by the Principle of Utility. Instead, we first ask what *set of rules* is optimal, from a utilitarian point of view. What rules should we prefer to have current in our society, if the people in our society are to flourish? Individual acts are then judged right or wrong according to whether they are acceptable or unacceptable by those rules. This new version of the theory is called *Rule-Utilitarianism,* to distinguish it from the original theory, now commonly called *Act-Utilitarianism.* Richard Brandt was perhaps the most prominent defender of Rule-Utilitarianism; he suggested that "morally wrong" means that an action

> would be prohibited by any moral code which all fully rational persons would tend to support, in preference to all others or to none at all, for the society of the agent, if they expected to spend a lifetime in that society.

Rule-Utilitarianism has no difficulty coping with the antiutilitarian arguments. An act-utilitarian, faced with the situation described by McCloskey, would be tempted to bear false witness against the innocent man because the consequences of *that particular act* would be good. But the rule-utilitarian would not reason in that way. He would first ask, "What general rules of conduct tend to promote the greatest happiness?" Suppose we imagine two societies, one in which the rule "Don't bear false

114    THE ELEMENTS OF MORAL PHILOSOPHY

witness against the innocent" is faithfully adhered to, and one in which this rule is not followed. In which society are people likely to be better off? From the point of view of utility, the first society is preferable. Therefore, the rule against incriminating the innocent should be accepted, and by appealing to this rule, we conclude that the person in McCloskey's example should not testify against the innocent man.

Analogous reasoning can be used to establish rules against violating people's rights, breaking promises, lying, and all the rest. Rules governing personal relationships—requiring loyalty to friends, loving care of one's children, and so on—can also be established in this manner. We should accept such rules because following them, as a regular practice, promotes the general welfare. But once having appealed to the Principle of Utility to establish the rules, we do not have to invoke the principle again to determine the rightness of particular actions. Individual actions are justified simply by appeal to the already-established rules.

Thus Rule-Utilitarianism cannot be convicted of violating our moral common sense. In shifting emphasis from the justification of acts to the justification of rules, the theory has been brought into line with our intuitive judgments to a remarkable degree.

**The Third Line of Defense: "Common Sense" Can't Be Trusted.**  Finally, a small group of contemporary utilitarians has had a very different response to the antiutilitarian arguments. Those arguments point out that the classical theory is at odds with ordinary notions of justice, individual rights, and so on; and this group responds: "So what?"  In 1961 the Australian philosopher J. J. C. Smart published a monograph entitled *An Outline of a System of Utilitarian Ethics;* reflecting on his position in that book, Smart said:

> Admittedly utilitarianism does have consequences which are incompatible with the common moral consciousness, but I tended to take the view "so much the worse for the common moral consciousness." That is, I was inclined to reject the common methodology of testing general ethical principles by seeing how they square with our feelings in particular instances.

Our moral common sense is, after all, not necessarily reliable. It may incorporate various irrational elements, including prejudices absorbed from our parents, our religion, and the general culture. Why should we simply assume that our feelings are always correct? And why should we reject a plausible, rational theory of ethics simply because it conflicts with those feelings? Perhaps it is the feelings, not the theory, that should be discarded.

In light of this, consider again McCloskey's example of the person tempted to bear false witness. McCloskey argues that it would be wrong to have a man convicted of a crime he did not commit because it would be unjust. But wait: Such a judgment serves *that man's* interests well enough, but what of the *other* innocent people who will be hurt if the rioting and lynchings continue? Surely we might hope that we never have to face a situation like this. All the options are terrible. But if we must choose between (a) securing the conviction of one innocent person and (b) allowing the deaths of several innocent people, is it so unreasonable to think that the first option, bad as it is, is preferable to the second?

And consider again the objection that Utilitarianism is too demanding because it would require us to use our resources to feed starving children rather than go to movies and buy cars and cameras. Is it unreasonable to believe that continuing our affluent lives is less important than those children?

On this way of thinking, Act-Utilitarianism is a perfectly defensible doctrine and does not need to be modified. Rule-Utilitarianism, by contrast, is an unnecessarily watered-down version of the theory, which gives rules a greater importance than they merit. There is a serious problem with Rule-Utilitarianism, which can be brought out if we ask whether its rules have *exceptions.* After the rule-utilitarian's "ideal social code" has been established, are its rules to be followed no matter what? There will inevitably be cases where an act that is prohibited by the code would nevertheless maximize utility, maybe even by a considerable amount. Then what is to be done? If the rule-utilitarian says that in such cases we may violate the code, it looks like he has fallen back into act-utilitarianism. On the other hand, if he says that we may not do the "forbidden" act, then, as Smart puts it, the utilitarian's original concern for promoting welfare has been replaced by an irrational "rule worship." What sort of utilitarian would allow the sky to fall for the sake of a rule?

Act-Utilitarianism engages in no such rule-worship. It is, however, recognized to be a radical doctrine that implies that many of our ordinary moral feelings may be mistaken. In this respect, it does what good philosophy always does—it challenges us to rethink matters that we have heretofore taken for granted.

If we consult what Smart calls our "common moral consciousness," it seems that many considerations other than utility are morally important. But Smart is right to warn us that "common sense" cannot be trusted. That may turn out to be Utilitarianism's greatest contribution. The deficiencies of moral common sense are obvious, once we think for only a moment. Many white people once felt that there is an important difference between whites and blacks, so that the interests of whites are somehow more important. Trusting the "common sense" of their day, they might have insisted that an adequate moral theory should accommodate this "fact." Today, no one worth listening to would say such a thing, but who knows how many other irrational prejudices are still a part of our moral common sense? At the end of his classic study of race relations, *An American Dilemma* (1944), the Swedish sociologist Gunnar Myrdal reminds us:

> There must be still other countless errors of the same sort that no living man can yet detect, because of the fog within which our type of Western culture envelops us. Cultural influences have set up the assumptions about the mind, the body, and the universe with which we begin; pose the questions we ask; influence the facts we seek; determine the interpretation we give these facts; and direct our reaction to these interpretations and conclusions.

Could it be, for example, that future generations will look back in disgust at the way affluent people in the 21st century enjoyed their comfortable lives while third-world children died of easily preventable diseases? Or at the way we slaughtered and ate helpless animals? If so, they might note that utilitarian philosophers of the day were criticized as simple-minded for advancing a moral theory that straightforwardly condemned such things.

**Chapter 5**

# Kantian Ethical Theory

Most people who drive automobiles occasionally exceed the posted speed limits, but assume you have an acquaintance who never does this. You ask the person why he or she never speeds, and the answer is, "I'm afraid I'll be caught by the police and have to pay a fine." This would be a consequentialist approach to speeding. This individual does not speed because of the fear of bad consequences. There is, however, another answer a person might give: "I do not speed because I respect the law. Sometimes I want to speed because I'm in a hurry, but because I respect the law I never do it." This is a very different answer; it is not concerned with either consequences or personal wants. The person's action is guided simply by respect for the law. It may seem odd that someone would respect the speeding laws, but assume that this person respects the law in general and therefore obeys all the laws, even the posted speed limits.

This example concerns the laws established by a government—the kind of law that I argued needs to be separated from ethics (see Chapter 1). We know this kind of law exists, but the German philosopher Immanuel Kant (1724–1804) argues that another kind of law also exists, *moral law*. It is not the law of any one country or society; moral law applies to all persons. Many people would intuitively agree with Kant. Their ethical insight is that *there are moral laws that apply to all persons*. This chapter discusses an ethical theory related to this insight and to the idea of acting from respect for the moral law.

In Chapter 1, I suggested that philosophers often work with this model of action:

$$Reasoning \rightarrow Action \rightarrow Consequences$$

Consequentialist ethical theories, such as ethical egoism claim that good and evil are related to the consequences that result from an action. In contrast, *deontological ethical theories* focus on the reasoning that precedes the action. The word "deontology" relates to the Greek word "deon," which translates roughly as "duty." Immanuel Kant is the most influential of the deontological philosophers. He believed persons had a duty to obey the moral law. Kant's ethical theory is extremely complicated.[1] I will not provide an exact explication of his ideas but instead discuss a simplified "Kantian ethics" centered around acting from respect for the moral law.

## Rules and Actions

The relation between rules and actions is essential to Kantian ethics. The key idea is that, for any action, we can identify a personal rule that guides the action. Suppose I send some money to a charity because I believe everyone ought to help those who are less fortunate. My reasoning might be described in this way. I performed the action (giving money to this charity) because I thought I should act from my personal rule: Everyone ought to help those who are less fortunate. The initial Kantian idea is that every action is guided by a personal rule. Consequently, Kantian theory states that if persons want to be ethical the personal rules that guide their actions must be able to be willed to be moral laws. It is not enough that by coincidence personal rules of action are consistent with these moral laws; persons must be acting because they could will their personal rules to be moral laws. Subsequent sections will explain this position.

## Developing the Kantian Ethical Insight

Consider once again the person who always obeys the speed limit laws. The person acknowledges that the laws exist and respects them; therefore, he or she obeys them. In theory the laws apply to everyone. That is, everyone is supposed to be equal with regard to the law. If I am caught going fifteen miles an hour over the speed limit, I should be treated the same way you would be treated if you were caught doing the same thing. The law exists, and everyone is equal in regard to it. The Kantian position on ethics is similar to this, except, of course, it refers to the moral law. *The Kantian ethical insight is that there are moral laws and that these laws apply to all persons.* If the moral law applies equally to everyone, all persons are moral equals in regard to the law. If the Kantian insight was filled out, it would state that (1) there are moral laws connected to reason, and (2) that all persons are equal in regard to the moral law and should be treated consistently in sufficiently similar situations. The moral law and the moral equality of persons or rational

**70**  *Chapter 5 / Kantian Ethical Theory*

beings are crucial to Kantian ethics. The idea of moral equality among persons means that moral laws equally bind all persons and that all persons count the same when we are applying moral laws. Assume that the rule "It is wrong to steal other people's property" can be willed to be a moral law. If persons are moral equals, they are all bound by the rule, and the rule protects all property. No one has a privileged ethical position that allows him or her to ignore the rule. Therefore, moral laws place obligations on everyone; that is, they are universal.

The ideas of moral equality and ethical consistency for persons are closely connected. Suppose that the rule "It is wrong to steal other people's property" is legitimate. If I believe two persons are moral equals and that they are in sufficiently similar situations, then I ought to act from the moral rule in a consistent way—I should refrain from stealing either person's property. If I do not act this way, I am being inconsistent in two ways. The first inconsistency concerns the rule; I am not consistently acting from the rule. The rule orders me not to steal, but in one case I act from it, and in a sufficiently similar case I disregard it. The second inconsistency relates to my attitude toward persons. I have said that persons are moral equals, but I treat them as if they were not moral equals, stealing from one and not from the other. Kantian ethics claims that persons ought to be consistent, both in acting from moral laws and in the treatment of persons. Moral equality and ethical consistency are key ideas in Kantian ethics.

## Rational Beings, Persons, and Moral Laws

According to Kantian ethics, moral laws are connected to reason, and they bind all free, rational beings. In this context, to be a "rational being" means, at least, to be capable of acting in accord with rational rules or principles. In more detail, a rational being must be able to deliberate, follow rules, make decisions, and support those decisions with reasons. Rational beings must also be able to understand the idea of the moral law and decide how to act based on reasoning about personal rules of action and moral laws. Finally, rational beings must be able to act from respect for the moral law. If a being cannot meet these criteria, he or she will not qualify as a rational being or a person under Kantian ethics.

Moral laws are perceived by persons as universal commands. Because moral laws command persons universally or absolutely, they must be followed without exceptions. They are not conditional rules. Conditional rules tell us what actions persons should take to attain some desired goal and have an "if–then" form: If you want to lose weight, then you ought to exercise and watch what you eat. The rule is conditional because it will only guide you to act if you want to lose weight. Therefore, conditional rules do not obligate everyone—only those people who desire to reach the goal. In contrast, legitimate moral rules or laws place an obligation on everyone regardless of their desires; they are universal.

If moral laws are a product of reason, then it is rational for a person to act from these moral laws. If a person violates the moral laws, he or she has acted inconsistently or irrationally. Persons are capable of being rational and ought to act rationally, presumably out of respect for their rationality. Therefore, ultimately, acting from respect for the moral law is based on acting from respect for rationality. Some might ask, "Why should rational beings act from respect for their rationality?" It is clearly possible and sometimes in our self-interest to act irrationally and inconsistently. As Kant himself acknowledged, persons are imperfectly rational beings. A Kantian would presumably say that we have given up a large part of our freedom and rationality if we do not act from respect for the moral law. We should endorse our nature as free, rational beings —not reject it by acting irrationally.

## The Ethical Standard of Kantian Ethics

Kantians use a basic moral law, principle, or ethical standard called the *Categorical Imperative* to determine the legitimate rules or more specific moral laws that ought to guide action. The Categorical Imperative is similar to an essential principle in many religions. In Christianity this principle is called the Golden Rule. One version of the Golden Rule is, "Do unto others as you would have them do unto you." The first formulation of the Categorical Imperative or ethical standard might be phrased: *Act only from those personal rules that you can at the same time will to be moral laws.* The difference between the Golden Rule and the first formulation of the Kantian Categorical Imperative is subtle, yet important, because the Kantian formula is less likely to lead to a subjective interpretation. I might interpret the Golden Rule as telling me to treat persons the way that I would like to be treated. This interpretation runs the risk of having someone understand it as the instruction to use his or her personal likes and dislikes as the ethical standard for how to treat everyone else. This would extend the person's subjective standard to everyone and would have the problems related to ethical subjectivism. In my opinion, this is not what was meant by the Golden Rule, and it is certainly not what Kant meant. Persons are to act from those personal rules that they could will to be ethical laws because they are rational, moral equals. The first formulation is related to the idea that the moral law is universal. If individuals follow the Categorical Imperative and act on personal rules that they could will to be moral laws, they will have acted ethically.

Kantian ethical theory identifies another version of the Kantian ethical standard that also relates to moral equality and consistency. The second formulation of the Categorical Imperative might be stated like this: *Act in regard to all persons in ways that treat them as ends in themselves and never simply as means to accomplish the ends of others.* Persons are free, rational beings who have various purposes and goals that they wish to accomplish. The second formulation of the Categorical Imperative or ethical standard acknowledges these characteristics when it refers to persons as ends in themselves. Kantian ethics demands that persons evaluate their personal rules and act only on those that they could will to be universal laws. Persons must also acknowledge that other persons should do the same thing because they are moral equals. They must never forget that persons are free and can reason and act, and they should never treat others merely as tools to accomplish their goals, the way they would use a hammer to fix something. For example, I cannot simply order you to help me repair my roof and expect you to do it regardless of whatever plans you may have. This disregards your status as a free, rational being who can make decisions and has goals and instead treats you merely as a means for me to get my roof fixed. I need to ask you to help me fix my roof. This leaves the decision up to you and acknowledges your status as a free being who can make decisions and has his or her own goals. I am still using you as a means to get my roof repaired, but not merely as a means. Rational beings can use persons to accomplish their ends, but they should never use them merely as means to accomplish those ends. Persons are moral equals and, therefore, must act only from personal rules that treat persons as ends in themselves, and never from rules that treat persons merely as means to accomplish their ends. If they do this, they will have acted ethically.

## Legitimate Moral Laws

How are persons to know the rules that they should will to be moral laws? To answer this question, Kantian ethics appeals to consistency, universalizability, and moral equality. First, individuals must determine the personal rule on which they propose to act. Second, they should only act from rules that are internally consistent. Third, they should only follow rules that are universal. Fourth, they should only act from rules that treat persons as moral equals. Finally, people should never act from rules that treat persons merely as means to accomplish the ends of others.

Consider this proposed rule: "I may promise to do something and then break that promise if it is in my self-interest to do so." Assume that I may break the promise for any self-interested reason, no matter how trivial. Therefore, based on willing this rule to be a moral law, everyone would make promises and then in many cases break them. This rule does not meet the consistency criterion because it is internally inconsistent. When I promise to do something, perhaps help you fix your roof, I am saying that I *will* do it. However, this rule is also stating that I *will not* do it if something trivial, but in my self-interest, arises. It is saying that I *will* help you fix your roof and that I *will not* help you. These two aspects of the rule are inconsistent and would make my promise to help you fix your roof meaningless. If this rule were extended to guide all promises, it would make promises in general meaningless. We would never know if the person were going to do the thing he or she had promised to do. Thus, this rule would not meet the first criterion because it is internally inconsistent.

Rational beings should also reject potential rules that are not universal and that do not treat persons as moral equals. Because we are moral equals, legitimate moral laws apply to all of us. A rule may be rejected if it is not universal, that is, if it does not apply to everyone. Suppose someone proposes the rule that "Only women should help those less fortunate than themselves." This rule should be rejected because it is not universal; it does not apply to all persons. The rule implies that women have a special ethical standing, but this is incorrect if all persons are moral equals. All legitimate moral laws treat persons as moral equals and hence apply to everyone. To be ethical, persons must follow only rules that they could will to be moral laws.

Moral agents should also reject potential rules that treat persons merely as means to accomplish the ends of others. Consider the proposed rule, "Whenever my lawn needs mowing, John should mow it for me." This rule disregards John's status as a free, rational being with ends and purposes of his own and considers him merely as a means for me to get my lawn mowed. It is irrational and unethical to treat John as merely a means when he is really a free, rational being. Thus, this potential rule could not be legitimately willed to be a moral law.

Kantians believe that many rules could be willed to be moral laws. One is that "Persons ought to keep their promises." First, keeping all of our promises is internally consistent because the rule, by its formulation, does not interfere with our doing that to which we have obligated ourselves. There might be a promise that is foolishly made—one which it turns out the person does not have the ability to keep—but the inability to keep this promise is a problem with the particular promise and not a necessary problem with the moral rule. Second, this moral rule is universal because it applies to everyone and all promises. Third, this moral rule also treats persons as moral equals because persons will be keeping their promises to everyone, rather than keeping them to some persons and not to others. Finally, it does not treat persons merely as means; by keeping my promise to someone, I respect the person's ends that may be related to the promise. Therefore, persons can will the rule to be a moral law.

Another example would be the rule that "It is unethical to enslave persons." This rule could be willed to be a moral law because it is internally consistent and would treat persons as moral equals and ends in themselves. Slaves meet the criteria as persons, but they are not treated as persons (as free, rational beings and moral equals). They are treated merely as means to satisfy the ends of their owners. If we claimed that slavery was ethical, we would be claiming that some persons (rational beings) ought not to be treated as persons (rational beings). This would be inconsistent and would violate the idea that rational beings must treat persons as moral equals. Conversely, the rule that slavery is unethical supports the idea that persons must always be treated as rational beings and moral equals, and as ends in themselves.

There is no other method to determine the rules that should guide action. Kantians cannot claim that the moral laws would be the rules that produce the best consequences. This is the position taken by rule utilitarianism (see Chapter 6). According to rule utilitarians, we should follow rules that maximize net happiness or human benefit for the greatest number of persons affected. In contrast, Kantians claim that the legitimacy of moral laws is not connected to consequences. Therefore, the Kantian ethical standard does not specify the kinds of consequences that must be produced. The rules that persons should will to be moral laws ought to be rules that fit the criteria of internal consistency, universalizability, and moral equality.

Kantian ethics would not provide a complete list of all the rules that could be willed to be moral laws. As rational beings, persons ought to evaluate their personal rules of action. It would be inconsistent and unethical to reject being a rational being and not to evaluate those personal rules. Of course, Kantians believe persons will all arrive at the same conclusions about which rules could be willed to be moral laws if they use reason correctly. The emphasis, however, is on the moral standard and the procedure used to identify the legitimate rules to guide action, not on identifying a specific set of moral laws.

When a person contemplates a morally significant action, he or she must be able to identify or arrive at a description of the action. From the description, the personal rule that would guide the action can be identified. For example, suppose that my contemplated action is helping you fix your roof, which is related to my promise to help you fix your roof. The rule that would guide my action if I help you is, "Persons ought to keep their promises." As discussed earlier, this rule could be willed to be a moral law; therefore, it is ethical for me to keep my promise and help you fix your roof. We would have to be able to know what counted and did not count as making a promise, the relevant personal rule, and whether that rule could be willed to be a moral law. In some cases, there may be more than one relevant rule. If both rules could be willed to be moral laws, the action is ethical. However, if one rule could be willed to be a moral law and the other could not, there would be a conflict. Conflicts between rules will be discussed further in the section on the problems with Kantian ethics.

## Justification for the Ethical Standard and Strengths of the Theory

An earlier section identified the two Kantian ethical standards or versions of the Categorical Imperative: (1) *Act only from those personal rules that you can at the same time will to be moral laws* and (2) *Act in regard to all persons in ways that treat them as ends in themselves and never simply as means to accomplish the ends of others.* In this section, we turn to justifications for the standards and corresponding strengths of Kantian ethics. These justifications and strengths relate to the three traditional ethical assumptions.

### Ethics Is Rational

The first justification for using the standard and corresponding strength of the Kantian ethical theory is that it makes ethics rational. The theory enables us to provide reasons to support our moral rules, and we can show why some reasons and rules are better than others. Kantians can discuss ethical issues, and if they are well intentioned, they ought to be able to arrive at mutual conclusions. For most people, a theory that makes ethics rational is stronger than a theory that makes it irrational because it enables us to better understand how to live and why we should live that way. It also enables us to reach agreements with other people over moral problems; therefore, we should be able to live together more successfully.

### The Moral Equality of Persons

The second justification for the ethical standard and related strength of the theory is that it asserts that persons are moral equals. This is a positive feature for many people because it prevents prejudiced attitudes like racism and sexism. Sexism, for example, claims that women are inferior to men. Although sexists may claim that women are physically and intellectually inferior, it is the implied claim that women are morally inferior that is most objectionable. If women are morally inferior, then they are not worth as much as men. Their interests can be legitimately sacrificed to serve the interests of men, or women can be forced to live their lives merely to benefit men. The Kantian ethical theory argues that all persons are rational beings and moral equals. No man can legitimately use a woman merely as the means to achieve his ends or those of another person. Thus, the Kantian ethical theory provides the reasoning to refute sexism, racism, and other prejudiced attitudes. This is a justification for using the ethical standard and a strength of the theory for many people.

### Universal Moral Guidelines

The third justification for using the ethical standard and corresponding strength of the theory is that it allows for the universalizability of moral guidelines and judgments. The moral guidelines or laws generated by the use to the Categorical Imperative ought to be the same for all rational beings. The example of the moral law "It is unethical to enslave persons" was discussed earlier. This is a legitimate moral law and ought to be lawful for all rational beings. These universal moral guidelines enable us to produce universalizable moral judgments. For example, "Enslaving illegal immigrants to work in New York City garment sweat shops is evil." This judgment is correct no matter what part of New York City and whatever time period. For many people, a theory that gives one the justification to declare that certain actions are universally good or bad is a stronger theory than one that does not do this. It is stronger because the capacity to make universal moral judgments provides a justification for taking firm and confident positions on various moral issues.

These strengths of the Kantian ethical theory make it seem to many like an improvement over the earlier theories. In a later section of the chapter, some problems with the theory will be discussed.

## Determining Morally Significant Actions

The legitimate ethical standard identified by Kantians provides a means of separating morally significant actions from those that are not morally significant. With respect to actions, any action performed from respect for the moral law is morally significant. It is also morally significant if we fail to act from respect for the moral law; for example, acting on self-interest in a situation relevant to a legitimate moral law would also be morally significant. If someone asks me a question, I ought to provide a truthful answer or refuse to answer. I should not lie even if it is in my self-interest to do so. It is morally significant if I tell a lie. In general, in Kantian ethics anything related to acting from respect for the moral law is morally significant.

## Kantian Ethics and the Traditional Ethical Assumptions

As has been shown in the previous section, Kantian ethical theory accepts the traditional ethical assumptions. It would claim that ethics is rational. We can use reason to reach theoretical and practical conclusions about ethics. We can also provide reasons to support moral laws and solutions to ethical problems, evaluate those reasons and solutions, and conclude that some of them are better than others. More specifically, we can evaluate personal rules and see if we could will them to be moral laws. Kantians would also agree that there are mutually acceptable solutions to moral problems, assuming we agree on the description of the proposed action and on the evaluation of the proposed rule.

Kantian ethics also accepts the view that all persons are moral equals and should be treated impartially. All persons are rational beings equally bound by the moral law, and, therefore, they are all moral equals. If "Breaking a promise is unethical" is a moral law, then all persons ought to keep their promises to everyone. No one has a special moral status that allows him or her to break promises and still be ethical. Thus, all persons must be treated impartially if a moral agent wants to act ethically.

Finally, Kantian ethics endorses the idea of universalizing moral guidelines and judgments. If one person can legitimately will the rule "Breaking a promise is unethical" to be a moral law, then any rational being can do so, and it would be unethical to break promises. The moral law applies equally to all of us. Assuming that we can will some rules to be moral laws, we can universalize our ethical evaluations connected to those laws.

## Kantian Ethics and the Basic Ethical Themes

Kantian ethics has a position on each of the four basic ethical themes. The first theme was represented by this question: *What kind of moral guidelines makes something good or bad: subjective, relative, or objective ones?* Kantians believe good and bad are objective because they depend on or are the product of considerations of reason that do not depend on the perceptions, judgments, or emotions of particular persons or the beliefs of a particular society. If a personal moral rule can be willed to be a moral law based on the Categorical Imperative, then that law is objective. Its justification is this use of reason, not considerations related

**78**  *Chapter 5 / Kantian Ethical Theory*

to societies. It also is not connected to the emotions or attitudes of specific individuals. The moral law is based on reason and has nothing to do with emotion. Thus, in the sense of "objective" as discussed in Chapter 1, any Kantian moral guideline is an objective one.

Another significant theme in ethics is indicated by this question: *What makes something good or bad; is it the consequences that are produced or the reasoning that leads up to it?* Kantian ethics asserts that the rightness or wrongness of something depends on the reasoning that guided it. The ethical evaluation of an action depends on whether or not the action was done because the personal rule that guided it could be willed to be a moral law.

The third theme is related to this question: *Are good and bad related to following general rules without exceptions or connected to separately evaluating each action, belief, and so on?* Kantians believe ethics involves following rules that could be willed to be moral laws. They allow no exceptions to acting from these rules; making an exception would mean that the moral agent had been inconsistent in acting from the moral law or that he or she had not treated persons as moral equals.

The fourth theme is connected to the proper focus of ethical attention: *Should the group, community, or majority of persons be the focus of ethics or should the focus be on the individual?* Kantians believe the focus of ethics should be the individual person, or rational being. Each person must evaluate his or her personal rules of action and act from those that he or she could will to be moral laws. If individuals use reason correctly, however, everyone will arrive at the same set of legitimate rules of action.

## Contrasting Kantian Ethics with Ethical Egoism

Kantian ethical theory and ethical egoism are very different theories (see Appendix 1) with very different ethical standards. Kantian ethical theory endorses the two forms of the Categorical Imperative: (1) act only from those personal rules that you can at the same time will to be moral laws, and (2) act in regard to all persons in ways that treat them as ends in themselves and never simply as means to accomplish the ends of others. Ethical egoism claims that what is good is what produces a net benefit for a particular individual and that what is bad is what produces a net harm for the individual. A similarity between the two theories relates to the first traditional ethical assumption: Both theories assume that ethics is rational. Kantian ethics differs in that it accepts impartiality, moral equality, and universalizability, whereas ethical egoism accepts none of these. In regard to the ethical themes, there is agreement on two themes, and disagreement on two others. The theories basically agree on the first theme. Kantians assert that good and bad are objective because they depend on general considerations of reason and not on society or the emotions and attitudes of specific individuals. Ethical egoism also claims that good and bad are objective because they relate to factual considerations related to harm and benefit to the individual. The two theories disagree on the second ethical theme. Egoism determines good and bad by looking at the consequences to the individual, whereas Kantian ethical theory looks at the reasoning that precedes an action. There is also disagreement on the third theme, with Kantians connecting good and bad to following general rules without exceptions and ethical egoists evaluating actions on a case-by-case basis. Finally, the theories agree that the focus of ethics should be on the individual, although Kantians focus on the individual willing moral laws and egoists concentrate on considerations of individual benefit. Thus, there are some similarities between the two theories, but a greater number of important differences as well.

## Problems with Kantian Ethics

Kantian ethical theory, historically, has been very important, but it does have some problems. In the next section, three of the more clear-cut of these problems will be discussed. The conclusion of the chapter will evaluate the theory in terms of the criteria from Chapter 1.

### Descriptions for Actions

One problem with Kantian ethical theory relates to the procedure for creating moral laws. Persons must be able to identify an action ("making a promise" or "killing an innocent person") and then decide on the rule that guides the action ("persons ought to keep their promises" or "it is unethical to kill innocent people"). This identification is essential; without it there will be no personal rule. Without the personal rule, there will be no way to determine ethical action because an action can only be ethical if it follows from a personal rule that could be willed to be a moral law. Kant seems to have assumed that there is only one correct description for an action and that each action only connects to one rule. Examples suggest otherwise. Suppose I contemplate taking some food from a grocery store to feed my starving children. What is the correct description of the action? Is it a case of stealing, of saving the lives of innocent people, or of caring for my children? There are certainly incorrect ways to describe this action (for example, taking a walk in the park), but which of the plausible descriptions is the one to use in determining the appropriate rule and ultimately whether the action is ethical? If we cannot identify a single description for the action, we are faced with

**80**    *Chapter 5 / Kantian Ethical Theory*

multiple personal rules. Is this the relevant rule? Whenever my children are starving and I can get no money for food, I ought to take the food from large stores. Is it this rule? It is unethical to steal the property of others. Is it this rule? Persons ought to try to save the lives of innocent people. Finally, is it this rule? We ought to care for our children. It seems that all of these rules (and perhaps others) apply to this case. The problem is that we do not know the proper description or rule. If we cannot identify the single relevant personal rule, we will not be able to decide how to act ethically because we will not know what rule to examine to see if it can be willed to be a moral law. If we cannot do this, we will not obtain help in solving the relevant moral problem. Although this is a serious criticism, the theory would still work in areas where there is no question about the correct description of the action. This criticism shows that the theory will have only limited success as an ethical theory.

## Conflicting Moral Laws

One way to solve the problem of not being able to identify a single description and rule is to declare that several descriptions and rules are relevant to any action. This, however, creates a new dilemma, the problem of conflicting moral laws. Suppose a person could will both of these rules to be moral laws: (1) It is unethical to steal, and (2) Persons ought to try to save the lives of innocent persons. In a case where children are starving and the only way to get food is by theft, which rule should we follow? Kantian theory does not provide the means to allow us to rank moral laws; hence, we will not know what is the ethical thing to do. In fact, even if there could be a legitimate ranking of moral laws, this would not be sufficient. There might be cases where we would have a conflict between a very serious violation of a less important moral law and a minor violation of a more important law.[2] Once again, the theory provides no way to resolve this problem. If persons do not know which rule to follow, they will not have help in solving moral problems. To the extent that conflicting rules arise, Kantian ethics will not be a successful ethical theory.

## Exceptions to Moral Laws

The third main difficulty with Kantian ethics is connected to the idea that Kantians allow no exceptions to moral laws. Using Kantian ethics, there can be no exceptions to legitimate moral laws because we must be consistent and treat persons as moral equals. Kant thought, for example, that persons should never lie, even if a lie might prevent someone from being hurt or even killed. This might seem ridiculous, but we must remember that Kantians are not concerned with consequences. They endorse respect for the moral law, not maximum benefit. When we disregard consequences, what could possibly motivate us to break our moral rule and lie? This aspect of the theory seems rigid and inflexible. If there can be no compromises, Kantian theory will not help us to solve many real moral problems.

In connection to this problem, there is a potential solution that Kantians could offer. They could claim that although moral laws need to be followed without exceptions there is no reason moral laws cannot have exceptions built into them. An example of such a rule might be: It is unethical to steal the property of others except when stealing is the only way to save the lives of innocent people. The only difficulty with this solution is that the exception built into the rule would have to be motivated by considerations related either to consistency or moral equality, and not to consequences. We might argue that we could incorporate this exception about saving the lives of innocent people by stealing into the previous law out of respect for the moral equality of those people whose lives are in danger. Unfortunately, while respecting the moral equality of the people whose lives are in danger, we are not respecting the moral equality of the people from whom we are stealing. A main problem with these exceptions to the rules is that they bring us back to the problem of conflicting moral laws. Why is it more important, based on Kantian ethics, to respect moral equality related to life than moral equality connected to property? Without some policy concerning the relative moral value of ethical laws, this strategy is doomed to fail. Once again, we see a criticism that leads to the conclusion that Kantian ethical theory will be only partially successful in helping us solve ethical problems.

These three problems with Kantian ethics have led many moral philosophers to reject it. Others, however, insist that Kant's work is the most important in the history of ethics and that the theory is the best one we have.

## Conclusion

The Kantian approach to ethics has been very influential. Many persons intuitively believe in the moral law and find acting from respect for that law compelling. Also, most people believe moral equality is an important element in ethics, and no ethical theory takes a stronger position on moral equality than Kantian ethics. Using the formulations of the Categorical Imperative, Kantian ethical theory identifies ethical guidelines, argues that these guidelines are better than those produced by other theories, and distinguishes guidelines that would prevent the unlimited pursuit of self-interest. Thus, it satisfies the first three criteria for a successful ethical theory.

The problems with Kantian ethics relate to the fourth criterion, that the theory must produce effective solutions to ethical problems. One problem with Kantian theory is related to the correct descriptions for actions. This is a serious problem although it is hard to determine how serious it is. To what extent do people disagree on what constitutes lying, theft, breaking promises, and so on? If the degree of disagreement is great, then Kantian ethics will not be very effective at all. The second problem—the inability to resolve conflicting moral laws—is probably the most serious and may be an adequate reason to reject the theory. Many serious moral issues—abortion, gun control, drug testing—involve such conflicts. These are the issues with which we need the most help, and Kantian theory is not equipped to provide that assistance. The third problem with allowing no exceptions to moral laws is a serious one for people who believe effective solutions can never be merely a matter of following rules. They require a more flexible theory that will consider exceptions to basic moral rules. Therefore, although Kantian ethical theory satisfies the first three criteria for a successful ethical theory, it has problems producing effective solutions to moral problems. Based on the criteria from Chapter 1, Kantian ethical theory is only partially successful as an ethical theory.

What are we to conclude about the partially successful Kantian ethical theory and the ethical insight related to it? Should we reject it as we rejected divine command theory, ethical relativism, ethical egoism, and emotivism? Kantian ethical theory seems stronger than these others and should not be rejected unless we can find a better theory. In the eighteenth and nineteenth centuries, a group of moral philosophers, called utilitarians, did believe they had an ethical theory superior to Kant's. In the next chapter, we will look at this utilitarian theory. It takes a completely different approach to ethics and avoids the problems that plague the Kantian view. Utilitarianism examines the actual consequences of actions to determine whether they are good or evil. Perhaps you will agree with the utilitarians that their ethical theory is superior to Kant's.

## QUESTIONS FOR REVIEW

*Here are some questions to help you review the main concepts in this chapter.*

1. What is the basic ethical insight connected to Kantian ethical theory?

2. How do moral laws and conditional rules function differently?

3. What are the two formulations of the Kantian ethical standard or Categorical Imperative? Do you think they are really saying the same thing, or do they have an important difference? Support your answer.

4. In general, how are persons to know what personal rules they should will to be moral laws?

5. Identify one potential rule that Kantians would reject, and explain why they would do so.

6. Identify one specific rule that Kantians would will to be a moral law, and explain why they would do so.

7. In your opinion, what is the most significant strength of Kantian ethical theory? Support your answer.

8. How do Kantians differentiate between what is and what is not morally significant?

9. What position do Kantians take on aspects of the traditional ethical assumptions?

10. What view does Kantian ethical theory take on each of the four ethical themes?

11. Identify one similarity and two differences between Kantian ethical theory and ethical egoism.

12. What do you think is the most significant problem with Kantian ethical theory? Support your answer.

13. Is Kantian ethical theory a successful ethical theory based on the criteria from Chapter 1? Support your answer.

### NOTES

1. A primary source for Kant's ideas on ethics is Immanuel Kant, *Groundwork of the Metaphysics of Morals,* translated by H. J. Paton (New York: Harper & Row, 1964).

2. This second aspect of the problem with conflicting moral laws, that even with a ranking there would still be a serious difficulty, was mentioned by one of the reviewers of the first edition of this text.

# Fundamental Principles of the Metaphysics of Morals

Immanuel Kant

Immanuel Kant was born in 1724 in Königsberg, Prussia, where he spent his entire life. As a boy he attended the Collegium Fridericanum, a school run by the Pietists (the Lutheran sect to which his family belonged). In 1740 he enrolled in the University of Königsberg, where he studied a wide variety of subjects, including theology, philosophy, mathematics, physics, and medicine. He withdrew from the university in 1747 to support himself by working as a private tutor for families in the Königsberg area. He resumed his studies in 1754 and completed his degree the following year. He then became a lecturer at the University of Königsberg, teaching such diverse subjects as mathematics, geography, mineralogy, and philosophy. Fifteen years later he was appointed Professor of Logic and Metaphysics. His writings—especially his monumental *Critique of Pure Reason* (1781)—brought him increasing fame, and students came from afar to hear him lecture. In 1797 he stopped lecturing but continued to write. He died in Königsberg in 1804 at the age of seventy-nine.

Kant's principal works, in addition to the *Critique of Pure Reason,* are *Prolegomena to Any Future Metaphysics* (1783), *Fundamental Principles of the Metaphysics of Morals* (1785), *Critique of Practical Reason* (1788), and *Critique of Judgment* (1790).

Our selection is taken from *Fundamental Principles of the Metaphysics of Morals,* a work whose aim, Kant explains in his preface, is "to seek out and establish the supreme principle of morality." According to Kant, the moral worth of an action is determined by one's motive, not by the consequences of the action. And the proper motive (what makes a will a *good* will) is to do one's duty simply because it is one's duty. To act out of duty means to act out of respect for the law, and to act out of respect for the law means to follow the "categorical imperative." This imperative states that our action should be "universalizable"—which means that the personal policy (maxim) on which our action is based must be one that we could consistently will that all persons follow. If our maxim cannot be universalized, the action is immoral. For example, the maxim of making a false promise to escape a difficulty cannot consistently be universalized because, if everyone followed it, promises would no longer be able to function as promises because no one would believe them. The categorical imperative is, for Kant, the ultimate criterion for determining the morality of any action.

According to Kant, the categorical imperative can be expressed in various equivalent ways, including the injunction that we should always treat persons (including ourselves) as ends in themselves, and never simply as means to an end. Returning to his example of making a false promise, he explains that such a promise is immoral because it uses the person lied to merely as means to obtain one's end.

▼

## First Section: Transition from the Common Rational Knowledge of Morality to the Philosophical

Nothing can possibly be conceived in the world, or even out of it, which can be called good without qualification, except a *good will*. Intelligence, wit, judgment, and the other talents of the mind, however they may be named, or courage, resolution, perseverance, as qualities of temperament, are undoubtedly good and desirable in many respects; but these gifts of na-ture may also become extremely bad and mischievous if the will which is to make use of them, and which, therefore, constitutes what is called *character*, is not good. It is the same with the gifts of fortune. Power, riches, honour, even health, and the general well-being and contentment with one's condition which is called *happiness*, inspire pride, and often presumption, if there is not a good will to correct the influence of these on the mind, and with this also to rectify the whole principle of acting and adapt it to its end. The sight of a being who is not adorned with a single feature of a pure and good will, enjoying unbroken prosperity, can never give pleasure to an impartial rational spectator. Thus a good will appears to constitute the indispensable condition even of being worthy of happiness.

There are even some qualities which are of service to this good will itself and may facilitate its action, yet which have no intrinsic unconditional value, but always presuppose a good will, and this qualifies the esteem that we justly have for them and does not permit us to regard them as absolutely good. Moderation in the affections and passions, self-control, and calm deliberation are not only good in many respects, but even seem to constitute part of the intrinsic worth of the person; but they are far from deserving to be called good without qualification, although they have been so unconditionally praised by the ancients. For without the principles of a good will, they may become extremely bad; and the coolness of a villain not only makes him far more dangerous, but also directly makes him more abominable in our eyes than he would have been without it.

A good will is good not because of what it performs or effects, not by its aptness for the attainment of some proposed end, but simply by virtue of the volition; that is, it is good in itself, and considered by itself is to be esteemed much higher than all that can be brought about by it in favour of any inclination, nay, even of the sum total of all inclinations. Even if it should happen that, owing to special disfavour of fortune, or the [stingy] provision of a stepmotherly nature, this will should wholly lack power to accomplish its purpose; if with its greatest efforts it should yet achieve nothing, and there should remain only the good will (not, to be sure, a mere wish, but the summoning of all means in our power); then, like a jewel, it would still shine by its own light, as a thing which has its whole value in itself. Its usefulness or fruitlessness can neither add to nor take away anything from this value. It would be, as it were, only the setting to enable us to handle it the more conveniently in common commerce or to attract to it the attention of those who are not yet connoisseurs, but not to recommend it to true connoisseurs or to determine its value. . . .

We have, then, to develop the notion of a will which deserves to be highly esteemed for itself and is good without a view to anything further, a notion which exists already in the sound natural understanding, requiring rather to be cleared up than to be taught, and which in estimating the value of our actions always takes the first place and constitutes the condition of all the rest. In order to do this, we will take the notion of *duty*, which includes that of a good will, although implying certain subjective restrictions and hindrances. These, however, far from concealing it or rendering it unrecognizable, rather bring it out by contrast and make it shine forth so much the brighter.

I omit here all actions which are already recognized as inconsistent with duty, although they may be useful for this or that purpose, for with these the question whether they are done *from duty* cannot arise at all, since they even conflict with it. I also set aside those actions which really conform to duty, but to which men have *no direct inclination,* performing them because they are impelled to it by some other inclination. For in this case we can readily distinguish whether the action which agrees with duty is done from duty or from a selfish view. It is much harder to make this distinction when the action accords with duty, and the subject has besides a *direct* inclination to it. For example, it is always a matter of duty that a dealer should not overcharge an inexperienced purchaser; and wherever there is much commerce the prudent tradesman does not overcharge, but keeps a fixed price for everyone, so that a child buys of him as well as any other. Men are thus honestly served; but this is not enough to make us believe that the tradesman has so acted from duty and from principles of honesty: his own advantage required it. It is out of the question in this case to suppose that he might besides have a direct inclination in favour of the buyers, so that, as it were, from love he should give no advantage to one over another. Accordingly, the action was done neither from duty nor from direct inclination, but merely with a selfish view.

On the other hand, it is a duty to maintain one's life; and, in addition, everyone has also a direct inclination to do so. But on this account the often anxious care which most men take for it has no intrinsic worth, and their maxim[1] has no moral import. They preserve their life *as duty requires,* no doubt, but not *because duty requires.* On the other hand, if adversity and hopeless sorrow have completely taken away the relish for life; if the unfortunate one, strong in mind, indignant at his fate rather than desponding or dejected, wishes for death, and yet preserves his life without loving it—not from inclination or fear, but from duty—then his maxim has a moral worth.

To be beneficent when we can is a duty; and besides this, there are many minds so sympathetically constituted that, without any other motive of vanity or self-interest, they find a pleasure in spreading joy around them and can take delight in the satisfaction of others so far as it is their own work. But I maintain that in such a case an action of this kind, however proper, however amiable it may be, has nevertheless no true moral worth, but is on a level with other inclinations, e.g., the inclination to honour, which, if it is happily directed to that which is in fact of public utility and accordant with duty, and consequently honourable, deserves praise and encouragement, but not esteem. For the maxim lacks the moral import, namely, that such actions be done from duty, not from inclination. Put the case that the mind of that philanthropist was clouded by sorrow of his own, extinguishing all sympathy with the lot of others, and that while he still has the power to benefit others in distress, he is not touched by their trouble because he is absorbed with his own. And now suppose that he tears himself out of this dead insensibility and performs the action without any inclination to it, but simply from duty; then first has his action its genuine moral worth. Further still; if nature has put little sympathy in the heart of this or that man; if he, supposed to be an upright man, is by temperament cold and indifferent to the sufferings of others, perhaps because in respect of his own he is provided with the special gift of patience and fortitude, and supposes, or even requires, that others should have the same—and such a man would certainly not be the meanest product of nature—but if nature had not specially framed him for a philanthropist, would he not still find in himself a source from whence to give himself a far higher worth than that of a good-natured temperament could be? Unquestionably. It is just in this that the moral worth of the character is brought out which is incomparably the highest of all, namely, that he is beneficent, not from inclination, but from duty. . . .

The second proposition[2] is: That an action done from duty derives its moral worth, not from the purpose which is to be attained by it, but from the maxim by which it is determined, and therefore does not depend on the realization of the object of the action, but merely on the *principle of volition* by which the action has taken place, without regard to any object of desire. It is clear from what precedes that the purposes which we may have in view in our actions, or their effects regarded as ends and springs of the will, cannot give to actions any unconditional or moral worth. In what, then, can their worth lie, if it is not to consist in the [relation of the will] to its expected effect? It cannot lie anywhere but in the principle of the will, without regard to the ends which can be attained by the action. For the will stands between its a priori principle, which is formal, and its a posteriori spring, which is material,[3] as between two roads; and as it must be determined by something, it follows that it must be determined by the formal principle of volition when an action is done from duty, in which case every material principle has been withdrawn from it.

The third proposition, which is a consequence of the two preceding, I would express thus: Duty is the necessity of acting from respect for the law. I may have *inclination* for an object as the effect of my proposed action, but I cannot have *respect* for it, just for this reason, that it is an effect and not an [activity] of will. Similarly, I cannot have respect for inclination, whether my own or another's; I can at most, if my own, approve it; if another's, sometimes even love it, that is, look on it as favourable to my own interest. It is only what is connected with my will as a principle, by no means as an effect—what does not subserve my inclination, but overpowers it, or at least, in case of choice, excludes it from its calculation—in other words, simply the law of itself, which can be an object of respect, and hence a command. Now an action done from duty must wholly exclude the influence of inclination, and with it every object of the will, so that nothing remains which can determine the will except objectively the law, and subjectively pure respect for this practical law, and consequently the maxim that I should follow this law even to the thwarting of all my inclinations.

Thus the moral worth of an action does not lie in the effect expected from it, nor in any principle of action which requires to borrow its motive from this expected effect. For all these effects—agreeableness of one's condition, and even the promotion of the happiness of others—could have been also brought about by other causes, so that for this there would have been no need of the will of a rational being; whereas it is in this alone that the supreme and unconditional good can be found. The preeminent good which we call moral can therefore consist in nothing else than *the conception of law* in itself, which certainly is only possible in a rational being, in so far as this conception, and not the expected effect, determines the will. This is a good which is already present in the person who acts accordingly, and we have not to wait for it to appear first in the result.

But what sort of law can that be, the conception of which must determine the will, even without paying any regard to the effect expected from it, in order that this will may be called good absolutely and without qualification? As I have deprived the will of every impulse which could arise to it from [obeying a specific] law, there remains nothing but the universal conformity of its actions to law in general, which alone is to serve the will as a principle, that is, I am never to act otherwise than [in such a way] *that I could also will that my maxim should become a universal law.* Here, now, it is the simple conformity to law in general, without assuming any particular law applicable to certain actions, that serves the will as its principle, and must so serve it, if duty is not to be a vain delusion and a chimerical notion. The common reason of men in its practical judgments perfectly coincides with this and always has in view the principle here suggested. Let the question be, for example: May I when in distress make a promise with the intention not to keep it? I readily distinguish here between the two significations which the question may have: whether it is *prudent,* or whether it is *right,* to make a false promise. The former may undoubtedly often be the case. I see clearly indeed that it is not enough to extricate myself from a present difficulty by means of this subterfuge, but it must be well considered whether there may not [afterwards] spring from this lie much greater inconvenience than that from which I now free myself. And as, with all my supposed cunning, the consequences cannot be so easily foreseen, [and trust in me] once lost may be much more injurious to me than any mischief which I seek to avoid at present, it should be considered whether it would not be more prudent to act herein according to a universal maxim, and to make it a habit to promise nothing except with the intention of keeping it. But it is soon clear to me that such a maxim will still only be based on the fear of consequences. Now it is a wholly different thing to be truthful from duty, and to be so from apprehension of injurious consequences. In the first case, the very notion of the action already implies a law for me; in the second case, I must first look about elsewhere to see what results may be combined with it which would affect myself. For to deviate from the principle of duty is beyond all doubt wicked; but to be unfaithful to my maxim of prudence may often be very advantageous to me, although to abide by it is certainly safer. The shortest way, however, and an unerring one, to discover the answer to this question whether a lying promise is consistent with duty, is to ask myself, Should I be content that my maxim (to extricate myself from difficulty by a false promise) should hold good as a universal law, for myself as well as for others, and should I be able to say to myself, "Every one may make a deceitful promise when he finds himself in a difficulty from which he cannot otherwise extricate himself"? Then I presently become aware that while I can will the lie, I can by no means will that lying should be a universal law. For with such a law there would be no promises at all, since it would be in vain to allege my intention in regard to my future actions to those who would not believe this allegation, or if they over-hastily did so, would pay me back in my own coin. Hence my maxim, as soon as it should be made a universal law, would necessarily destroy itself.

I do not, therefore, need any far-reaching penetration to discern what I have to do in order that my will may be morally good. Inexperienced in the course of the world, incapable of being prepared for all its contingencies, I only ask myself: Can you also will that your maxim should be a universal law? If not, then it must be rejected, and that not because of a disadvantage accruing from it to myself or even to others, but because it cannot enter as a principle into a possible universal legislation—and reason extorts from me immediate respect for such legislation. I do not indeed as yet discern on what this respect is based (this the philosopher may inquire), but at least I understand this, that it is an estimation of the worth which far outweighs all worth of what is recommended by inclination, and that the necessity of acting from pure respect for the practical law is what constitutes duty, to which every other motive must give place, because it is the condition of a will being good in itself, and the worth of such a will is above everything. . . .

### Second Section: Transition from Popular Moral Philosophy to the Metaphysics of Morals

. . . In this study we may not merely advance by the natural steps from the common moral judgment (in this case, very worthy of respect) to the philosophical, as has been already done, but also from a popular philosophy, which goes no further than it can reach by groping with the help of examples, to metaphysics (which does not allow itself to be checked by anything empirical, and—as it must measure the whole extent of this kind of rational knowledge—goes as far as ideal conceptions, where even examples fail us), we must follow and clearly describe the practical faculty of reason, from the general rules of its determination to the point where the notion of duty springs from it.

Everything in nature works according to laws. Rational beings alone have the faculty of acting according to the *conception* of laws, that is, according to principles; [in other words, they] have a will. Since the deduction of actions from principles requires reason, the will is nothing but practical reason. If reason infallibly determines the will, then the actions of such a being which are recognized as objectively necessary are subjectively necessary also; that is, the will is a faculty to choose only that which reason, independent of inclination, recognizes as practically necessary, that is, as good. But if reason of itself does not sufficiently determine the will; if the latter is subject also to subjective conditions (particular impulses) which do not always coincide with the objective conditions; in a word, if the will does not *in itself* completely accord with reason (which is actually the case with men); then the actions which objectively are recognized as necessary are subjectively contingent, and the determination of such a will according to objective laws is *obligation*. That is to say, the relation of the objective laws to a will that is not thoroughly good is conceived as the determination of the will of a rational being by principles of reason, but which the will from its nature does not of necessity follow.

The conception of an objective principle, in so far as it is obligatory for a will, is called a *command* (of reason), and the formula of the command is called an *imperative*. . . .

Now all imperatives command either *hypothetically* or *categorically*. The former represent the practical necessity of a possible action as means to something else that is willed (or at least which one might possibly will). The categorical imperative would be that which represented an action as necessary of itself without reference to another end, that is, as objectively necessary.

Since every practical law represents a possible action as good, and on this account, for a subject who is practically determinable by reason, necessary; [therefore,] all imperatives are formulas determining an action which is necessary according to the principle of a will good in some respects. Now if the action is good only as a means to something else, then the imperative is *hypothetical;* if it is conceived as good in itself and consequently as being necessarily the principle of a will which of itself conforms to reason, then it is *categorical* . . . .

When I conceive a hypothetical imperative in general, I do not know beforehand what it will contain until I am given the condition. But when I conceive a categorical imperative, I know at once what it contains. For as the imperative contains besides the law only the necessity that the maxim shall conform to this law, while the law contains no conditions restricting it, there remains nothing but the general statement that the maxim of the action should conform to a universal law, and it is this conformity alone that the imperative properly represents as necessary.

There is therefore but one categorical imperative, namely this: *Act only on that maxim whereby you can at the same time will that it should become a universal law.*

Now if all imperatives of duty can be deduced from this one imperative as from their principle, then, although it should remain undecided whether what is called duty is not merely a vain notion, yet at least we shall be able to show what we understand by it and what this notion means.

Since the universality of the law according to which effects are produced constitutes what is properly called *nature* in the most general sense (as to form), that is, the existence of things so far as it is determined by general laws, the imperative of duty may be expressed thus: *Act as if the maxim of your action were to become by your will a universal law of nature.*

We will now enumerate a few duties, adopting the usual division of them into duties to ourselves and to others, and into perfect and imperfect duties.[4]

1. A man reduced to despair by a series of misfortunes feels wearied of life, but is still so far in possession of his reason that he can ask himself whether it would not be contrary to his duty to himself to take his own life. Now he inquires whether the maxim of his action could become a universal law of nature. His maxim is: From self-love I adopt it as a principle to shorten my life when its longer duration is likely to bring more evil than satisfaction. It is asked then simply whether this principle founded on self-love can become a universal law of nature. Now we see at once that a system of nature of which it should be a law to destroy life by means of the very feeling whose special nature it is to impel to the improvement of life would contradict itself, and therefore could not exist as a system of nature; hence that maxim cannot possibly exist as a universal law of nature, and consequently would be wholly inconsistent with the supreme principle of all duty.

2. Another finds himself forced by necessity to borrow money. He knows that he will not be able to repay it, but sees also that nothing will be lent to him unless he promises stoutly to repay it in a definite time. He desires to make this promise, but he has still so much conscience as to ask himself: Is it not unlawful and inconsistent with duty to get out of a difficulty in this way? Suppose, however, that he resolves to do so, then the maxim of his action would be expressed thus: When I think myself in want of money, I will borrow money and promise to repay it, although I know that I never can do so. Now this principle of self-love or of one's own advantage may perhaps be consistent with my whole future welfare; but the question now is, Is it right? I change then the suggestion of self-love into a universal law, and state the question thus: How would it be if my maxim were a universal law? Then I see at once that it could never hold as a universal law of nature, but would necessarily contradict itself. For supposing it to be a universal law that everyone, when he thinks himself in a difficulty, should be able to promise whatever he pleases, with the purpose of not keeping his promise; the promise itself would become impossible, as well as the end that one might have in view in it, since no one would consider that anything was promised to him, but would ridicule all such statements as vain pretences.

3. A third finds in himself a talent which, with the help of [cultivation] might make him a useful man in many respects. But he finds himself in comfortable circumstances and prefers to indulge in pleasure rather than to take pains in enlarging and improving his happy natural capacities. He asks, however, whether his maxim of neglect of his natural gifts, besides agreeing with his inclination to indulgence, agrees also with what is called duty. He sees then that a system of nature could indeed subsist with such a universal law although men (like the South Sea islanders) should let their talents rest, and resolve to devote their lives merely to idleness, amusement, and propagation of their species—in a word, to enjoyment; but he cannot possibly *will* that this should be a universal law of nature, or be implanted in us as such by a natural instinct. For, as a rational being, he necessarily wills that his faculties be developed, since they serve him and have been given him for all sorts of possible purposes.

4. A fourth, who is in prosperity, while he sees that others have to contend with great wretchedness and that he could help them, thinks: What concern is it of mine? Let everyone be as happy as heaven pleases, or as he can make himself; I will take nothing from him nor even envy him, only I do not wish to contribute anything to his welfare or to his assistance in distress. Now no doubt if such a mode of thinking were a universal law, the human race might very well subsist, and doubtless even better than in a state in which everyone talks of sympathy and good will, or even takes care occasionally to put it into practice, but, on the other side, also cheats when he can, betrays the rights of men, or otherwise violates them. But although it is possible that a universal law of nature might exist in accordance with that maxim, it is impossible to will that such a principle should have the universal validity of a law of nature. For a will which resolved this would contradict itself, inasmuch as many cases might occur in which one would have need of the love and sympathy of others, and in which, by such a law of nature, sprung from his own will, he would deprive himself of all hope of the aid he desires.

These are a few of the many actual duties, or at least what we regard as such, which obviously fall into two classes on the one principle that we have laid down. We must be *able to will* that a maxim of our action should be a universal law. This is the canon of the moral appreciation of the action generally. Some actions are of such a character that their maxim cannot without contradiction be even *conceived* as a universal law of nature, far from it being possible that we should will that it should be so. In others this intrinsic impossibility is not found, but still it is impossible to will that their maxim should be raised to the universality of a law of nature, since such a will would contradict itself. It is easily seen that the former violate strict or rigorous (inflexible) duty; the latter only laxer (meritorious) duty. Thus it has been completely shown by these examples how all duties depend as regards the nature of the obligation (not the object of the action) on the same principle. . . .

. . . Man, and generally any rational being, exists as an end in himself, not merely as a means to be arbitrarily used by this or that will, but in all his actions, whether they concern himself or other rational beings, must be always regarded at the same time as an end. All objects of the inclinations have only a conditional worth; for if the inclinations and the wants founded on them did not exist, then their object would be without value. But the inclinations themselves, being sources of want, are so far from having an absolute worth for which they should be desired, that, on the contrary, it must be the universal wish of every rational being to be wholly free from them. Thus the worth of any object which is to be acquired by our action is always conditional. Beings whose existence depends not on our will but on nature's, have nevertheless, if they are nonrational beings, only a relative value as means, and are therefore called *things*. Rational beings, on the contrary, are called *persons* because their very nature points them out as ends in themselves, that is, as something which must not be used merely as means, and so far therefore restricts freedom of action (and is an object of respect). These, therefore, are not merely *subjective* ends, whose existence has a worth *for us* as an effect of our action, but *objective* ends, that is, things whose existence is an end *in itself*. [This kind of end is one] for which no other can be substituted, which they should subserve merely as means; for otherwise nothing whatever would possess absolute worth. But if all worth were conditioned and therefore contingent, then there would be no supreme practical principle of reason whatever.

If, then, there is a supreme practical principle or, in respect of the human will, a categorical imperative, it must be one which, being drawn from the conception of that which is necessarily an end for everyone because it is an end in itself, constitutes an *objective* principle of will, and can therefore serve as a universal practical law. The foundation of this principle is: *Rational nature exists as an end in itself.* Man necessarily conceives his own existence as being so: so far, then, this is a *subjective* principle of human actions. But every other rational being regards its existence similarly, just on the same rational principle that holds for me; so that it is at the same time an objective principle, from which as a supreme practical law all laws of the will must be capable of being deduced. Accordingly, the practical imperative will be as follows: *So act as to treat humanity, whether in your own person or in that of any other, in every case as an end, never as a means only.* We will now inquire whether this can be practically carried out.

[Let us return to] the previous examples.

First, under the head of necessary duty to oneself: He who contemplates suicide should ask himself whether his action can be consistent with the idea of humanity as an end in itself. If he destroys himself in order to escape from painful circumstances, he uses a person merely as a means to maintain a tolerable condition up to the end of life. But a man is not a thing, that is to say, something which can be used merely as means, but must in all his actions be always considered as an end in himself. I cannot, therefore, dispose in any way of a man in my own person so as to mutilate him, to damage or kill him. . . .

Secondly, as regards necessary duties, or those of strict obligation, towards others: He who is thinking of making a lying promise to others will see at once that he would be using another man merely as a means, without the latter containing at the same time the end in himself. For he whom I propose by such a promise to use for my own purposes cannot possibly assent to my mode of acting towards him, and therefore cannot himself contain the end of this action. This violation of the principle of humanity in other men is more obvious if we take in examples of attacks on the freedom and property of others. For then it is clear that he who transgresses the rights of men intends to use the person of others merely as means, without considering that as rational beings they ought always to be esteemed also as ends, that is, as beings who must be capable of containing in themselves the end of the very same action.

Thirdly, as regards contingent (meritorious) duties to oneself: It is not enough that the action does not violate humanity in our own person as an end in itself; it must also *harmonize* with it. Now there are in humanity capacities of greater perfection which belong to the end that nature has in view in regard to humanity in ourselves as the subject: to neglect these might perhaps be consistent with the *maintenance* of humanity as an end in itself, but not with the *advancement* of this end.

Fourthly, as regards meritorious duties towards others: The natural end which all men have is their own happiness. Now humanity might indeed subsist although no one should contribute anything to the happiness of others, provided he did not intentionally withdraw anything from it; but after all, this would only harmonize negatively, not positively, with humanity as an end in itself, if everyone does not also endeavour, as far as in him lies, to forward the ends of others. For the ends of any subject that is an end in himself, ought as far as possible to be my ends also, if that conception is to have its full effect with me.

---

▶ NOTES

1. *maxim:* the personal policy on which a person acts. In the case described here, the maxim would be to follow one's inclination to preserve one's life. Kant later contrasts a maxim with *universal law,* which binds all rational creatures. A maxim is *subjective* principle, while universal law is an *objective* principle. [D.C.A., ed.]

2. The first proposition [not identified as such by Kant] was that to have moral worth an action must be done from duty. [T.K.A., trans.]

3. *A priori* means "independent of experience" (literally, in Latin, "from what comes earlier"); *a posteriori* means "dependent on experience" ("from what comes later"). Duty is an a priori principle of the will be-

cause it binds prior to any experience; the incentive ("spring") of action is a posteriori because it depends on the person's experience. Kant here draws a further contrast between duty and incentive: Duty is a *formal* principle because it refers to the general form any action should take; incentive is *material* because it involves the situation ("matter") of a particular action. [D.C.A.]

4. In Kant's terminology, a *perfect duty* is one that prohibits a specific action, while an *imperfect duty* commands us to achieve some general goal without specifying what means we are to use. Kant's following four examples illustrate, respectively, (1) a perfect duty to ourselves (not to commit suicide), (2) a perfect duty to others (not to make false promises), (3) an imperfect duty to ourselves (to develop our talents), and (4) an imperfect duty to others (to help those in need). [D.C.A.]

**Chapter 4**

# *Ethical Egoism and Ethical Subjectivism*

The previous chapter showed the difficulty in identifying the actual ethical guidelines of a society. Without clear moral guidelines provided by society, it would appear that we should be unable to make ethical evaluations or judgments, yet people make them all the time. If someone breaks into my house and steals my stereo equipment, I am furious and quick to tell anyone who will listen that the person who did it is a jerk who should be caught and punished. I got a lot of pleasure out of listening to my stereo, and now I cannot do that. The loss of my stereo has harmed me, and I am angry about it. Obviously, I think the theft was morally bad or wrong. Individuals seem to have no trouble making ethical evaluations and, therefore, perhaps legitimate moral guidelines are related to something about particular individuals instead of something about societies. For many people, this idea that legitimate moral judgments necessarily connect to something about particular individuals seems intuitively correct. They would endorse the ethical insight that *legitimate moral guidelines necessarily have something to do with particular individuals.*

To develop this insight, we must discover what it is about particular individuals that relates to good and bad. In the above example, I claimed that the loss of my stereo harmed me. I got a lot of pleasure out of listening to it, and now I cannot do that. My loss of pleasure harms me. We might connect harm to the individual with something being morally bad. If harm to the individual is bad, then benefit to the individual

48

should be good. Therefore, the initial claim related to a theory associated with individuals is that whatever harms individuals is bad or wrong and whatever benefits them is right or good.

## Ethical Egoism

The idea that moral good and bad relate to harm and benefit to an individual is an essential component of an ethical theory called ethical egoism. *Ethical egoism* claims that to act ethically moral agents should act in their own self-interest and maximize benefit for themselves. *The ethical standard of ethical egoism is that what is good for an individual is what produces a net benefit for that individual, and what is bad is what produces a net harm for that individual.* Individuals have only one fundamental moral duty: to maximize net benefit and minimize net harm to themselves. They have no basic moral obligation to other people. Ethical egoism leads to the conclusion that there is no difference between "good for me" and "good." Whatever is beneficial for me is morally good, no matter what the effects on others may be. Other people's harm and benefit simply should not count in our moral considerations. If it is beneficial for me to assault you and steal your money because I need it, I know that I can do it without being caught, and I will not be bothered by bad feelings about it afterward, then it is morally good to do it. The fact that you are injured and lose your money is irrelevant.

This version of ethical egoism is making a claim about how everyone should act: Everyone should act based on their self-interest. You will act to maximize benefit to you, and I will act to maximize benefit to myself. This ethical position does not mean that a person can never act in a way that would benefit someone else. If helping someone else is the best way to maximize benefit to me, then I ought to help that person. If I depend on another person for a ride to work each day, it would be consistent with ethical egoism for me to lend that person a hundred dollars to get the car fixed. Although I am temporarily out the hundred dollars, I gain the significant benefit of being able to go to work and make money. In this case, I should help the person because that is the best way to maximize benefit to myself. Therefore, an ethical egoist may have secondary moral obligations to other people that are related to the basic moral obligation to maximize benefit to himself or herself. I ought to loan the other person money for repairs because I am obligated to maximize benefit to myself. An egoist does not have to be a selfish person. If the best way to maximize benefit to myself is to be generous to others, then I should do that. Perhaps my generosity will be repaid by that person being generous to me, and I will achieve a net advantage. Egoists may be concerned about world poverty, the environment, and other global problems. Their basic reason for being concerned with these problems, however, is that they believe their concern will produce benefits for them.

Ethical egoism does not claim that I should always do what is pleasant. I should be rational about what is best for me. Sometimes I may have to do something unpleasant or painful to achieve a greater benefit in the future. I may regard exercising for an hour every day as unpleasant, but as an ethical egoist, I should do it because it would produce significant benefits for me. As this example implies, egoists do not have to concern themselves solely with short-term consequences. An egoist needs to think about whether a short-term harm, like the pain of getting a cavity filled, will produce a greater amount of long-term benefit, such as a healthy tooth.

Ethical egoism is a consequentialist ethical theory because it determines good and bad based on the consequences to the individual. If the consequences of an action are only benefits, then the action is good. If the consequences are only harms, then it is bad. If the consequences include both benefits and harms, then the egoist must determine whether there is a net benefit or harm. Thus, egoism involves calculations of potential or actual benefit and harm. The object of these calculations is to determine the actions that produce the greatest amount of net benefit for the individual.

## Justification for the Ethical Standard and Strengths of the Theory

An ethical theory should provide an ethical standard to determine good and bad and offer some justification for that standard. The ethical standard was presented in an earlier section, and now the justification will be considered.

### The Natural Inclination to Be Self-Interested

The best justification for using the ethical standard and a corresponding strength of the theory is that the standard and theory seem to fit people's natural inclination to be self-interested. By self-interested, we usually mean that people want to promote their own well-being or maximize benefits to themselves. They tend to look out for their own well-being first, and then consider the well-being of other persons later. Ethical egoism endorses this self-interested attitude and asserts that self-interested actions are the only ethical ones. Thus, one justification for using this standard is that it is consistent with people's inclinations. A theory that is consistent with human nature has an advantage over a theory that is at odds with human nature because people will be more inclined to accept it. This consistency with people's natural inclinations is a strength of the theory.

### Respect for the Individual

Another justification for the standard and a corresponding strength of the theory is that it respects the individual. As philosophers like Friedrich Nietzsche and popular thinkers like Ayn Rand have argued, we must endorse the integrity of the individual and not obligate the individual to serve others. To obligate Rose to help John is to devalue Rose's life because it means she must live at least a small part of her life for John's benefit. The egoist would claim that she should live for her own benefit, not for someone else's. Also, theories that obligate people to help others do not necessarily limit that help to a small amount. People might find themselves obligated to spend all their time helping others. Thus, in one sense their lives are of no value, only the lives of these other people matter. The egoist position is that every individual has an equal right to pursue his or her benefit and that people should not be devalued and obligated to serve others. For some people, this respect for the individual is a reason to use this standard and a strength of the theory.

### Content and Efficiency

A third strength of the theory is that it gives good and bad a clear content: benefit and harm to the individual. This content also seems to promote simplicity and ethical efficiency. That is, we can identify and compare potential harm and benefit to one person with relative efficiency. Certainly ethical egoism is simpler and more efficient than a theory that tries to identify and compare the benefits and harms to everyone affected by an action. The egoist will only have to determine the harms and benefits to one person, whereas the utilitarian will have to identify all the people who are affected by an action and then discover all of the harms and benefits to each of these people. It is much easier for the egoist to make an ethical judgment than for the utilitarian to do so. Thus, another strength of egoism is that it is more efficient than some other theories.

## Morally Significant Actions

A theory should also delineate morally significant actions from ones that are not morally significant. For an ethical egoist, morally significant actions are ones that either benefit or harm the particular individual. When someone steals my stereo, it is morally significant because I have been harmed. Wearing a blue-striped white shirt rather than a plain white one with my blue suit is not morally significant because the choice of shirts does not benefit or harm me.

## Ethical Egoism and the Traditional Ethical Assumptions

Ethical egoism accepts only one of the traditional assumptions associated with ethical theories: It assumes that ethics is rational. Ethical egoism assumes that we can use reason to reach theoretical and practical conclusions about ethical matters, including why we should be ethical egoists. More specifically, people can provide reasons based on harm and benefit to the individual to support egoistic solutions to ethical problems, these reasons can be evaluated, and some solutions will be better than others. Ethical egoism does not endorse moral equality and impartiality. The individual is the only one whose harm and benefit matter; thus, he or she is morally superior to everyone else. The individual certainly does not have to treat people impartially. Friends and family should be given special treatment because that will presumably result in more benefit to the individual. Finally, ethical egoism does not assume that any ethical evaluations can be universalized. Because people are different, what maximizes net benefit for an individual in a particular situation may not maximize net benefit for another person in the same situation. In any case, the individual is only concerned with his or her own moral evaluations, not with extending those evaluations to other people.

## Ethical Egoism and the Basic Ethical Themes

In addition to the traditional assumptions connected to ethical theories, the basic ethical themes about moral good and bad can also be related to ethical egoism in an effort to obtain a better understanding of the theory. The first theme can be represented by this question: *What kind of moral guidelines makes something good or bad: subjective, relative, or objective ones?* This is an interesting issue. The ethical egoist's guidelines are clearly not relative because they do not depend on society. It would seem that the ethical egoist's moral guidelines should be subjective because they are related to something about particular individuals. Chapter 1, however, defined "subjective moral guidelines" as ones that are necessarily a product of the emotions or attitudes of specific individuals. Ethical egoism does not relate good and bad to emotions or attitudes but instead to supposedly objective considerations of harm and benefit to the individual. If it is a fact that telling the truth in this situation will harm me, then it is bad for me to do it. Thus, although this may seem odd, ethical egoism claims that good and bad are objective because they are based on factual considerations of harm and benefit.

Another significant theme in ethics is this: *What makes something good or bad; is it the consequences that are produced or the reasoning that leads up to it?* As stated earlier, ethical egoism is a consequentialist theory. Good and bad are based on consequences to particular individuals.

The third theme relates to this question: *Are good and bad related to following general rules without exceptions or connected to separately evaluating actions, beliefs, and so on?* People who believe we should guide our behavior by general rules feel that these rules should have no exceptions. People who want to evaluate things separately believe we must always be open to the possibility that we can appropriately make an exception to even the best moral rule. They want to evaluate each action as independently as possible based on some criterion or criteria. The criterion may be similar to a rule, but if it is, then the criterion is the only rule that they will always endorse. Ethical egoism could endorse either of these approaches depending on which one maximized overall benefit. Clearly, egoists have one moral rule with no exceptions: The individual ought to maximize net benefit to himself or herself. An individual egoist could take either approach, however, depending on which one would do the best job of maximizing overall benefit for that individual.

The fourth important theme relates to the proper focus of ethical attention and benefit: *Are good and bad primarily related to the group, community, or majority of people or should the focus be on the individual?* Ethical egoism is focused on the individual. The group, community, or majority of people are irrelevant except to the extent that they affect the individual.

## Contrasting Ethical Egoism with Ethical Relativism

Ethical egoism and ethical relativism are very different theories, but they do have some similarities (see Appendix 1). Egoism originates with the insight that moral guidelines are necessarily connected to something about specific individuals, whereas ethical relativism asserts that guidelines relate to actual societies. The ethical standards differ in a corresponding way. The ethical standard for egoism relates good and bad to benefit and harm to the individual, whereas ethical relativism connects good and bad to the actual moral guidelines of a society. In relation to the traditional ethical assumptions, the theories have only one common position: Egoism and ethical relativism both assume that people are not moral equals. The two theories differ with regard to the other ethical assumptions. Ethical egoism assumes that ethics is rational, whereas ethical relativism makes the production of moral guidelines mysterious and arbitrary. Egoism does not assume that ethical evaluations can be universalized, but ethical relativism claims that a person should use the moral guidelines of his or her society to judge everything. In regard to the themes related to good and bad, the two theories differ on everything. Egoism claims that good and bad are objective because they are based on factual considerations, whereas ethical relativism asserts that good and bad are relative to society. Egoism determines good and bad by focusing on consequences, whereas ethical relativism endorses following general rules without exceptions. Egoism focuses on either following rules or evaluating actions separately depending on which course would maximize net benefit to the individual. Ethical relativism is committed to following general rules without exceptions. Finally, egoism relates good and bad to the individual, whereas ethical relativism connects them to the society or group. In summary, the two theories have many important differences, and only one similarity.

## Problems with Ethical Egoism

There are a number of problems with ethical egoism, three of which are discussed in this section. The concluding section on ethical egoism relates these problems to the criteria from Chapter 1.

### Determining the Consequences and Doing the Calculations

The first problem with ethical egoism is one that is found in all consequentialist theories; it involves the difficulty in identifying all the consequences or harms and benefits that follow from an action. Whether an action is good or bad depends on the beneficial and harmful consequences. Therefore, the egoist must identify all the consequences of an action. The effects of actions are often widespread, however, and it is difficult to identify all of them. Also, when someone tries to determine whether or not a proposed action is ethical, the individual must predict future consequences. Predicting the future is notoriously difficult, and an incorrect prediction will produce a faulty moral judgment. Thus, one problem with ethical egoism is that it will be hard to make accurate moral judgments in cases where the consequences are difficult to identify or predict.

Another problem with ethical egoism is related to doing the calculations. Ethical egoism involves weighing or comparing the harms and benefits of an action to determine whether there is a net harm or benefit. It also involves comparing the harms and benefits of alternative courses of action to determine which is best. It is difficult to do this, however, when the harms and benefits are very different kinds of things. Perhaps I could make ten thousand dollars by taking advantage of a friend in a business deal. It will cost me a friend, but I will make a lot of money. As an egoist, I should do whatever benefits me the most, but which action produces more benefit? Is the person's friendship or the ten thousand dollars more beneficial to me? It is hard to weigh these two because they are such different kinds of things. If ethical egoists cannot successfully weigh the competing sets of consequences, they will not be able to solve moral problems.

### Inconsistency

A second and more serious problem is that, in a sense, ethical egoism is inconsistent. The inconsistency involves the two basic principles of ethical egoism. The first principle is that what is good for an individual is what produces the greatest net benefit for that individual. The second is that everyone ought to act based on his or her self-interest. You will act to maximize benefit to you, and I will act to maximize benefit to me. These two principles are difficult to reconcile. If what is good for me is what produces the greatest net benefit for me, then it is not good for me for everyone to act based on his or her self-interest. I will gain more benefit from your actions if you act in my best interest rather than in your best interest. As an ethical egoist, I would reject the second principle of ethical egoism—that everyone should act based on their self-interest—and claim that everyone ought to act so as to maximize net benefit to me. This is, of course, not a very plausible scenario. It would be against people's natural inclinations to disregard their benefit and simply act for my benefit. Thus, ethical egoism is either inconsistent or it goes against people's natural inclination to be self-interested instead of being in accord with it.

### Living Together Successfully

The final problem with ethical egoism is related to one of the basic purposes of ethics as identified by this book. One purpose of ethics is to help us solve moral problems and live successfully with each other. Ethical egoism would not help us accomplish this purpose. Ethical egoism asserts that what is good is what maximizes net benefit for the individual. Other people's harm and benefit, in itself, simply does not count. Therefore, egoism would legitimize even the most harmful and antisocial acts as long as they benefited the individual. Harming others and committing antisocial acts is not an effective way to live successfully with other people. Ethical egoism cannot assist us to successfully resolve conflicts of interest between people because it gives the individual a superior moral status to everyone else. Other people are merely the means to achieve the individual's benefit. It is doubtful that a person could live successfully with other people if he or she thought of them merely as a means to achieving his or her own self-interest.

## Evaluation of Ethical Egoism

The previous section discussed several problems with ethical egoism. At this point, however, we should consider whether or not ethical egoism would be a successful ethical theory based on the criteria in Chapter 1. First, can ethical egoism identify some ethical guidelines? The theory does identify a basic ethical guideline: People should act based on their self-interest and maximize net benefit to themselves. We can use this guideline to evaluate particular cases; for example, that in this situation I should lie if it will produce more benefit than harm for me. Second, the theory can also show that some ethical guidelines are better than others. "I should lie whenever it benefits me" is a better guideline than "I should always tell the truth no matter what the consequences may be" because the first one will maximize net benefit to me. Skipping to the fourth criterion, ethical egoism can help us solve some moral problems, but the difficulty in identifying all the consequences and doing the calculations will limit its effectiveness to some degree. The theory does not, however, satisfy the third criterion. Nothing in the guidelines identified by the theory prohibits the unlimited pursuit of self-interest. Indeed, individuals ought to pursue self-interest in any and all ways that really maximize benefit to them. It would permit acts that are harmful to others or to society in general if these acts really benefit the individual ethical egoist. Therefore, ethical egoism is not a successful ethical theory based on the criteria from Chapter 1. It does not identify ethical guidelines that would control the unlimited pursuit of self-interest and help us to live together successfully.

Most philosophers reject ethical egoism because it can be used to validate brutal and harmful behavior. If the egoist would receive a net benefit from killing you and stealing your money, then it is ethical for him or her to do it. This does not seem to be an adequate approach to ethics because it clearly would not help us live together more successfully.

## Ethical Subjectivism

The second half of this chapter investigates another ethical theory focused on the individual. Consider once again the example at the beginning of the chapter. Someone breaks into my house and steals my stereo equipment. Upon discovery of the theft, I am furious and quick to tell anyone who will listen that the person who did it is a jerk who should be caught and punished. Ethical egoism focuses on the harm to me, but we might also consider my attitude or emotional reaction. I am angry that my stereo has been stolen. Perhaps good and bad are related to our attitudes and emotions. *Ethical subjectivism* can be used to identify any theory that claims that the emotions or attitudes of individuals are the source of ethical guidelines. If a particular individual has a positive attitude or emotional response to something, it is ethical. If he or she has a negative attitude or emotional response to it, it is unethical. The specific version of ethical subjectivism that will be considered in this chapter is called emotivism.

## Emotivism

The philosopher Charles Stevenson produced a version of ethical subjectivism called *emotivism*. Stevenson argued that good and evil (or, to be more precise, moral judgments or expressions) are related to the attitudes of specific individuals.[1] Stevenson's theory is not really an ethical theory in the sense of the term used in this text. His theory is about the nature of moral judgments, not about producing and justifying an ethical standard. We can, however, build a simple ethical theory about how to live using Stevenson's ideas.

Stevenson's theory is based on the idea that there are different kinds of language with different functions or uses. Some language is used to describe possible facts. For example, the sentence "The book's cover is green" states a possible fact—that the book's cover is green. The proposition expressed by the sentence is true if, and only if, the book's cover really is green. Thus, the statement is true if it corresponds accurately to an actual fact. Descriptive language states or describes possible facts and can be true or false.

Moral language does not describe possible facts. It has two functions, the first of which is to express positive and negative attitudes. Stevenson uses the word "attitude" to indicate psychological dispositions of being for or against something. These expressions of attitudes have an emotional aspect and an *emotive* meaning. The phrase "Lying is evil" expresses the person's disapproval of stealing. It is like saying, "Lying, boo!" "Giving to charity is good" expresses approval and is the same as "Giving to charity, yea!" Examples of moral language are similar, but not identical, to exclamations, such as "Hurrah" or "Damn." Because moral expressions are like exclamations, they cannot be true or false. "Hurrah" cannot be true or false, and neither can "Lying is evil." Stevenson's idea is that ethical judgments express a particular individual's attitudes of being for or against things.

58   *Chapter 4 / Ethical Egoism and Ethical Subjectivism*

It is important to understand that according to Stevenson moral language does not report attitudes—it expresses them. In contrast to Stevenson's view, someone else might claim that the expression "Lying is evil" reported my negative feeling about lying. This would mean that my expression is another kind of descriptive language. Instead of reporting things about the world, such as the color of book covers, it reports people's attitudes about actions. Thus, moral language could be true or false depending on whether or not it was an accurate report of the person's attitude. Suppose that Rose has a negative attitude about lying, but says "Lying is ethical." Her statement is false because it is an incorrect report of her attitude. Thus, based on this "reporting view," moral language reports people's attitudes about actions and can be true or false. This "reporting view" account of moral language is not Stevenson's view.

Perhaps Stevenson declined to endorse the "reporting view" of moral language because he realized that it misrepresented the nature of ethical argument and disagreement. If you say "abortion is wrong" and I insist that it is ethical, we are disagreeing about the moral status of abortion. Using the "reporting view," however, there would be no disagreement. You are reporting your attitude and I am reporting mine. Both of our claims are true, and there is no disagreement between us even though the claims themselves seem to contradict each other. This view misrepresents ethical disagreement. When we make our different claims, we are making different claims about abortion, not merely about our attitudes. We are disagreeing about the moral status of abortion. I think you are wrong and I am right; I do not think that both claims could be true. Therefore, this "reporting view" seems seriously flawed because it greatly distorts the nature of ethical disagreement.

Stevenson's view avoids this problem. When you say "Abortion is wrong," you are expressing your negative attitude about abortion. When I claim it is ethical, I am expressing my positive attitude. Thus, we have a real disagreement over the status of abortion. For you it is the kind of thing that produces negative feelings, whereas for me it is the kind of thing that creates positive feelings. Thus, our moral disagreement is not only about our different attitudes but also about the nature of abortion. This produces a less distorted view of ethical discourse and disagreement.

According to Stevenson, the second aspect of moral language is that it possesses a prescriptive function. That is, moral language prescribes certain actions or is used to influence people to act in certain ways. In relation to this aspect of moral language, when I say "Stealing is evil," I am trying to keep you from stealing. When I say "Giving to charity is good," I am encouraging you to give to charity. This second aspect of moral language suggests that examples of moral language are similar to commands as well as to exclamations. When I say "Stealing is evil," it is similar, although not identical, to commanding you: "Do not steal." I am commanding you to do or not do a certain kind of action. Based on Stevenson's ideas, moral language attempts to influence people not by appealing to considerations of facts or reason but instead by encouraging them to develop a similar attitude. It is an emotional appeal, not a rational one. Moral language has a prescriptive function because it is used to encourage certain attitudes and kinds of actions in other people.

This second aspect of moral language increases the disagreement between the people in the earlier example. When you say "Abortion is wrong," you are trying to influence women not to have abortions. When I say it is ethical, I am attempting to influence women to have abortions. Thus, once again we are disagreeing about the moral status of abortion. You urge people not to have abortions, and I assert that it is an acceptable kind of action. Stevenson's view seems to create a less distorted view of moral disagreement than the "reporting view."

Stevenson claims that moral language is different from descriptive or fact-stating language. Moral language does not state possible facts. It has both emotive and prescriptive aspects because it expresses an attitude and tries to influence others. Stevenson's position concerns the nature of moral language, but in the next section I will attempt to use it as the basis for a simple ethical theory.

## Emotivism as an Ethical Theory

Based on Stevenson's ideas, we can create a very simple theory about how one ought to live. Although Stevenson might have been unwilling to endorse it, this theory is similar to a view put forward by some ethics students. Based on this "emotive ethical theory," moral obligation could be related to attitudes or emotional responses. If someone has a positive attitude or emotional response to something, it is good. If a person has a negative attitude or emotional response to it, it is bad. Thus, the ethical standard would be that *what is good for an individual is what produces a positive attitude or emotional response in that individual, and what is bad is what produces a negative attitude or emotional response.* Presumably my outrage or anger at having my stereo stolen would count as the appropriate kind of attitude or emotional response and would make the action of stealing my stereo a bad one. Therefore, good and bad would necessarily depend on particular individuals.

The emotive ethical theory might assert that attitudes and emotional responses to actions are involuntary. A person does not collect the facts about the action, evaluate them, and then decide how to feel. This would make good and bad ultimately dependent on facts about particular persons, as in ethical egoism. The attitudes or emotional responses are simply involuntary responses to actions. The individual is confronted with an action and experiences a certain response. In any case, how the attitudes and emotional responses arise is morally irrelevant; only the attitudes about or emotional responses to actions would matter.

In the emotive ethical theory, all persons would use their attitudes or emotional responses as the basis for moral judgments. This theory asserts that ethics is not related to facts or reasoning but to attitudes or emotional responses. Any other view of ethical judgments, such as ethical relativism or ethical egoism, is based on the wrong considerations.

## Justification for the Ethical Standard and Strengths of the Theory

The previous section presented the ethical standard of the emotive ethical theory. This section offers some justifications for using this ethical standard and some corresponding strengths of the ethical theory.

### Moral Disagreement

The best justification for the ethical standard of the emotive ethical theory is that it explains why we have such a large amount of disagreement over ethical matters. When we disagree over factual matters, such as the distance to the moon, we can collect data and reason about them. With accurate observations and measurements, we can often resolve these factual disagreements. Ethical issues, such as the debate over abortion, seem more difficult. People can agree about the facts but still disagree on the issue. For some reason, solving ethical problems is more than a matter of collecting facts and reasoning about them. The emotive ethical theory explains why this is the case. Ethical matters are related to attitudes and emotions; therefore, collecting data and reasoning are useless. It is very difficult to resolve emotional differences. People simply feel whatever they feel. Also, emotions are notoriously inconsistent, varying from person to person for no apparent reason and changing for a particular individual over time. I may feel one way about something today and another way about the same thing tomorrow. Thus, one justification for using this standard is that it explains the large amount of disagreement over ethical issues. The ability to explain this matter is seen by some people as a strength of the theory.

### The Difference between Science and Ethics

A second way to justify using this standard and a related strength of the theory is similar, although not identical, to the first one. The emotive ethical theory provides a plausible explanation for the difference between science and ethics. Science operates in a certain way involving hypothesis, experimentation, and theories. It rests primarily on observation. Ethics seems quite different. Moral philosophers rarely do experiments, nor do they make many observations of the physical world around them. Why are these two areas of human endeavor so different? The emotive ethical theory provides an answer to this question. Ethics is unlike science because science deals with observables, whereas ethics deals with attitudes and emotional responses, which cannot always be observed. This ability to explain the difference between science and ethics is one reason to use this standard and a strength of the theory.

### Moral Certainty and Confidence

The final justification for using the standard and a corresponding strength of the emotive ethical theory is that it produces moral certainty and confidence. Presumably, individuals know their own attitudes and can identify their emotional responses with certainty. Therefore, individuals can be certain about and confident in their moral judgments because these judgments depend only on their attitudes or emotional responses. Also, no one else knows these attitudes and emotional responses as well as the individual, so the person can be confident that he or she cannot be effectively challenged. Thus, a justification for using this standard and a corresponding strength of the theory is that it provides moral certainty and confidence.

## Morally Significant Actions

An ethical theory should also delineate morally significant actions from ones that are not morally significant. For a proponent of the emotive ethical theory, a morally significant action is one that elicits an attitude or emotional response. The theft of my stereo was morally significant because I was angry about it. Other actions, such as filling my car's tank with gasoline, would not be morally significant because I would not have any attitude or emotional response toward them at all.

## Emotive Ethical Theory and the Traditional Ethical Assumptions

Emotive ethical theory would not accept any of the traditional assumptions associated with ethical theories. First, it does not assume that ethics is rational. Ethical guidelines and judgments relate to involuntary attitudes or emotional responses, not to considerations based on reason. Emotivists would not assume that we could use reason to reach theoretical and practical conclusions about ethical matters. Only the attitudes or emotional responses matter, and they are not necessarily rational. Emotive ethical theory also does not endorse impartiality and moral equality. Each individual's attitudes and emotional responses determine good and bad for him or her; the attitudes of others or the effects of our actions on them are irrelevant. Thus, the individual is morally superior to everyone else and does not have to treat people impartially. Finally, emotive ethical theory does not assume that any ethical evaluations can be universalized. Good and bad relate to a particular individual's attitudes or emotional responses. Other people may have very different dispositions and responses and make very different moral judgments. Thus, we cannot assert that another person should make the same judgment in a similar situation. Although moral language has a prescriptive element, there is no intention to or possibility of influencing every existing person with a particular expression.

## Emotive Ethical Theory and the Basic Ethical Themes

In an effort to better comprehend the emotive ethical theory, let's examine how the basic ethical themes about moral good and bad can be related to it. The first theme can be represented by this question: *What kind of moral guidelines makes something good or bad: subjective, relative, or objective ones?* As was stated in an earlier section, emotivism is one kind of ethical subjectivism. The moral guidelines of the emotive ethical theory are subjective because they are based on the particular attitudes or emotional responses of specific individuals. Emotivist guidelines are not relative because they do not depend on society. They are also not objective, in the way that term was used in Chapter 1, because they are not a product of objective considerations of fact and/or reason that do not depend on the perceptions, emotions, or judgments of particular persons.

Another significant theme in ethics is this: *What makes something good or bad; is it the consequences that are produced or the reasoning that leads up to it?* This contrast is not really appropriate for the emotive ethical theory because good and bad are clearly not based on reasoning. In one sense, labeling an act as good or bad might be said to be based on consequences. If an action produces a positive attitude or emotional response, it is good. Some might say that the emotional response is a consequence of the action, but this seems to distort the meaning of "consequences" as discussed in Chapter 1. The best answer would seem to be neither; good and bad are based on attitudes, not on consequences or reasoning.

The third theme relates to this question: *Are good and bad related to following general rules without exceptions or connected to separately evaluat-*

*ing actions, beliefs, and so on?* People who believe we should guide our behavior by general rules feel that these rules should have no exceptions. People who want to evaluate things separately believe we must always be open to the possibility that we can appropriately make an exception to even the best moral rule. They want to evaluate each action as independently as possible based on some criterion or criteria. The criterion may be similar to a rule, but if it is, then the criterion is the only rule that they will always endorse. The emotive ethical theory does not propose that we follow general rules. Each action is evaluated based on the attitude or emotional response connected to it. Thus, actions are evaluated individually.

The fourth important theme relates to the proper focus of ethical attention and benefit: *Are good and bad primarily related to the group, community, or majority of people or should the focus be on the individual?* The emotive ethical theory is focused on the individual. The group, community, or majority of people are morally irrelevant. Only the attitudes and emotional responses of the individual matter. Even if the attitudes were somehow a product of society, this would be morally irrelevant because it is the attitudes themselves that matter, not why the individual has those attitudes.

## Contrasting the Emotive Ethical Theory with Ethical Egoism

Both the emotive ethical theory and ethical egoism relate moral guidelines to something about specific individuals, but they are very different theories (see Appendix 1). The ethical standard for egoism relates good and bad to benefit and harm to the individual, whereas the emotive ethical theory joins good and bad to individuals' attitudes and emotional responses. In regard to the traditional ethical assumptions, the two theories agree that people are not moral equals and that moral judgments cannot be universalized. The theories disagree, however, on whether ethics is rational. The emotive ethical theory assumes it is not, and ethical egoism claims the reverse. Related to the themes concerning good and bad, the theories have some similarities and some differences. First, emotive ethical theory asserts that good and bad are subjective, whereas ethical egoism claims that they are objective. Second, both theories claim that good and bad are related to specific individuals, not to the group, majority of people, or society. Third, ethical egoism relates good and bad to consequences, not to reasoning before the action, whereas the emotive ethical theory connects good and bad to attitudes rather than to either consequences or reasoning. Finally, ethical egoism focuses on either following rules or evaluating actions separately, depending on which would maximize net benefit to the individual. The emotive ethical theory relates good and bad to specific actions. Although the two theories relate to the same ethical insight, they have important differences.

## Problems with the Emotive Ethical Theory

This section discusses three of the many problems with emotivism. The final section of the chapter provides an overall evaluation and reviews why most philosophers reject the theory.

### Moral Language

One problem with emotive ethical theory is that it is based on Stevenson's view of moral language, which many philosophers believe is misguided. Stevenson argues that moral language always has an emotive and a prescriptive element: It expresses an attitude and prescribes a certain kind of conduct. I cannot adequately analyze and evaluate Stevenson's view of language here, but one criticism of it can be summarized. Stevenson claims that every example of moral language has emotive and prescriptive aspects, yet many examples refute this. In a discussion of different kinds of theft, Rose might say, "Although I don't feel sorry for the companies, it is clear that stealing from large stores is still unethical." There is no emotional aspect to this expression at all. Rose is not bothered by retail theft from large stores; she is just acknowledging that it is still unethical. In a similar manner, someone could use a moral expression without prescribing anything. For example, John might say, "Although I would never tell a woman she had to give birth to a child, I personally believe abortion is wrong." John is not prescribing that anyone refrain from getting an abortion. He is simply stating his personal position, which, for some reason, he is unwilling to extend to any pregnant woman. There is no prescriptive element to his expression. If Stevenson had stated that moral expressions sometimes have emotive and prescriptive elements, there would be no problem. When he claims that they always do, he is mistaken. If Stevenson's view of moral language is misguided, then the ethical theory based on it is suspect.

### Ethics as Mysterious and Arbitrary

Another serious problem with emotive ethical theory is that it makes ethical guidelines and ethical judgments mysterious and arbitrary. If I ask why you think euthanasia is unethical, as an emotivist, you will answer, "Because I have a bad attitude toward disconnecting from life support someone in the last stages of dying from a disease." If I ask why you hold this negative attitude, you would have to reply that why does not matter. Nothing except the actual attitude is morally relevant. Therefore, we are left with these mysterious attitudes and with no explanation for why we have the ones we do. Consequently, we have no real explanation for why we have the ethical guidelines that we do. In addition to these matters being mysterious, any attitude or ethical guideline would be as good as any other one. Thus, the attitudes and moral guidelines are arbitrary. A theory that makes moral guidelines and moral judgments mysterious and arbitrary is not a very valuable theory for many people.

### Preventing the Unlimited Pursuit of Self-Interest

The final problem is that emotive ethical theory implies that any conduct can be ethical. If a person has a positive attitude or emotional response when contemplating rape, then rape is ethical for that person. There is no way to objectively declare rape to be evil because only individual attitudes and emotional responses are morally significant. Any action, no matter how brutal or cruel, could be ethical. The third criterion for a successful moral theory stated that an ethical theory must identify moral guidelines that would prohibit the unlimited pursuit of self-interest. Clearly, the emotive ethical theory cannot satisfy this criterion. It would legitimate even the most harmful or antisocial conduct if the person had a positive emotional response or a positive attitude toward that behavior. Allowing people to act in harmful and antisocial ways is not appropriate if we want to solve moral problems and live together successfully. This tendency of the theory to legitimatize any conduct is a serious problem for many philosophers.

## Evaluation of the Emotive Ethical Theory

The emotive ethical theory has both strengths and weaknesses. Most philosophers reject this theory, and if it is examined in the context of the criteria from Chapter 1, it would be discarded. First, can emotive ethical theory identify some ethical guidelines? If we believe moral language has a prescriptive function, and if we are not too rigid or exclusive about what counts as "ethical guidelines," the answer is that emotive ethical theory can identify some moral guidelines. Moral expressions or judgments are attempts to influence particular people either to do or not to do various things, and these attempts could be viewed as ethical guidelines. According to emotive ethical theory, individuals produce the ethical guidelines, and the theory informs us about how to identify them.

Second, can emotive ethical theory show that some ethical guidelines are better than others? If the attitudes and emotional responses of particular individuals determine the ethical guidelines, then any moral guideline would be legitimate if it were related to a judgment that actually expressed an attitude. The moral guideline related to the specific attitude is better than others for the particular individual—but not for people in general. If we want an ethical theory to show that some moral guidelines are better than others for all of us, emotive ethical theory cannot help us.

Third, can emotive ethical theory help us live together successfully? Emotive ethical theory cannot satisfy this criterion. It would legitimate even the most harmful or antisocial conduct if the person had a good attitude toward that behavior. A theory that does not prohibit brutal and cruel actions cannot help us to live together successfully.

Finally, can emotive ethical theory help us solve ethical problems? If solving ethical problems simply means that we can arrive at personal solutions, then emotive ethical theory can help solve moral problems. My attitudes and emotional responses can guide me in solving ethical problems. If I have a positive attitude toward stealing a book and no negative attitude toward the possible legal consequences of doing so, then I should do it. If solving ethical problems includes being able to support my solutions with reasons that other people would understand and might even endorse, then emotive ethical theory cannot help us solve moral problems in a satisfactory way. My only reason for saying that stealing the book was good is that I had a good attitude toward doing it. Why I have the attitude is morally irrelevant. Thus, in a personal sense emotive ethical theory satisfies the fourth criterion, but in an interpersonal sense it does not.

Based on the serious problems with at least two of the four criteria, emotive ethical theory would not be a successful ethical theory. It would not show that some moral guidelines were better than others, and it would not help us solve moral problems and live together successfully.

## Conclusion

In this chapter, I have discussed two approaches to ethics that relate legitimate moral guidelines to something about particular individuals. Neither of these theories is successful in the context of meeting the criteria outlined in Chapter 1. My conclusion is that we should also reject the "ethical insight" that legitimate moral guidelines necessarily have something to do with particular individuals. In Chapters 2 and 3, we considered God and society as the sources of legitimate moral guidelines. In this chapter, we investigated whether legitimate moral guidelines had their source in specific individuals. All of these approaches to ethics have proved unsuccessful. In Chapter 5, we will turn to a theory that relates legitimate moral guidelines to reason and that exemplifies the three traditional ethical assumptions of rationality, impartiality, and universalizability. Perhaps an approach to ethics more in line with traditional ethical assumptions will be more successful.

## QUESTIONS FOR REVIEW

*Here are some questions to help you review the main concepts in this chapter.*

1. Explain how ethical egoism and ethical subjectivism relate to the same moral insight.

2. Explain the difference in the ethical standards of ethical egoism and the emotive ethical theory.

3. Why does ethical egoism initially seem to be consistent with people's natural inclinations? Explain the problem that calls this consistency into question.

4. In your view, what is the greatest strength of ethical egoism? What is the greatest strength of the emotive ethical theory?

5. In your opinion, what is the most serious problem with ethical egoism? What is the most serious problem with emotivism?

6. How does Stevenson think "moral language" differs from "descriptive language"? What problem does the author suggest exists with Stevenson's view of moral language?

7. If you had to choose between ethical egoism and the emotive ethical theory, which one would you choose? Why is this the better theory?

8. Compare and contrast ethical egoism and the emotive ethical theory on the traditional moral assumptions.

9. Compare and contrast ethical egoism and the emotive ethical theory on the themes connected to good and bad.

10. In terms of the criteria from Chapter 1, is ethical egoism a successful ethical theory? Explain why, or why not.

11. In terms of the criteria from Chapter 1, is the emotive ethical theory a successful ethical theory? Explain why, or why not.

## NOTE

1. Charles L. Stevenson, *Ethics and Language* (New Haven: Yale University Press, 1944).

# Beyond Good and Evil

Friedrich Nietzsche

Friedrich Nietzsche was born in Röcken, Prussia, in 1844. After graduating from the Lutheran boarding school at Pforta in 1864, he enrolled in the University of Bonn to study theology. There he began to doubt his Christian faith (he eventually became an atheist and harsh critic of Christianity) and in 1865 transferred to the University of Leipzig to study classical philology (Greek and Latin language and literature) and music. He was recognized as a brilliant student of philology, and at the age of twenty-four, before he had even finished his doctorate, he was offered the chair of classical philology at the University of Basel in Switzerland. The University of Leipzig quickly granted his degree, and Nietzsche assumed the professorship at Basel in 1869. Ten years later, because of his increasingly bad health, Nietzsche resigned his position. For the next ten years, half blind and in unremitting pain, he wandered through Switzerland, Germany, and Italy in search of a cure. His mental health began to deteriorate as well; in 1889 he collapsed on the streets of Turin, Italy, completely insane. He died in Weimar in 1900.

Nietzsche's principal works are *The Birth of Tragedy out of the Spirit of Music* (1872), *Human, All Too Human* (1878), *The Gay Science* (1882), *Thus Spoke Zarathustra* (1883–1885), *Beyond Good and Evil* (1886), and *On the Genealogy of Morals* (1887).

Our selection is from *Beyond Good and Evil*, a book consisting of about three hundred aphorisms on various subjects. The topic of Chapter 9, from which our reading comes, is "What Is Noble?" According to Nietzsche, to be noble means to see oneself as the center and origin of all value. In fact, the terms "good" and "bad" originally designated simply what the aristocracy did and did not value. For Nietzsche, "life *is* precisely the will to power," and historically members of the aristocracy exercised their will to power by exploiting common people and using them as they saw fit. Nietzsche calls the morality of the ruling aristocracy a "master morality." He contrasts this kind of morality with "slave morality," which arose when common people tried to make their inferior and despicable lives more bearable by exalting as virtues such qualities as kindness, sympathy, selflessness, patience, and humility (the cornerstones of Christian morality). Slave morality gave rise to the pair of terms "good" and "evil," which Nietzsche contrasts with the "good" and "bad" of master morality. In slave morality, "good" refers to the slaves' (false) values, and "evil" to the (legitimate and noble) values of the rulers. Since rulers are not in the inferior position of slaves, they need not subscribe to slave values and are "beyond good and evil."

Nietzsche bemoans the fact that modern civilization, with its democratic and egalitarian tendencies, is replacing life-affirming master morality with life-denying slave morality. Yet there are still elements of master morality in some souls, and it is to these souls that Nietzsche's praise of "what is noble" is addressed.

▼

### Chapter 9: What Is Noble?

**257** Every elevation of the type "man" has hitherto been the work of an aristocratic society—and so will it always be—a society believing in a long scale of gradations of rank and differences of worth among human beings, and requiring slavery in some form or other. Without the *pathos of distance*, such as grows out of the incarnated difference of classes, out of the constant outlooking and downlooking of the ruling caste on subordinates and instruments, and out of their equally constant practice of obeying and commanding, of keeping down and keeping at a distance—that other more mysterious pathos could never have arisen, the longing for an ever new widening of distance within the soul itself, the formation of ever higher, rarer, further, more extended, more comprehensive states—in short, just the elevation of the type "man," the continued "self-surmounting of man," to use a moral formula in a supermoral sense. To be sure, one must not resign oneself to any humanitarian illusions about the history of the origin of an aristocratic society (that is to say, of the preliminary condition for the elevation of the type "man"): the truth is hard. Let us acknowledge unprejudicedly how every higher civilisation hitherto has *originated!* Men with a still natural nature—barbarians in every terrible sense of the word, men of prey, still in possession of unbroken strength of will and desire for power—threw themselves upon weaker, more moral, more peaceful races (perhaps trading or cattle-rearing communities), or upon old mellow civilisations in which the final vital force was flickering out in brilliant fireworks of wit and depravity. At the commencement, the noble caste was always the barbarian caste. Their superiority did not consist first of all in their physical, but in their psychical power—they were more *complete* men (which at every point also implies the same as "more complete beasts").

**258**  Corruption—as the indication that anarchy threatens to break out among the instincts, and that the foundation of the emotions, called "life," is convulsed—is something radically different according to the organisation in which it manifests itself. When, for instance, an aristocracy like that of France at the beginning of the Revolution flung away its privileges with sublime disgust and sacrificed itself to an excess of its moral sentiments, it was corruption—it was really only the closing act of the corruption which had existed for centuries, by virtue of which that aristocracy had abdicated step by step its lordly prerogatives and lowered itself to a *function* of royalty (in the end even to its decoration and parade-dress). The essential thing, however, in a good and healthy aristocracy is that it should *not* regard itself as a function either of the kingship or the commonwealth, but as the *significance* and highest justification [of it]—that it should therefore accept with a good conscience the sacrifice of a legion of individuals who, *for its sake,* must be suppressed and reduced to imperfect men, to slaves and instruments. Its fundamental belief must be precisely that society is *not* allowed to exist for its own sake, but only as a foundation and scaffolding by means of which a select class of beings may be able to elevate themselves to their higher duties, and in general to a higher existence—like those sun-seeking climbing plants in Java (they are called *Sipo matador*), which encircle an oak so long and so often with their arms, until at last, high above it, but supported by it, they can unfold their tops in the open light and exhibit their happiness.

**259** To refrain mutually from injury, from violence, from exploitation, and to put one's will on a par with that of others—this may result in a certain rough sense in good conduct among individuals when the necessary conditions are given (namely, the actual similarity of the individuals in amount of force and degree of worth, and their co-relation within one organisation). As soon, however, as one wished to take this principle more generally, and if possible even as *the fundamental principle of society*, it would immediately disclose what it really is—namely, a will to the *denial* of life, a principle of dissolution and decay. Here one must think profoundly to the very basis and resist all sentimental weakness: life itself is *essentially* appropriation, injury, conquest of the strange and weak, suppression, severity, obtrusion of peculiar forms, incorporation, and at the least (putting it most mildly), exploitation. But why should one forever use precisely these words on which for ages a disparaging purpose has been stamped? Even the organisation within which, as was previously supposed, the individuals treat each other as equal—it takes place in every healthy aristocracy—must itself, if it be a living and not a dying organisation, do all that towards other bodies, which the individuals within it refrain from doing to each other: it will have to be the incarnated will to power, it will endeavour to grow, to gain ground, attract to itself and acquire ascendency—not owing to any morality or immorality, but because it *lives*, and because life *is* precisely will to power. On no point, however, is the ordinary consciousness of Europeans more unwilling to be corrected than on this matter; people now rave everywhere, even under the guise of science, about coming conditions of society in which "the exploiting character" is to be absent. That sounds to my ears as if they promised to invent a mode of life which should refrain from all organic functions. "Exploitation" does not belong to a depraved, or imperfect and primitive society: it belongs to the *nature* of the living being as a primary organic function; it is a consequence of the intrinsic will to power, which is precisely the will to life. Granting that as a theory this is a novelty—as a reality it is the *fundamental fact* of all history: let us be so far honest towards ourselves!

**260** In a tour through the many finer and coarser moralities which have hitherto prevailed or still prevail on the earth, I found certain traits recurring regularly together and connected with one another, until finally two primary types revealed themselves to me, and a radical distinction was brought to light. There is *master morality* and *slave morality*—I would at once add, however, that in all higher and mixed civilisations, there are also attempts at the reconciliation of the two moralities; but one finds still oftener the confusion and mutual misunderstanding of them, indeed, sometimes their close juxtaposition—even in the same man, within one soul. The distinctions of moral values have either originated in a ruling caste, pleasantly conscious of being different from the ruled—or among the ruled class, the slaves and dependents of all sorts. In the first case, when it is the rulers who determine the conception "good," it is the exalted, proud disposition which is regarded as the distinguishing feature, and that which determines the order of rank. The noble type of man separates from himself the beings in whom the opposite of this exalted, proud disposition displays itself: he despises them. Let it at once be noted that in this first kind of morality the antithesis "good" and "bad" means practically the same as "noble" and "despicable"—the antithesis "good" and "evil" is of a different origin. The cowardly, the timid, the insignificant, and those thinking merely of narrow utility are despised; also the distrustful, with their constrained glances, the self-abasing, the dog-like kind of men who let themselves be abused, the mendicant flatterers, and above all the liars—it is a fundamental belief of all aristocrats that the common people are untruthful. "We truthful ones" the nobility in ancient Greece called themselves. It is obvious that everywhere the designations of moral value were at first applied to *men* and were only derivatively and at a later period applied to *actions;* it is a gross mistake, therefore, when historians of morals start with questions like, "Why have sympathetic actions been praised?" The noble type of man regards *himself* as a determiner of values; he does not require to be approved of; he passes the judgment, "What is injurious to me is injurious in itself"; he knows that it is he himself only who confers honour on things; he is a *creator of values.* He honours whatever he recognises in himself: such morality is self-glorification. In the foreground there is the feeling of plenitude, of power, which seeks to overflow, the happiness of high tension, the consciousness of a wealth which would give and bestow. The noble man also helps the unfortunate, but not—or scarcely—out of pity, but rather from an impulse generated by the superabundance of power. The noble man honours in himself the powerful one, him also who has power over himself, who knows how to speak and how to keep silence, who takes pleasure in subjecting himself to severity and hardness, and has reverence for all that is severe and hard. "Wotan placed a hard heart in my breast," says an old Scandinavian saga: it is thus rightly expressed from the soul of a proud Viking. Such a type of man is even proud of *not* being made for sympathy; the hero of the saga therefore adds warningly: "He who has not a hard heart when young, will never have one." The noble and brave who think thus are the furthest removed from the morality which sees precisely in sympathy, or in acting for the good of others, or in *désintéressement,*[1] the characteristic of the moral; faith in oneself, pride in oneself, a radical enmity and irony towards "selflessness," belong as definitely to noble morality as do a careless scorn and precaution in presence of sympathy and the "warm heart." It is the powerful who *know* how to honour; it is their art, their domain for invention. The profound reverence for age and for tradition (all law rests on this double reverence), the belief and prejudice in favour of ancestors and unfavourable to newcomers, is typical in the morality of the powerful. And if, reversely, men of "modern ideas" believe almost instinctively in "progress" and the "future" and are more and more lacking in respect for old age, the ignoble origin of these "ideas" has complacently betrayed itself thereby. A morality of the ruling class, however, is more especially foreign and irritating to present-day taste in the sternness of its principle that one has duties only to one's equals, that one may act towards beings of a lower rank, towards all that is foreign, just as seems good to one, or "as the heart desires," and in any case "beyond good and evil." It is here that sympathy and similar sentiments can have a place. The ability and obligation to exercise prolonged gratitude and prolonged revenge (both only within the circle of equals), artfulness in retaliation, *raffinement*[2] of the idea in friendship, a certain necessity to have enemies (as outlets for the emotions of envy, quarrelsomeness, arrogance—in fact, in order to be a good *friend*): all these are typical characteristics of the noble morality, which, as has been pointed out, is not the morality of "modern ideas" and is therefore at present difficult to realise, and also to unearth and disclose. It is otherwise with the second type of morality, *slave morality*. Supposing that the abused, the oppressed, the suffering, the unemancipated, the weary, and those uncertain of themselves, should moralise; what will be the common element in their moral estimates? Probably a pessimistic suspicion with regard to the entire situation of man will find expression, perhaps a condemnation of man, together with his situation. The slave has an unfavourable eye for the virtues of the powerful; he has a scepticism and distrust, a refinement of distrust of everything "good" that is there honoured—he would persuade himself that the very happiness there is not genuine. On the other hand, those qualities which serve to alleviate the existence of sufferers are brought into prominence and flooded with light; it is here that sympathy, the kind, helping hand, the warm heart, patience, diligence, humility, and friendliness attain to honour; for here these are the most useful qualities and almost the only means of supporting the burden of existence. Slave morality is essentially the morality of utility. Here is the seat of the origin of the famous antithesis "good" and *"evil"*—power and dangerousness are assumed to reside in the evil, a certain dreadfulness, subtlety, and strength, which do not admit of being despised. According to slave morality, therefore, the "evil" man arouses fear; according to master morality, it is precisely the "good" man who arouses fear and seeks to arouse it, while the bad man is regarded as the despicable being. The contrast attains its maximum when, in accordance with the logical consequences of slave morality, a shade of depreciation—it may be slight and well-intentioned—at last attaches itself even to the "good" man of this morality; because, according to the servile mode of thought, the good man must in any case be the *safe* man: he is good-natured, easily deceived, perhaps a little stupid, *un bonhomme.*[3] Everywhere that slave morality gains the ascendency, language shows a tendency to approximate the significations of the words "good" and "stupid." A last fundamental difference: the desire for *freedom*, the instinct for happiness and the refinements of the feeling of liberty belong as necessarily to slave morals and morality, as artifice and en-thusiasm in reverence and devotion are the regular symptoms of an aristo-cratic mode of thinking and estimating. Hence we can understand without further detail why love *as a passion*—it is our European speciality—must ab-solutely be of noble origin. As is well known, its invention is due to the Provençal poet-cavaliers, those brilliant ingenious men of the *"gai saber,"*[4] to whom Europe owes so much, and almost owes itself.

**261** Vanity is one of the things which are perhaps most difficult for a noble man to understand: he will be tempted to deny it, where another kind of man thinks he sees it self-evidently. The problem for him is to rep-resent to his mind beings who seek to arouse a good opinion of themselves which they themselves do not possess—and consequently also do not "de-serve"—and who yet *believe* in this good opinion afterwards. This seems to him on the one hand such bad taste and so self-disrespectful, and on the other hand so grotesquely unreasonable, that he would like to consider vanity an exception and is doubtful about it in most cases when it is spoken of. He will say, for instance: "I may be mistaken about my value, and on the other hand may nevertheless demand that my value should be acknowl-edged by others precisely as I rate it—that, however, is not vanity (but self-conceit, or, in most cases, that which is called 'humility,' and also 'mod-esty')." Or he will even say: "For many reasons I can delight in the good opinion of others, perhaps because I love and honour them and rejoice in all their joys, perhaps also because their good opinion endorses and strengthens my belief in my own good opinion, perhaps because the good opinion of others, even in cases where I do not share it, is useful to me, or gives promise of usefulness—all this, however, is not vanity." The man of noble character must first bring it home forcibly to his mind, especially with the aid of history, that, from time immemorial, in all social strata in any way dependent, the ordinary man *was* only that which he *passed for*; not being at all accustomed to fix values, he did not assign even to himself any other value than that which his master assigned to him (it is the peculiar *right of masters* to create values). It may be looked upon as the result of an extraordinary atavism[5] that the ordinary man, even at present, is still always *waiting* for an opinion about himself, and then instinctively submitting himself to it; yet by no means only to a "good" opinion, but also to a bad and unjust one (think, for instance, of the greater part of the self-apprecia-tions and self-depreciations which believing women learn from their con-fessors, and which in general the believing Christian learns from his church). In fact, conformably to the slow rise of the democratic social order (and its cause, the blending of the blood of masters and slaves), the originally noble and rare impulse of the masters to assign a value to them-selves and to "think well" of themselves will now be more and more encour-aged and extended. But it has at all times an older, ampler, and more radically ingrained propensity opposed to it—and in the phenomenon of "vanity" this older propensity overmasters the younger. The vain person rejoices over *every* good opinion which he hears about himself (quite apart from the point of view of its usefulness, and equally regardless of its truth or falsehood), just as he suffers from every bad opinion: for he subjects himself to both, he *feels* himself subjected to both, by that oldest instinct of subjection which breaks forth in him. It is "the slave" in the vain man's blood, the remains of the slave's craftiness—and how much of the "slave" is still left in woman, for instance!—which seeks to *seduce* to good opinions of itself; it is the slave, too, who immediately afterwards falls prostrate himself before these opinions, as though he had not called them forth. And to repeat it again: vanity is an atavism. . . .

**265**    At the risk of displeasing innocent ears, I submit that egoism belongs to the essence of a noble soul—I mean the unalterable belief that to a being such as "we," other beings must naturally be in subjection, and have to sacrifice themselves. The noble soul accepts the fact of his egoism without question, and also without consciousness of harshness, constraint, or arbitrariness therein, but rather as something that may have its basis in the primary law of things. If he sought a designation for it, he would say: "It is justice itself." He acknowledges under certain circumstances, which made him hesitate at first, that there are other equally privileged ones; as soon as he has settled this question of rank, he moves among those equals and equally privileged ones with the same assurance, as regards modesty and delicate respect, which he enjoys in intercourse with himself—in accordance with an innate heavenly mechanism which all the stars understand. It is an *additional* instance of his egoism, this artfulness and self-limitation in intercourse with his equals (every star is a similar egoist). He honours *himself* in them; and in the rights which he concedes to them, he has no doubt that the exchange of honours and rights, as the *essence* of all intercourse, belongs also to the natural condition of things. The noble soul gives as he takes, prompted by the passionate and sensitive instinct of requital, which is at the root of his nature. The notion of "favour" has, *inter pares*,[6] neither significance nor good repute; there may be a sublime way of letting gifts, as it were, light upon one from above, and of drinking them thirstily like dewdrops; but for those arts and displays the noble soul has no aptitude. His egoism hinders him here: in general, he looks "aloft" unwillingly—he looks either *forward*, horizontally and deliberately, or downwards; *he knows that he is on a height*. . . .

**272**    Signs of nobility: never to think of lowering our duties to the rank of duties for everybody; to be unwilling to renounce or to share our responsibilities; to count our prerogatives, and the exercise of them, among our *duties*. . . .

**287** What is noble? What does the word "noble" still mean for us nowadays? How does the noble man betray himself, how is he recognised under this heavy overcast sky of the commencing plebeianism, by which everything is rendered opaque and leaden? It is not his actions which establish his claim (actions are always ambiguous, always inscrutable); neither is it his "works." One finds nowadays among artists and scholars plenty of those who betray by their works that a profound longing for nobleness impels them; but this very *need of* nobleness is radically different from the needs of the noble soul itself, and is in fact the eloquent and dangerous sign of the lack thereof. It is not the works, but the *belief* which is here decisive and determines the order of rank—to employ once more an old religious formula with a new and deeper meaning. It is some fundamental certainty which a noble soul has about itself, something which is not to be sought, is not to be found, and perhaps, also, is not to be lost. *The noble soul has reverence for itself.*

▶ NOTES

1. *désintéressement:* unselfishness (French) [D.C.A., ed.]
2. *raffinement:* refinement (French) [D.C.A.]
3. *un bonhomme:* a simple-minded person; literally, "a good person" (French) [D.C.A.]
4. *gai saber:* the art of the troubadours (a fourteenth-century French term that means, literally, "the merry science") [D.C.A.]
5. *atavism:* recurrence of a trait that appeared in one's remote ancestors [D.C.A.]
6. *inter pares:* among equals (Latin) [D.C.A.]

# Chapter 8

# *Virtue Ethics*

One way to determine good and bad is in relation to a goal, a purpose, or a function—something good helps accomplish the goal, promotes achieving the purpose, or helps carry out the function. If the primary function of my university is to educate students, then something that clearly promotes their education would be good relative to that function. For example, skill in teaching is good because it promotes the education of students. If the university had a different primary goal, perhaps to maximize profit, different things would be good. For example, skill in persuading students to pay higher tuition would be good. The idea of good and bad being dependent on a goal, a purpose, or a function is often present in corporations, institutions, and organizations. Many corporations develop a statement of purpose and encourage employees to develop skills and techniques that will promote achieving that purpose. A purpose allows us to evaluate other things in relation to the purpose, but it does not allow us to assess the purpose itself.

In Chapter 1, I stated that the most important function of ethical theories is to help us solve moral problems and live together successfully. The criteria for evaluating a successful ethical theory reflect this basic goal. This goal-oriented approach can be applied to persons as well as to ethical theories. What is the goal of all (or almost all) persons? One plausible answer is that the goal is to live the "good life." People want to live well, to flourish, and to be successful, although they may have different ideas of what allows them to do so. This may be a good opportunity to ask yourself, "What is my idea of the good life?" Would you need to have successful relations with family members, with friends, or with colleagues? Would you have to be healthy, wealthy, or famous, or a great success in your career? Would you require pleasure, excitement, happiness, devotion, or tranquility? Many elements could be important parts

**135**

of the good life, and your list may be very different from someone else's. Whatever elements you selected, the goal is to live the good life, and whatever promotes or produces the good life is good, whereas whatever detracts from or degrades it is bad.

The Greek philosopher Aristotle (384–322 B.C.E.) uses a goal-oriented approach and a view of the good life to develop a "virtue ethics" based on the distinctive function of human beings. He assumes that all human beings have a basic function or purpose and that a good person is one who is successful at accomplishing it. The key to living the good life, according to Aristotle, is developing certain virtues, such as practical wisdom, courage, and generosity. Thus, his approach to moral good and bad is often called "virtue ethics." Many people would intuitively agree that the virtues help people to live well. Thus, the basic ethical insight associated with virtue ethics is that *the virtues help persons to achieve well-being or to live the good life.* The additional ethical idea that makes Aristotle's virtue ethics distinctive is that there is a basic human function and that the virtues help us to accomplish that function.

## Virtue Ethics, Well-Being, and Reasoning

Virtue ethics, as presented in this chapter, is based on the ideas of Aristotle. This ethical theory emphasizes character and being a good person instead of performing good actions and claims that the virtues are essential to being a good person. There are many possible definitions for virtues, but the one used in this chapter must cover both intellectual and moral virtues. Therefore, *virtues* are character traits that promote the well-being of the person who has them.

Aristotle begins the *Nicomachean Ethics* with a discussion about the goals of human action.[1] He observes that the end, goal, or purpose for an action is always something that is good or that appears to be good. Some goals are means to achieve other ends, and some are ends in themselves. Aristotle is interested in whether there is some ultimate end shared by all human beings. Is there some goal or end that is not a means to anything else but is the ultimate end of all other goals? An answer to this question would reveal the ultimate end for all human beings, not just the ultimate end for some particular person. He believes there is general agreement about the highest of all the goods achievable by action and states:

> Verbally there is very general agreement; for both the general run of men and people of superior refinement say that it is happiness, and identify living well and faring well with being happy; but with regard to what happiness is they differ, and the many do not give the same account as the wise.[2]

The word being translated as "happiness" is the word *eudaimonia*. This word might also be translated as "well-being," or "flourishing." "Happiness" is the usual translation, but I believe this is misleading because for many people happiness implies pleasure. Aristotle rejects the life of pleasure and asserts that the ultimate end is a well-lived life. The well-lived life includes not only pleasure and happiness but also health, longevity, achievement, moral excellence, knowledge, wisdom, and other qualities. Therefore, the ultimate human purpose should be designated as "well-being," which is the concept I will use here.

Aristotle is interested in what constitutes the well-being of humans as opposed to what makes up the well-being of other living things. He observes that some people equate human well-being with pleasure, or wealth, or honor. They also often change their ideas based on their situation; for example, they think well-being is health when they are sick, but wealth when they are poor. Aristotle rejects lives based on pleasure, wealth, and honor as lives that necessarily produce well-being. After rejecting these, he says, "Presumably, however, to say that happiness [well-being] is the chief good seems a platitude, and a clearer account of what it is is still desired. That might perhaps be given, if we could first ascertain the function of man."[3] Aristotle believes human well-being is related to the basic or characteristic function of human beings. Just as a good flute player or sculptor is one who successfully fulfills the distinctive function of a flute player or sculptor, a good human being is one who successfully fulfills the characteristic function of a human being.

Aristotle's idea is that there is a distinctive or proper function for human beings and that that function is related to human well-being. He concludes that the human function is connected to the capacity of humans that he thinks no other living thing possesses—the ability to reason. The essence of reasoning, for Aristotle, is acting in accordance with a rational principle. Therefore, the ultimate good of human beings is well-being, which is realized through excellence in the function that is characteristic to human beings. That function is reasoning or acting in accordance with a rational principle. Human well-being or a well-lived life will be achieved through excellence in reasoning or successfully acting in accordance with rational principles. It is not really necessary to limit this characteristic function to human beings, although Aristotle does so. If there are other beings who also possess reason as their basic function, then this form of well-being would be appropriate for them as well.

Aristotle was primarily interested in good lives or good characters rather than specific good actions. To determine if a person had achieved well-being, the person's complete character or life would have to be examined. In this context, *character* can be considered to be the combination of mental and moral qualities or traits that distinguish an individual. Aristotle would look for excellence in reasoning displayed in all the aspects of character and life. This excellence is not possible unless an individual possesses the virtues. Therefore, it is essential to understand the virtues that a person of good character would possess.

## Intellectual Virtues

How does one achieve excellence in reasoning or the ability to reason well? First, reasoning well means being able to use reason to investigate things and to understand them. Aristotle claims that the proper end of this kind of reasoning is truth:

> Let it be assumed that the states by virtue of which the soul possesses truth by way of affirmation or denial are five in number, i.e. art, knowledge, practical wisdom, philosophic wisdom, comprehension; for belief and opinion may be mistaken.[4]

These five virtues by which people achieve excellence in reasoning and truth may be called the *intellectual virtues*. By "art," Aristotle means knowledge and skill in the arts, which allows a person to produce excellent material things, such as statues or pottery. By "knowledge," he means acquiring knowledge that deals with things that are universal, necessary, and eternal. This knowledge is arrived at by logic and observation. "Practical wisdom" involves excellence in deliberation about the means of achieving a good end, that is, the ability to make sound judgments about the conduct of life. It relates to discovering the appropriate actions to promote well-being as well as controlling the passions that might interfere with these appropriate actions (more will be said about controlling the passions later). "Philosophic wisdom" involves knowledge of the ultimate things, such as the first cause of the universe. Finally, by "comprehension," he means understanding. He claims that understanding and practical reasoning are about the same objects, but there is an important difference between them. "For practical wisdom issues commands, since its end is what ought to be done or not to be done; but understanding only judges."[5] These intellectual virtues are essential to excellence in reasoning, and excellence in reasoning is crucial to well-being.

## Moral Virtues and Vices

Aristotle believes virtue is connected to reasoning well. Therefore, to be virtuous we must not allow our emotions or passions to interfere with our reasoning. We sometimes see a situation where someone is too upset to think clearly; to reason well, we must avoid this. Aristotle claims that a person's emotional response is partly the result of teaching or training in accord with reason. People are taught to feel certain ways in certain situations. This produces habitual responses that are in accord with reason. Thus, a person's emotional response to a situation can be developed in accord with reason through teaching and can also be controlled by using reason.

Intellectual virtue is connected to knowledge and wisdom, but Aristotle claims that "moral virtue" is related to actions and the emotions or passions that accompany them. He states that an excess, a deficit, or an intermediate amount of emotion accompanies actions. An excess or a deficit amount of passion may interfere with acting rationally and choosing the ethical action. Aristotle believes the virtuous person feels a moderate amount of emotion in many situations and chooses the mean in regard to certain actions. He observes:

> Excellence, then, is a state concerned with choice, lying in a mean relative to us, this being determined by reason and in the way in which the man of practical wisdom would determine it. Now it is a mean between two vices, that which depends on excess and that which depends on defect; and again it is a mean because the vices respectively fall short or exceed what is right in both passions and actions, while excellence both finds and chooses that which is intermediate.[6]

The moral virtues are related to feeling a moderate amount of emotion and acting based on the mean. Each virtue is a mean between two vices that involve feeling excess and deficit amounts of emotion and acting inappropriately. An example of a virtue that involves moderation is courage. Courage involves feeling the right amount of fear and confidence when acting in dangerous or difficult situations. In battle, for example, the coward feels too much fear and not enough confidence, whereas the rash person feels too little fear and too much confidence. The coward runs away, and the rash person attacks the enemy foolishly. Neither of these is the ethical or rational action. Courage involves feeling a moderate amount of fear and confidence; this allows the person to act in a rational way. Aristotle calls the virtues connected to moderate emotional responses "moral virtues." The moral virtues also fit the definition of virtues as traits of character that promote the well-being of the person who has them. For example, courage is the disposition to feel the proper amount of fear and confidence in a dangerous or difficult situation, and this disposition promotes the person's well-being.

Moral virtues usually involve emotions and actions wherein excess and deficiency of emotion are wrong. This might lead us to conclude that the vices are always excesses or deficits of an emotion, but this is not true. He observes:

> But not every action nor every passion admits of a mean; for some have names that already imply badness, e.g. spite, shamelessness, envy, and in the case of actions adultery, theft, murder; for all of these and suchlike things imply by their names that they are themselves bad, and not excesses or deficiencies of them. It is not possible, then, ever to be right with regard to them; one must always be wrong.[7]

These unethical emotions, such as spite, involve feelings that are evil in any amount, and the unethical actions, such as adultery, are evil, regardless of the feeling that accompanies them. Thus, Aristotle's ethics has a significant objective aspect to it. The intellectual virtues also provide a large objective element because they are always good. There is a subjective element to Aristotle's ethics as well, however, because the mean or proper amount of emotion depends upon a particular individual. The right amount of emotion for a person to feel in a particular situation may vary from person to person depending on the person's nature. Each person must determine the mean in connection with a rational principle that a person of practical wisdom would use for that particular person in that particular situation. The person of practical wisdom is someone who is able to reason correctly about ethical problems and can determine the correct course of action to take.

Aristotle discusses a variety of virtues that involve feeling the right amount of emotion and choosing the mean in regard to action, although for modern readers some of these "emotions" may seem more like attitudes or orientations (see Summary of Some of Aristotle's Moral Virtues). Only some of the virtues he discusses will be enumerated here. Courage is one of his virtues, but was discussed earlier. Another is temperance or self-control, which is moderation in regard to the passion involved with actions motivated by pleasure. An excess of this passion is self-indulgence. Aristotle thinks a deficiency of the desire for pleasure is rarely found. A third virtue is generosity, a mean amount of the emotion and the appropriate actions connected to giving and taking money or gifts. The excess of the passion and action is extravagance and the deficiency is stinginess. In connection with actions related to feelings of anger, people who feel the appropriate amount of anger and act properly are considered to be amiable, another virtue. Those who feel too much anger and act inappropriately are wrathful, and those who feel too little are apathetic. Aristotle also thinks that truthfulness is a virtue where the person has found the mean between being boastful and being self-deprecating. A person who observes the mean in amusing others may be called witty. Someone who goes to excess is a buffoon, and someone who is deficient is humorless. In regard to the emotion and actions related to pleasing others, the virtue is friendliness, whereas excess is obsequiousness and a deficiency is quarrelsomeness or grouchiness. The

### SUMMARY OF SOME OF ARISTOTLE'S MORAL VIRTUES

| Area | Defect | Excess | Mean or Virtue |
|---|---|---|---|
| Fear and confidence in dangerous situations | Cowardice | Recklessness | Courage |
| Desire for pleasure | Hardly ever found | Self-indulgence | Self-control (Temperance) |
| Giving and receiving money and things | Stinginess | Extravagance | Generosity |
| Getting angry | Apathy | Wrathfulness | Amiability |
| Telling the truth | Self-deprecation | Boastfulness | Truthfulness |
| Amusing others | Boorishness | Buffoonery | Wittiness |
| Pleasing others | Grouchiness or quarrelsomeness | Obsequiousness | Friendliness |

common element in all the virtues is that in each of them reason or practical wisdom controls the amount of emotion a person feels and the actions he or she takes.

*Moral virtues* are traits of character concerned with choice that involve moderation in action and emotion; this moderation is determined by a rational principle as discovered by a person of practical wisdom. Therefore, the intellectual virtue of practical reason and the moral virtues are closely related. The origin of action is choice, and the source of choice is desire and reasoning connected to achieving some goal or end. Virtuous action depends on practical wisdom guiding our choices and controlling our emotions.

## The Ethical Person

For the most part, Aristotle thinks people acquire the virtues through education and training. There is also the possibility of emulating a virtuous person. We need to look at a virtuous person for anything resembling an Aristotelian ethical standard. In virtue ethics, the ethical standard will not be a rule or principle that designates ethical actions. Instead, the ethical standard will be *a person who possesses the virtues and does not possess the vices.* In another sense, the ethical standard will be a person who is living the good life. This person can be an actual virtuous individual or a nonexisting ideal person. In either case, the virtuous person will act as a model for others to emulate. If you want to obtain well-being or be an ethical person, you should strive to acquire the virtues, eliminate the vices, and be like the model or ideal person.

What would the virtuous person be like? The first aspect of the ideal or ethical person is that he or she would possess the intellectual virtues. He or she would be wise, knowledgeable, and capable of understanding. This claim that an ethical person is wise, knowledgeable, and capable of understanding may seem to be an odd claim to contemporary people. Many ancient Greek philosophers, however, believed a wise, knowledgeable, and understanding person was living a better life than a foolish and ignorant individual. Knowledge helps persons live better lives because knowledge opens up more opportunities and helps persons make better decisions. The virtuous person will be knowledgeable in a range of areas. Practical wisdom, the tendency or disposition to make sound judgments about the conduct of life, allows the virtuous person to make effective and fulfilling decisions and judgments and to act in appropriate ways. That person will also be able to live a better life than will a foolish person. Understanding will enable the virtuous person to judge correctly, which will lead to a better life than that of someone who judges incorrectly. If we consider knowledge, wisdom, and understanding as character traits, and if these traits can help us live better lives, then these traits fit the definition of virtues. They are character traits that promote the well-being of the person who has them.

As well as having the intellectual virtues, an ethical person must also have the moral virtues. He or she must be courageous, self-controlled, generous, amiable, truthful, witty, friendly, and so on. The common element in all these virtues is that the person does not allow excesses and deficiencies of emotion to interfere with reasoning well or to lead to intemperate actions. In addition to having the virtues, the virtuous person must not have the vices, avoiding emotions such as shamelessness and envy and actions such as adultery, theft, and murder.

Aristotle claims that being a good person involves more than action. First, people must know what they are doing. This relates to the intellectual virtue, knowledge. Second, they must choose the action because it is virtuous and choose it as an end in itself. This relates to practical wisdom. Third, the action must be the expression of their character and must be accompanied by the proper feeling or emotion. This relates to moral virtue. Good people know what they are doing and choose to feel or do something because it is virtuous. Their feelings and actions flow from their character, and their emotions do not interfere with being virtuous. The good person has achieved well-being. Aristotle thought that being a good person and obtaining well-being would only be possible in the presence of certain other factors, such as health, longevity, some degree of material prosperity, and living in a flourishing city. Without these things we would not really be able to live good lives. Thus, the good person must possess a good character and be living the good life. This is such a large requirement, however, one might ask whether there really are any good people. Whether there actually are or are not people who fit the description, anyone can strive to become a good person by trying to become more like Aristotle's model person. The closer one approximates the good person, the better one is.

Aristotle's ethics is different from Kantian ethics, utilitarianism, or moral rights theory. All of these theories focus on actions, either by concentrating on the reasoning that preceded them or the consequences that resulted from them. Aristotle is concerned with character and a person's whole life. Good people have a wide variety of virtues and do not have the vices. Aristotle's view of a good or virtuous person is essential to his theory and constitutes the main ethical standard available to him.

## Justification for the Ethical Standard and Strengths of the Theory

There are a number of justifications for using a model of a good person as an ethical standard, and each of them suggests a related strength of Aristotle's ethical theory.

### An Ethical Theory that Is Not Simplistic

The first justification for the ethical standard is that we should use it because it is not simplistic. Ethics is a comprehensive and complex investigation. The legitimate object of that investigation should be being a good person and living the good life rather than just performing good actions. The focus on performing good actions used by most other ethical theories oversimplifies ethics. Thus, one justification is that Aristotle's ethics is the one theory that does not distort ethics by oversimplifying it. The related strength of the theory is that a theory that corresponds better to the comprehensive and complex nature of ethics is superior to a simplistic one.

### A Practical Ethical Theory

A second justification is that Aristotle's ethics is practical. A person simply needs to find a good person and emulate him or her. This is a fairly common practice and one that is presumably practical. Many people try to emulate the lives of others. People try to live like Christ, a saint, the Buddha, Mohatma Gandhi, Mother Teresa, Martin Luther King Jr., or someone else whom they see as the epitome of goodness. It is a relatively practical endeavor because one can study the person's life and then try to emulate it. The related strength of the theory is that a practical theory is better than one that is impractical because the practical theory will do a better job of helping people solve moral problems and live together successfully.

### A Theory Consistent with Human Nature

The final justification for using this standard connects to Aristotle's assumption that there is a basic human function—reasoning—and that the well-lived life involves reasoning well. Being a virtuous person will help an individual accomplish the basic human function successfully. If this is correct, then Aristotle's ethical standard is the appropriate one to use because it is consistent with our common human nature and will help us achieve excellence in regard to that nature. The related strength of the theory is that a theory that is consistent with human nature and helps people to achieve excellence in respect to that nature is a better theory that one that is not.

There are a few interesting strengths to virtue ethics theory and also some significant problems, which will be discussed later. Although the theory originates in ancient Greece, it has some adherents today. These philosophers primarily value its holistic nature and its presumed practicality.

## Determining Morally Significant Actions

It is difficult to know exactly how virtue ethics would separate the ethically significant from what is not ethically significant. Aristotle does not discuss this matter because he is focused on character, not actions. One possible answer is that everything that promotes or detracts from well-being might be morally significant. The well-lived life involves knowledge, practical wisdom, feeling the right emotions, and also education, good habits, health, reasonable longevity, and so on. Thus, the range of the ethically significant is enormous. This theory will presumably have a larger set of morally significant actions than any other ethical theory.

## Virtue Ethics and the Traditional Ethical Assumptions

Aristotle would definitely agree with the first of the traditional ethical assumptions: that ethics is rational. He would embrace the notion that persons can reach theoretical and practical conclusions about ethical matters. They can also provide reasons to support ethical guidelines and solutions to moral problems. These reasons and solutions can be evaluated, and some will prove to be better than others. He would also acknowledge that well-intentioned people who share a similar view of human well-being and the basic human function could discuss ethical problems and arrive at mutually acceptable solutions.

The question of impartiality and moral equality is a difficult one for virtue ethics. Aristotle does not seem to have considered persons as moral equals. He endorsed slavery and believed slaves could not achieve the same well-being as citizens as long as they were enslaved. Hence, they were not the moral equals of citizens. For Aristotle, reasoning well and being virtuous depend on opportunity and education. People who lack opportunities and who may be poorly educated will not be the moral equals of those who have more opportunities and are well educated unless they can develop virtuous habits through other means, such as acquiring informal education or emulating ethical persons. Aristotle would at least claim that it would be harder for slaves to live well than for citizens to do so. He also believed a person who is born with a physical or mental disability is morally inferior to a person without such a condition. People with serious mental defects will not have the same opportunities for knowledge and practical wisdom and hence will be hindered in achieving well-being. Similarly, people with serious physical disabilities will not be able to achieve the full degree of well-being and therefore are morally inferior. Finally, Aristotle thought that women are intellectually inferior to men and thus could not achieve the degree of well-being open to males. Therefore, women are also not moral equals. Although Aristotle rejects moral equality and impartiality, does every version of virtue ethics have to do so? If an ethical person is one who is successful at fulfilling the basic function of rational beings (reasoning), then any rational being could, in theory, be ethical by being virtuous or reasoning well. People incapable of complete rationality would still be morally inferior however. Thus, we must conclude that Aristotle's virtue ethics and any theory strictly based on his ideas would not regard all persons as moral equals.

In a similar manner, it is difficult to reach a conclusion about universalizing moral judgments. Aristotle supported universal judgments about actions such as adultery, theft, and murder. He probably would also have claimed that we could universalize judgments connected to the intellectual virtues. He would not have universalized judgments about the actions that flow from moral virtues, such as courage and generosity, and certainly not about what constitutes a moderate amount of emotion. He would claim that the mean with respect to emotion is not the same for everyone in a similar situation. With regard to Aristotle's ideas, we can observe that there are a limited number of moral judgments, for example, ones related to theft, adultery, and murder, which could be universalized.

## Virtue Ethics and the Basic Ethical Themes

Relating virtue ethics to the four basic ethical themes is more difficult than doing so with the other theories. These themes work well with ethical theories focused on actions. Because virtue ethics relates to character, the themes will not be entirely appropriate. For the sake of comparison, however, I will discuss these themes in connection with virtue ethics. The first theme was represented by this question: *What kind of guidelines makes something good or bad: subjective, relative, or objective ones?* Aristotle believes some specific actions may be said to be objectively evil: murder, adultery, and theft. He also claims that certain vices are always evil: envy, shamelessness, and spite. Some virtues, such as practical wisdom, are always good. However, the moral virtues are not objective because the actual amount of emotion that constitutes the moderate amount varies from person to person in similar situations. For example, courage, as it relates to feeling the proper amount of fear and confidence, is subjective. The proper amount of emotion depends on the particular individual. Thus, the moral guidelines that create good and bad are, to a large extent, objective, but there are also subjective moral guidelines that produce other aspects of good and bad.

Another significant theme in ethics was indicated by this question: *What makes something good or evil; is it the consequences that are produced or the reasoning that leads up to it?* Ethical action, with respect to the moral virtues, is primarily related to the proper amount of emotion, not to consequences or reasoning. Therefore, in one sense, this question is not appropriate for Aristotle's ethics. The proper amount of emotion, however, is related to using reason to control the emotions and, therefore, we might say that moral action relates to reasoning. In general, Aristotle thinks that the good life is a life of excellence in reasoning. However, we might also say that virtue ethics is concerned with consequences. Ethical action is related to overall well-being, which is the ultimate goal of human virtue. All ethical actions are a means to achieve the ultimate end of well-being; hence, virtue ethics is also concerned with consequences. The best answer, then, is probably that virtue ethics is concerned with both reasoning and consequences.

The third theme is related to this question: *Are good and bad related to following general rules without exceptions or connected to separately evaluating each action, belief, and so on?* This question misses the point by an even wider margin than the previous one. Proponents of virtue ethics claim that people are not virtuous if they merely act virtuously. Virtuous people have good characters. Even if we do look at action, we see that it has several aspects. Virtuous people know what they are doing, they choose to do something because it is virtuous, and their feeling and actions flow from their character. The last part is crucial; ethical action flows from an ethical character, and an ethical character is a matter of good education and good habits. Ethical people do not need to follow general rules or evaluate individual actions because they have developed a good character and good habits. They act ethically in a spontaneous way, which is a product of character. Thus, the proper answer to this question would seem to be, neither.

The fourth theme is connected to the proper focus of ethical attention: *Are good and bad primarily related to the group, community, or majority of persons, or should the focus be on the individual?* Once again, it is difficult to answer this question definitively. The well-being that concerns Aristotle is the well-being of the individual. The goal of ethics is to discover the best life for an individual to live. Ethics, however, cannot be a matter of an individual acting in isolation. The virtuous person is necessarily social. He or she must live in a flourishing society and receive a proper education. Well-being cannot be achieved in isolation; it must be achieved together. Thus, virtue ethics includes both elements: individuals and the community. The goal of ethics is well-being for the individual, but well-being is necessarily social. Therefore, for lack of a better answer, we might say that virtue ethics involves both the individual and the community.

## Contrasting Virtue Ethics with Moral Rights Theory

Virtue ethics is radically different from moral rights theory and other theories presented here (see Appendix 1). We find four major differences between virtue ethics and moral rights theory even before we look at the traditional ethical assumptions and the basic ethical themes.

The most important difference is the assumption by Aristotle that there is a distinctive human function. Proponents of moral rights theory do not make this assumption. A second major difference is that virtue ethics is more interested in the person's character than in rights and actions. Aristotle's idea is that good actions will flow from a person with a good character. Next, virtue ethics connects the ethical life to factors such as education, health, living in a flourishing state, and theoretical wisdom, which proponents of moral rights theory would say are not essential parts of ethics. Virtue ethics has a wider view of ethical life because it is involved with social, intellectual, and physical factors as well as with making decisions and acting. Finally, the theories have very different ethical standards. Virtue ethics uses the moral model of a good or virtuous person as its ethical standard, whereas moral rights theory claims that people act unethically if they violate another person's right or rights and ethically if an action is in accord with a right or rights.

Virtue ethics and moral rights theory agree on the traditional ethical assumption that ethics is rational. The theories differ, however, regarding whether people are moral equals. Moral rights theory clearly states that all human beings are moral equals and possess moral rights. Virtue ethics claims that all persons are not moral equals because people with physical and mental disabilities, slaves, and persons who are educationally deprived will not be able to achieve complete well-being. Finally, moral rights theory claims that many moral judgments can be universalized, whereas Aristotle would probably claim that a fewer number could be. Because the theories have such different ethical standards, they take very different approaches to making moral judgments and universalizing them.

In connection with the first ethical theme, virtue ethics relates some moral guidelines to objective considerations and others to subjective ones. Moral rights theory endorses only objective ethical guidelines. Regarding the second theme, moral rights theory focuses on the reasoning that precedes action, but virtue ethics looks at both reasoning and consequences. In relation to the third theme, moral rights theory endorses not violating moral rights, a course that is similar to following rules without exceptions. Virtue ethics does not center on either following general rules or evaluating actions; rather, ethical action flows from a good character. Finally, moral rights theory concentrates on the individual, whereas virtue ethics is concerned with both individuals and with the groups in which those individuals must live to achieve well-being.

## Problems with Virtue Ethics

Virtue ethics has a number of strengths, which were discussed earlier. Unfortunately, the theory also has some serious problems, which are discussed in this section.

### Lack of Effective Ethical Guidelines

Aristotle's ethical theory does identify moral guidelines and does argue that some ethical guidelines are better than others. It also identifies ethical guidelines that would prohibit the unlimited pursuit of self-interest. An important problem with the theory, however, is that the ethical guidelines it presents seem inadequate to really help us solve many moral problems. This point relates to criterion four: a successful ethical theory must help us solve ethical problems. Aristotle provides only minimal guidelines about what actions should not be performed: for example, murder, theft, and adultery. Beyond these limited prohibitions, he offers little effective help. Discussion of the intellectual virtues does not help us solve particular ethical problems. Knowledge is required to work out ethical problems, but knowledge alone is not enough to solve them. Practical wisdom is the tendency or disposition to make sound judgments about the conduct of life, and it would certainly lead to successful solutions to ethical problems. However, practical wisdom remains mysterious for Aristotle. The concept of practical wisdom is never extended to identify the solutions to ethical problems that would follow from practical wisdom. The moral virtues provide no specific guidelines related to actions either. Aristotle presents the idea of a moderate amount of feeling, but the amount of feeling does not help us solve moral problems concerning how we should act. Regardless of what we feel, we need help in knowing what to do. In addition, there is not even objective guidance about the proper amount of feeling since the mean is relative to the individual. Aristotle specifies no objective moderate amount of fear and confidence in dangerous and difficult situations that would produce an objective account of courage. In the case of an ethically significant choice, we might have several choices that could be accompanied by a moderate amount of emotion, and several moderate amounts of emotion that might accompany an ethical choice by diferent individuals.

There can be no effective moral guidelines for virtue ethics unless a moral person can be identified, studied, and used as a moral model. The problem is that we are not sure whom to use as our moral model. There are many candidates for a moral person to emulate, and there are numerous differences between these candidates. Aristotle had one vision of the moral person; perhaps he would have identified Socrates. A modern philosopher might reject Socrates, however, and suggest someone else. There does not seem to be an adequate way to resolve this problem of the appropriate moral model. In general, Aristotle has not provided us with ethical guidelines that are adequate to help us solve many moral problems. Therefore, in light of its inability to completely satisfy criterion four, virtue ethics is not an entirely successful ethical theory.

Aristotle would not have viewed this lack of adequate ethical guidelines as a serious problem because he believed good actions would necessarily flow from good character and that education was necessary for the development of good character. He thought education would enable persons to develop the good habits needed to live well. If persons can live well as a result of possessing good habits, then they have no need for more precise ethical guidelines. This does not solve the problem, however; it only pushes it back one level. Aristotle has not provided educators with adequate ethical guidelines or a person to use as a moral model so that they would know how to educate the citizens to achieve good habits.

## Moral Luck

A second problem concerns Aristotle's view that an ethical life contains a variety of components, some of which are beyond the moral agent's control. Well-being requires health, a reasonably long life, and living in a healthy society. None of these requirements is completely within the control of the agent. This produces a version of the problem of moral luck. If the well-being of the individual depends on these factors, then an element of luck enters the moral realm. It is a matter of luck whether I am born a healthy citizen in a flourishing society or a sickly slave in a society on the verge of collapse. Many philosophers would claim that the ability to be a good person should be completely in the control of the moral agent; virtue ethics is seriously flawed in this regard. This problem relates to the fourth criterion for evaluating ethical theories. If I live in an unsuccessful society, I will be less likely to develop a good character. If I do not develop a good character, I will be unable to solve ethical problems successfully. A successful ethical theory is supposed to help us solve moral problems, but Aristotle's theory cannot help us solve ethical problems if we have bad luck. We solve ethical problems successfully because we have good character, and good character depends on luck because many of the social, physical, and intellectual factors necessary to develop a good character are beyond the control of the individual.

## The Fundamental Human Function

The final problem does not relate directly to any of the criteria for a successful moral theory, but it is probably the major reason people reject Aristotle's ethical theory. Aristotle argues that his ethical guidelines are the appropriate ones because they will help us to successfully accomplish the basic human function. He assumes the existence of a basic human function because of his assumption that everything has a basic function. However, Aristotle offers no compelling reasons to accept the position that everything has a basic function and that there is a distinctive human function. In the absence of such reasons, we are free to reject these ideas. If we reject the concept that there is a basic function for human beings, then we would also reject Aristotle's justification for choosing his ethical guidelines and his ethical guidelines.

Even if a person did accept the notion of a basic human function, he or she might not agree with Aristotle that the function was being rational. Aristotle claims that the basic human function must be related to whatever it is that only humans possess, and he thinks that humans alone are rational. Therefore, the human function is rationality. A couple of problems surface in regard to this. First, rationality might not be the exclusive possession of human beings. Our conclusion depends on how rationality is defined. Perhaps a gorilla that can learn to use sign language to communicate about a wide variety of things is rational. If rationality is not an exclusively human possession, then Aristotle's reason for choosing it is based on a mistake. Another problem is that the basic human function might not be related to something only humans possess; perhaps humans share their basic function with other species. It has been suggested that the fundamental human function, like that of any living organism, is to reproduce and pass on its genetic code. If our basic function is shared with other species, then Aristotle's decision to base ethics on our exclusive, basic function is mistaken because humans have no such exclusive, basic function. Finally, even if the basic function is an exclusive human possession, that function might not be being rational. Some Christians believe the fundamental human purpose is to love God and other human beings. Using Aristotle's reasoning, we might argue that the basic human function is to love God and other human beings because we are the only ones who can do so. There are many reasons to reject the most basic part of Aristotle's ethical theory, and subsequently, his ethical guidelines.

## Conclusion

Although virtue ethics begins with an interesting insight, serious problems are revealed with the theory as it is investigated. The theory's greatest strength is that it expands beyond ethical rules and actions the morally significant aspects of being a person. It is also interesting because it illustrates the functional or goal-oriented approach to ethics. One of its main weaknesses is the absence of a convincing justification for the notion of a basic human function that should ground ethical guidelines. This lack of justification illustrates a crucial problem for all functionalist ethical approaches—justification of the purpose or function is typically the weakest part of the theory. Because the theory evaluates everything in terms of the function, it has trouble evaluating the purpose or function itself. In regard to the criteria for a successful ethical theory, virtue ethics can provide some ethical guidelines. It can also argue that these guidelines are better than others. The guidelines endorsed by the theory would seem to prohibit the unlimited pursuit of self-interest. The main problem with the theory relates to criterion four, that the theory must be effective in helping us solve ethical problems. This theory's ethical guidelines are inadequate to help us solve many ethical problems, and it has a serious problem with moral luck. Based on the criteria in Chapter 1, Aristotle's virtue ethics would not be a completely successful ethical theory.

Many philosophers reject Aristotle's virtue ethics based on the distinctive human function of rationality. While discarding Aristotle's distinctive human function, they accept virtue ethics in general, but base it on some different account of the good life. Certainly there is nothing inherently wrong with a goal-oriented approach to good and bad. There is also nothing mistaken about the ethical insight that if we choose the relevant virtues they will help us to achieve the good life. The problem is not so much the goal-oriented approach as it is the selection of the goal. There is nothing internal to a generic version of virtue ethics that requires us to choose a certain goal or vision of the good life.

At this point, four partially successful ethical theories have been discussed: Kantian ethics, utilitarianism, moral rights theory, and virtue ethics. All four assume that ethics is rational, and all have been, to some degree, unsuccessful. One theory, ethical subjectivism, which did not make this assumption, was also unsuccessful. In the next chapter, we look at another theory that does not assume that ethics is rational, the ethics of care. In fact, the ethics of care also rejects the other traditional ethical assumptions of impartiality and universalizability. It is worth investigation because it represents such a different approach to moral guidelines.

## QUESTIONS FOR REVIEW

*Here are some questions to help you review the main concepts in this chapter.*

1. What is the ethical insight associated with virtue ethics? What additional idea helps make Aristotle's version of virtue ethics distinctive?

2. In your opinion, what is the good life? What elements would it necessarily contain?

3. What, in general, are virtues?

4. In Aristotle's opinion, what is the distinctive function of human beings?

5. What are the intellectual virtues? How do they help persons achieve well-being?

6. What are the moral virtues? Provide a detailed explanation of Aristotle's account of courage to illustrate a moral virtue. How would courage help persons to achieve well-being?

7. What is the ethical standard for virtue ethics?

8. In your opinion, what is the best justification for using the Aristotelian ethical standard? Discuss the related strengths of the theory.

9. Would virtue ethics endorse any aspects of the traditional ethical assumptions?

10. What position would virtue ethics take on each of the four ethical themes?

11. Identify three major differences between virtue ethics and moral rights theory.

12. Which problem with virtue ethics do you think is the most serious? Explain why.

13. Would virtue ethics be a successful ethical theory based on the criteria in Chapter 1? Explain why, or why not.

14. Do you believe there is a basic human function shared by all people? If so, what is it?

15. Who is your model of a good or virtuous person? If you had to choose someone to emulate, who would it be? Explain why you chose the person you did.

16. What is character? How would you describe your character? If you wanted to improve your character, how would you go about doing so? How would you know that you were headed in the right direction?

## NOTES

1. Aristotle, *Nicomachean Ethics,* in *The Complete Works of Aristotle,* edited by Jonathan Barnes (Princeton, NJ: Princeton University Press, 1984).
2. Ibid., pp. 1730–1731.
3. Ibid., p. 1735.
4. Ibid., p. 1799.
5. Ibid., p. 1805.
6. Ibid., p. 1748.
7. Ibid.

# Nicomachean Ethics

Aristotle

Aristotle was born in the town of Stagira in northern Greece in 384 B.C.E. At the age of seventeen, he went to Athens to study at Plato's Academy, where he remained until Plato's death twenty years later. He then spent three years in the city of Assos in Asia Minor and two years in Mytilene on the island of Lesbos. In 343 or 342, he accepted the invitation of King Philip II of Macedon to become the tutor of his thirteen-year-old son, Alexander (later known as Alexander the Great). After a few years at the royal court in Pella, Aristotle returned to Stagira. In 335 he went back to Athens, where he founded a school called the Lyceum. When Alexander died in 323, strong anti-Macedonian sentiment arose in Athens. Because of his connections with Macedon, Aristotle thought it prudent to leave Athens. He went to Chalcis on the island of Euboea, where he died the following year of a stomach ailment.

Aristotle is the author of two very different kinds of philosophical writings: polished works, intended for the general reading public, and notes from which he lectured, intended for circulation among his students and associates. The polished works have been entirely lost except for a few fragments; what has survived are the notes from his lectures on a wide variety of topics, including logic, biology, physics, psychology, metaphysics, and ethics.

Our selection is taken from the first two books of the set of notes known as the *Nicomachean Ethics*. Here Aristotle argues that the ultimate goal everyone seeks is happiness and that being moral is a necessary part of a happy life. Happiness, Aristotle contends, consists in living rationally. Living rationally requires that two parts of a person's soul function well: the intellectual (strictly rational) part and the part containing emotions and desires (while emotions and desires are not in themselves rational, they can obey reason).

These two parts of the soul function well if they possess their proper virtues (excellences, good inner dispositions). *Intellectual virtues* are those qualities that enable the strictly rational part of the soul to carry out its function; *moral virtues* (virtues of character) are those qualities that enable emotions and desires to fulfill their proper functions. Aristotle argues that a person who lives in accordance with the intellectual and moral virtues attains happiness and is moral.

Intellectual virtues include such qualities as wisdom and intelligence; moral virtues include such traits as courage and temperance (self-control). Aristotle defines moral virtue as a state of character that aims at the mean between extremes—the extremes of having an excess or a deficiency of emotion or desire. Both excess and deficiency are vices; virtue lies in the middle. For example, regarding the emotion of confidence, foolhardiness and cowardice are vices and courage is the virtue. Aristotle explains that the way to acquire a moral virtue is to perform repeatedly the appropriate acts; to become a temperate person, for example, one must frequently exercise acts of self-control.

▼

*The Nicomachean Ethics of Aristotle,* trans. J. E. C. Welldon. New York: Macmillan, 1892 (updated stylistically).

**Book I**

**Chapter 1**[1]

Every art and every scientific inquiry, and similarly every action and purpose, may be said to aim at some good. Hence the good has been well defined as that at which all things aim. But it is clear that there is a difference in the ends;[2] for some ends are activities, and others are products beyond the mere activities. Also, where there are certain ends beyond the actions, the products are naturally superior to the activities.

Since there are various actions, arts, and sciences, the ends are also various. Thus the end of medicine is health; of shipbuilding, a vessel; of strategy, victory; and of household management, wealth. It often happens that a number of such arts or sciences that fall under a single science, as the art of bridle-making and all the other arts concerning the equipment of horses fall under horsemanship, and as every military action falls under strategy. And in the same way other arts or sciences fall under other faculties. But in all these cases the ends of the master arts or sciences, whatever they may be, are more desirable than those of the subordinate arts or sciences, since it is for the sake of the former that the latter are sought. It makes no difference to the argument whether the activities themselves are the ends of the actions, or something else beyond the activities, as in the above-mentioned sciences.

**Chapter 2**

If it is true that in the sphere of action there is an end that we wish for its own sake, and for the sake of which we wish everything else, and that we do not desire all things for the sake of something else (if that is so, the process would go on to infinity and our desire will be empty and futile), it is clear that this will be the good, namely the supreme good. Does it not follow that the knowledge of this supreme good is of great importance for the conduct of life, and that, if we know it, we will be like archers who have a target to aim at, and will have a better chance of attaining what we want?

If this is the case, we must try to comprehend, at least in outline, the nature of the supreme good and the science to which it belongs. It would seem to belong to the most authoritative science, the master science; and this science is politics.[3] For politics is what determines what sciences are necessary in states, and what kind of sciences should be learned, and how far they should be learned by particular people. We perceive too that the sciences that are held in the highest esteem—for example, strategy, household management, and rhetoric—are subordinate to politics. But since it makes use of the other practical sciences, and also legislates things to be done and to be left undone, it follows that its end will include the ends of all the other sciences, and will therefore be the true good of human beings. For although the good of an individual is the same as the good of a state, the good of the state, whether in attainment or in preservation, is evidently greater and more perfect. For while in an individual by himself it is something to be thankful for, it is nobler and more divine in a nation or state. These then are the objects at which the present inquiry aims, and it is in a sense a political inquiry.

## Chapter 3

Our statement of these matters will be adequate if it is made with all the clearness that the subject matter admits, for it would be as wrong to expect the same degree of accuracy in all kinds of discourse as it would be to expect it in all manufactured items. Things noble and just, which are the subjects of investigation in politics, exhibit so great a diversity and uncertainty that they are sometimes thought to have only a conventional, and not a natural, existence. There is the same sort of uncertainty in regard to good things, since injuries often result from them; thus there have been cases in which people were ruined by wealth or by courage. Since our subjects and our premises are of this nature, we must be content to indicate the truth roughly and in outline; and since our subjects and premises are true generally but not universally, we must be content to arrive at conclusions that are only generally true. It is right to receive particular statements in the same spirit; for an educated person will expect accuracy in each subject only to the extent that the nature of the subject allows. One might as well accept probable reasoning from a mathematician as require demonstrative proofs from a rhetorician. . . .

## Chapter 4

Since every kind of knowledge and every moral purpose aims at some good, what in our view is the good at which politics aims, and what is the highest of all goods achievable by action? With regard to its name, there is a general agreement: The masses and the cultured classes agree in calling it happiness, and conceive that "to live well" or "to do well" is the same thing as "to be happy." But they do not agree regarding the nature of happiness, nor do the masses give the same account of it as the philosophers. The former define it as something visible and palpable, such as pleasure, wealth, or honor; different people give different definitions of it; and often the same person gives different definitions at different times. When a person has been ill, happiness is health; when he is poor, it is wealth; and if he is conscious of his own ignorance, he envies people who use grand language above his own comprehension. Some philosophers, on the other hand, have held that, besides these various goods, there is an absolute good that is the cause of goodness in them all.[4] It would perhaps be a waste of time to examine all these opinions; it will be enough to examine the most popular ones, or those that seem more or less reasonable. . . .

## Chapter 5

. . . It seems reasonable to derive men's conception of the good or of happiness from their lives. Ordinary or vulgar people conceive it to be pleasure, and accordingly approve a life of enjoyment. For there are three prominent lives: the life of pleasure, the political life, and, thirdly, the contemplative life. The mass of men show themselves to be completely slavish, choosing the life of cattle, but they get a hearing because so many persons in authority share the tastes of Sardanapallus.[5] Cultivated and practical people, on the other hand, identify happiness with honor, since honor is the general end of political life. But this appears too superficial for our present purpose, for honor seems to depend more on the people who pay it than on the person to whom it is paid, and we have an intuitive feeling that the good is something that is proper to a man himself and cannot easily be taken away from him. It seems too that the reason why men seek honor is to be confident of their own goodness. Accordingly they seek it from the wise and those who know them well, and they seek it on the ground of virtue—and so it is clear that, in their judgment at least, virtue is superior to honor. It would perhaps be right then to look upon virtue rather than honor as being the end of the political life. And virtue, it appears, lacks completeness; for it seems that a man can possess virtue and yet be asleep or inactive throughout life. Moreover, he may experience the greatest calamities and misfortunes. But no one would call such a life a life of happiness, unless he were maintaining a paradox. It is not necessary to dwell further on this subject, since it is sufficiently discussed in popular philosophical treatises. The third life is the contemplative, which we will investigate later on.[6]

The life of money-making is in a sense a life of constraint, and it is clear that wealth is not the good we are looking for, since money is merely useful, as means to something else. It would be a more reasonable view therefore that the things mentioned before[7] are ends, since they are valued for their own sake. Yet they too are apparently not the good, though much argument has been employed to show that they are. We may now dismiss this subject. . . .

**Chapter 7**

Let us return to the good that we are seeking and consider what its nature may be. For it is clearly different in different actions or arts: It is one thing in medicine, another in strategy, and so on. What then is the good in each of these instances? It is presumably that for the sake of which all else is done. In medicine this is health; in strategy, victory; in domestic architecture, a house; and so on. But in every action and purpose it is the end, for it is for the sake of the end that people do everything else. If, then, there is a certain end of all action, it will be this that is the good attainable by action; and if there are several such ends, it will be these.

Our argument has arrived by a different path at the same conclusion as before, but we must try to elucidate it still further. There seem to be several ends, and since we desire some of these—for example, wealth, flutes, and instruments generally—as means to something else, it is evident that they are not all final ends. But the highest good is clearly something final. Hence if there is only one final end, this will be the object that we are seeking; and if there are more than one, it will be the most final of them. We speak of that which is sought after for its own sake as more final than that which is sought after as a means to something else; we speak of that which is never desired as a means to something else as more final than things desired both in themselves and as means to something else; and we speak of a thing as absolutely final if it is always desired in itself and never as a means to something else. It seems that happiness above all answers to this description, since we always desire happiness for its own sake and never as a means to something else, whereas we desire honor, pleasure, intellect, and every virtue partly for their own sakes (for we desire them independently of what might result from them), but partly also for the sake of happiness, because we think that they will be means to happiness. Happiness, on the other hand, no one desires for the sake of these things, nor indeed as a means to anything else at all.

We come to the same conclusion if we start from the consideration of self-sufficiency, if we may assume that the final good is self-sufficient. When we speak of self-sufficiency, we do not mean that a person leads a solitary life all by himself, but that he has parents, children, a wife, friends, and fellow citizens in general, since man is naturally a social being. But here it is necessary to prescribe some limit; for if the circle be extended so as to include parents, descendants, and friends of friends, it will go on indefinitely. Leaving this point, however, for future investigation, we define the self-sufficient as that which, taken by itself, makes life desirable and lacking in nothing. And this is our conception of happiness.

We conceive happiness to be the most desirable of all things, and not merely as one among other good things. If it were one among other good things, the addition of the smallest good would increase its desirableness; for the addition would make it a greater good, and the greater of two goods is always the more desirable. It appears, then, that happiness is something final and self-sufficient, the end of all action.

Perhaps, however, it seems to be a platitude to say that happiness is the supreme good; what we need to do is to define its nature more clearly. The best way to arrive at such a definition is probably to ascertain the function of a human being. For, as with a flute player, a sculptor, or any artisan, or in fact anyone who has a definite function and action, his goodness seems to lie in his function, so it would seem to be with man, if indeed man has a definite function. Can we say that while a carpenter and a shoemaker have definite functions and actions, man, unlike them, is naturally functionless? The reasonable view is that, just as the eye, the hand, the foot, and similarly every part of the body each has a definite function, so man may be regarded as having a definite function apart from all these. What, then, can this function be? It is not life; for life is apparently something that man shares with the plants, and it is something peculiar to man that we are looking for. Therefore we must exclude the life of nutrition and growth. There is next what may be called the life of sensation. But this too is apparently shared by man with horses, cattle, and all other animals. There remains what I may call the practical life of the rational part of man's being. But the rational part is twofold: It is rational partly in the sense of being obedient to reason, and partly in the sense of possessing reason and intelligence. The practical life too may be conceived of in two ways,[8] and we must understand by it the life of activity, since this seems to be the more proper meaning of the term.

The function of a human being, then, is an activity of soul in accordance with reason, or not independent of reason. The function of a person of a certain kind, and of such a person who is *good* of his kind—for example, the function of a harpist and the function of a *good* harpist—are in our view generically the same. This view is true of people of all kinds without exception. The superiority in excellence[9] of the good one is simply an addition to the function; for it is a function of a harpist to play the harp, and of a good harpist to play the harp well. If this is so, and if we define the function of a human being as a kind of life, and this life as an activity or action of the soul in conformity with reason; if the function of a good person is such activity or action of a good and noble kind; and if everything is successfully performed when it is performed in accordance with its proper excellence—if all this is so, it follows that the human good is an activity of soul in accordance with virtue or, if there are multiple virtues, in accordance with the best and most complete virtue. But it is necessary to add "in a complete life." For just as one swallow or one day does not make a spring, so one day or a short time does not make someone fortunate or happy. . . .

**Chapter 13**

Since happiness is an activity of soul in accordance with complete virtue, it is necessary to examine the nature of virtue. For this will perhaps be the best way of studying happiness. . . .

The soul has two parts, one irrational and the other possessing reason. . . . It seems that of the irrational part of the soul, one part is shared by all living things—namely, the vegetative part. I mean the part of the soul that causes nutrition and growth. We may assume that this faculty of the soul exists in all things that receive nutrition, even in embryos; and that it exists in things that are fully grown, since it is more reasonable to suppose that it is the same faculty than that is a different one. It is clear then that the virtue or excellence of this faculty is not distinctively human but is shared by man with all living things. . . .

There seems to be another natural principle of the soul that is irrational and yet in a sense shares in reason. For in a continent or incontinent person we praise the reason and that part of the soul that possesses reason, since it exhorts men rightly and exhorts them to the best conduct. But it is clear that there is in them another principle that is naturally different from reason and fights and contends against reason. For just as the paralyzed parts of the body, when we intend to move them to the right, are drawn away in a contrary direction to the left, so it is with the soul: The impulses of incontinent people run contrary to reason. But there is this difference, however, that while in the body we see that part that is drawn astray, in the soul we do not see it. But it is probably right to suppose with equal certainty that there is in the soul too something different from reason that opposes and thwarts it, although the sense in which it is distinct from reason is immaterial. But it appears that this part too shares in reason, as we said. In a continent person it obeys reason, at least; and in a temperate or courageous person it is probably still more obedient, being absolutely harmonious with reason.

It appears then that the irrational part of the soul is itself twofold; for the vegetative faculty does not participate at all in reason, but the faculty of appetite or of desire in general participates in it more or less, insofar as it is submissive and obedient to reason. It is obedient in the sense in which we speak of "paying attention" to a father or to friends, but not in the sense in which we speak of "paying attention" to mathematics. All correction, rebuke, and exhortation show that the irrational part of the soul is in a sense subject to the influence of reason. But if we are to say that this part too possesses reason, then the part that possesses reason will have two divisions, one possessing reason absolutely and in itself, the other listening to it as a child listens to its father.

Virtue or excellence admits of a distinction that depends on this difference. For we speak of some virtues as intellectual and of others as moral. Wisdom, intelligence and prudence are intellectual virtues, while generosity and temperance are moral virtues. For when we describe a person's character, we do not say that he is wise or intelligent but that he is gentle or temperate. Yet we praise a wise man too for his disposition, and praiseworthy dispositions we call virtues.

**Book II**

**Chapter 1**

Virtue or excellence, then, is of two kinds, intellectual and moral. Intellectual virtue is both originated and fostered mainly by teaching, and therefore it demands experience and time. Moral virtue, on the other hand, is the outcome of habit, and accordingly its name "moral" *(ēthikē)* is derived by a slight variation from "habit" *(ethos)*. From this fact it is clear that no moral virtue is implanted in us by nature, for law of nature cannot be altered by habituation. Thus a stone naturally tends to fall downward, and it cannot be habituated or trained to rise upward, even if we were to try to train it by throwing it upward ten thousand times. Nor can fire be trained to sink downward, nor anything else that follows one natural law be trained to follow another. Virtues arise in us neither by nature nor contrary to nature. Nature gives us the capacity of receiving them, and that capacity is perfected by habit.

With regard to the various natural powers that belong to us, we first acquire the proper faculties and afterwards display the activities. This is clearly so with the senses. It was not by seeing frequently or hearing frequently that we acquired the senses of seeing or hearing; on the contrary, it was because we possessed the senses that we made use of them, not by making use of them that we obtained them. But the virtues we acquire by first exercising them, as is the case with all the arts, for it is by doing what we ought to do when we have learned the arts that we learn the arts themselves. For example, we become builders by building and harpists by playing the harp. Similarly it is by doing just acts that we become just, by doing temperate acts that we become temperate, by doing courageous acts that we become courageous. The experience of states is a witness to this truth, for legislators make the citizens good by training the habits. This is the object that all legislators have at heart. If a legislator does not succeed in it, he fails to achieve his purpose, and it constitutes the distinction between a good polity and a bad one.

The causes and means by which any virtue is produced and those by which it is destroyed are the same, and it is equally so with any art. For it is by playing the harp that both good and bad harpists are produced; and the case of builders and all other artisans is similar, since it is by building well that they will be good builders and by building badly that they will be bad builders. If it were not so, there would be no need for anybody to teach them; they would all be born good or bad in their various trades. The case of the virtues is the same. It is by acting in transactions that take place between people that we become either just or unjust. It is by acting in the face of danger and by habituating ourselves to fear or courage that we become either cowardly or courageous. It is much the same with our desires and angry passions. Some people become temperate and gentle, and others become licentious and passionate, according to the way they conduct themselves in particular circumstances. In a word, moral dispositions are the results of activities corresponding to the dispositions themselves. It is our duty therefore to give a certain character to the activities, since dispositions depend on the differences of the activities. Accordingly, it is no small matter how children are trained in habits in their early days; it is an important matter—in fact, it is all-important. . . .

### Chapter 4

A difficulty may be raised by our statement that people must become just by doing what is just and temperate by doing what is temperate: If they do what is just and temperate, they are already just and temperate, in the same way that people who do what is grammatical and musical are already grammarians and musicians.

But is not the answer that it is different in the case of the arts? For a person may do something that is grammatical either by chance or at the suggestion of somebody else; hence he will not be a grammarian unless he not only does what is grammatical but does it in a grammatical manner, that is, in virtue of the grammatical knowledge that he possesses.

There is another point of difference between the arts and the virtues. The productions of art have their excellence in themselves. It is enough therefore that when they are produced, they are of a certain character. But actions in accordance with virtue are not, for example, justly or temperately performed because they are in themselves just or temperate. It is necessary that the agent at the time of performing them should satisfy certain conditions: First, he should know what he is doing; second, he should deliberately choose to do it and to do it for its own sake; and third, that he should do it as an instance of a settled and immutable disposition. If it is a question whether a person possesses any art, these conditions (except indeed the condition of knowledge) are not taken into account; but if it is a question of possessing the virtues, mere knowledge is of little or no avail, and it is the other conditions, which are the results of frequently performing just and temperate actions, that are not of slight but of absolute importance. Accordingly, deeds are said to be just and temperate when they are of a kind that just or temperate person would do, and a just and temperate person is not merely one who does these deeds but one who does them in the way that just and the temperate people do them. . . .

### Chapter 6

It is not enough to state merely that virtue is a disposition; we must also describe the character of that disposition. It must be laid down that every virtue or excellence has the effect of producing a good condition of that of which it is a virtue or excellence, and of enabling it to perform its function well. Thus the excellence of the eye makes the eye good and makes it function well, since it is by the excellence of the eye that we see well. Similarly, the excellence of a horse makes it excellent and makes it good at racing, carrying its rider, and facing the enemy. If this is true for all things, then the virtue or excellence of man is a disposition that makes a man good and enables him to perform his proper function well. We have already explained how this will be the case, but another way of making it clear will be to study the nature or character of this virtue.

In everything, whether it is continuous or divisible, it is possible to take a greater, a smaller, or an equal part, and this can be done either in respect to the thing itself or relatively to us. The equal part is a mean between excess and deficiency. By the mean in respect to the thing itself, I understand that which is equally distant from both extremes; and this is one and the same thing for everyone. By the mean relative to us, I understand that which is neither too much nor too little; but this is not one thing, nor is it the same for everyone. Thus, if 10 is too much and 2 is too little, we take 6 as a mean in respect to the thing itself, since 6 is as much greater than 2 as it is less than 10. This is a mean in arithmetical proportion. But the mean relative to us must not be ascertained in this way. It does not follow that if 10 pounds of food is too much for a man to eat and 2 is too little, a trainer will order him 6 pounds. For this amount may itself be too much or too little for the person who is to take it: It will be too little, for example, for Milo,[10] but too much for a beginner in gymnastics. It will be the same with running and wrestling; the right amount will vary with the individual. This being so, everyone who understands his business avoids both excess and deficiency;

he seeks and chooses the mean—not the absolute mean, but the mean relative to us.

Every science, then, performs its function well if it looks to the mean and refers the works that it produces to that standard. This is why it is usually said of successful works that it is impossible to take anything from them or to add anything to them; excess or deficiency is fatal to excellence but the mean ensures it. Good artists too, as we say, have an eye to the mean in their works. But virtue, like nature itself, is more accurate and better than any art; therefore virtue will aim at the mean. (I speak of moral virtue, since it is moral virtue that is concerned with emotions and actions, and it is these that admit of excess and deficiency and the mean.) Thus it is possible to go too far, or not to go far enough, in respect to fear, courage, desire, anger, pity, and pleasure and pain generally; and the excess and the deficiency are both wrong. But to experience these emotions at the right times and on the right occasions and toward the right persons and for the right causes and in the right manner is the mean and the best—and this is characteristic of virtue. Similarly there may be excess, deficiency, or the mean in regard to actions. But virtue is concerned with emotions and actions, and here excess is an error and deficiency is a fault, whereas the mean is successful and praiseworthy—and both success and praiseworthiness are characteristics of virtue. It appears then that virtue is a mean, insofar at least as it aims at the mean.

There are many different ways of going wrong; for evil is in its nature infinite, to use the Pythagorean[11] image, but good is finite. But there is only one possible way of going right. Accordingly the former is easy and the latter difficult; it is easy to miss the target but difficult to hit it. This again is a reason why excess and deficiency are characteristics of vice and the mean characteristic of virtue. "Good is simple, but evil is manifold."[12]

Virtue then is a state of deliberate moral purpose consisting in a mean relative to us, the mean being determined by reason, or as a prudent man would determine it. It is a mean, first, as lying between two vices, the vice of excess on the one hand and the vice of deficiency on the other; and second because, whereas the vices either fall short of or go beyond what is proper in the emotions and actions, virtue not only discovers the mean but embraces it. Accordingly, virtue regarded in its essence or theoretical conception is a mean, but regarded from the point of view of the best and the right, it is an extreme.

But not every action or every emotion admits of a mean. There are some whose very name implies wickedness, for example, the emotions of malice, shamelessness, and envy; and the actions of adultery, theft, and murder. All these, and others like them, are censured as being intrinsically wicked, not the excess or deficiency of them. It is never possible then to be right in respect to them; they are always wrong. Right or wrong in such actions as adultery does not depend on our committing them with the right person, at the right time, or in the right manner; on the contrary, it is wrong to do anything of the kind at all. It would be equally wrong to suppose that there can be a mean or an excess or deficiency in unjust, cowardly, or licentious conduct; for if there were, there would be a mean of an excess or of a deficiency, an excess of an excess and a deficiency of a deficiency. But just as in temperance and courage there can be no excess or deficiency because the mean is, in a sense, an extreme; so too in these cases there cannot be a mean or an excess or deficiency. These acts are wrong, no matter how they are done. For it is a general rule that an excess or deficiency does not admit of a mean, and that a mean does not admit of excess or deficiency.

**Chapter 7**

It is not enough to lay this down as a general rule; we must apply it to particular cases. In reasoning about actions, general statements are less exact than particular statements, although they are broader. For all action refers to particulars, and it is essential that our theories should harmonize with the particular cases to which they apply. We must take particular virtues, then, from the chart.[13]

In regard to feelings of fear and confidence, courage is the mean. On the side of excess, the person whose fearlessness is excessive has no name (as often happens), but he whose confidence is excessive is foolhardy, while he whose fear is excessive and whose confidence is deficient is a coward.

In respect to pleasures and pains—although not of all pleasures and pains, and to a less extent in respect to pains than to pleasures—the mean is temperance and the excess is licentiousness. Since we never find people who deficient in regard to pleasures, such people have received no name, but we may call them insensible.

In respect to the giving and taking of money, the mean is generosity, and the excess and deficiency are prodigality and stinginess. Here the excess and deficiency take opposite forms; for while the prodigal man is excessive in spending and deficient in taking, the stingy man is excessive in taking and deficient in spending.

For the present we are giving only a rough and summary account of the virtues, and that is sufficient for our purpose.

---

► NOTES

1. The chapter divisions in Welldon's translation have been revised to follow the chapter divisions in the Greek edition in the Oxford Classical Text, edited by Ingram Bywater (Oxford, England: Clarendon Press, 1894), which has become standard. [D. C. ABEL, EDITOR]

2. *ends:* goals [D. C. ABEL]

3. To the Greeks, the city-state *(polis)* was the most advanced form of community, and politics was the enterprise of achieving the good of the city-state. [D. C. ABEL]

4. Aristotle here refers primarily to Plato, under whom he studied for twenty years. [D. C. ABEL]

5. Sardanapallus is the Greek name of King Ashurbanipal of Assyria (668–627 B.C.E.), who was famous for his sensual indulgence. [D. C. ABEL]

6. Aristotle discusses the theoretical life in Book X of the *Nicomachean Ethics* (not included in our reading). [D. C. ABEL]

7. *things mentioned before:* namely, pleasure, honor, and virtue [D. C. ABEL]

8. The practical life of reason can be spoken of in a passive sense, as merely possessing the ability to reason, or in an active sense, as actually exercising this ability. [D. C. ABEL]

9. Depending on the context, the translator renders the Greek word *aretē* as "excellence" (as here) or "virtue." At times he uses the double translation "virtue or excellence." As Aristotle explains later (Book II, Chapter 6), *aretē* is the quality that makes a thing be in good condition and enables it to perform its function well. [D. C. ABEL]

10. Milo of Croton was a famous Greek wrestler of the sixth century B.C.E. [D. C. ABEL]

11. Pythagoras (about 580–500 B.C.E.) was a Greek philosopher and mathematician. [D. C. ABEL]

12. A line—perhaps Pythagorean—of unknown authorship [W. E. C. WELLDON, TRANSLATOR]

13. Aristotle evidently refers to a chart that he used when presenting this material to his students. [D. C. ABEL]

CHAPTER **12**

# Feminism and the Ethics of Care

But it is obvious that the values of women differ very often from the values which have been made by the other sex; naturally, this is so. Yet it is the masculine values that prevail.

VIRGINIA WOOLF, *A ROOM OF ONE'S OWN* (1929)

## 12.1. Do Women and Men Think Differently about Ethics?

The idea that women and men think differently has traditionally been used to justify subjugating one to the other. Aristotle said that women are not as rational as men, and so women are naturally ruled by men. Kant agreed, adding that for this reason women "lack civil personality" and should have no voice in public life. Rousseau tried to put a good face on it by emphasizing that men and women merely possess different virtues; but of course it turned out that men's virtues fit them for leadership, whereas women's virtues fit them for home and hearth.

Against this background, it is not surprising that the burgeoning women's movement of the 1960s and '70s rejected the idea of psychological differences between women and men altogether. The conception of men as rational and women as emotional was dismissed as a mere stereotype. Nature makes no mental or moral distinction between the sexes, it was said; and when there seem to be such differences, it is only because women have been conditioned by an oppressive system to behave in "feminine" ways.

More recently, however, feminist thinkers have reconsidered the matter, and some have concluded that women do indeed think differently than men. But, they add, women's ways of

160

thinking are not inferior to men's; nor do the differences justify subordinating anyone to anyone else. On the contrary, female ways of thinking yield insights that have been missed in male-dominated areas. Thus, by attending to the distinctive approach of women, progress can be made in subjects that were stalled. Ethics is said to be a leading candidate for this treatment.

**Kohlberg's Stages of Moral Development.** Consider the following problem, devised by the educational psychologist Lawrence Kohlberg. Heinz's wife was near death, and her only hope was a drug that had been discovered by a pharmacist who was selling it for an exorbitant price. The drug cost $200 to make, and the pharmacist was selling it for $2,000. Heinz could raise only $1,000. He offered this to the druggist, and when his offer was rejected, Heinz said he would pay the rest later. Still the druggist refused. In desperation, Heinz considered stealing the drug. Would it be wrong for him to do that?

This problem, known as "Heinz's Dilemma," was one of several used by Kohlberg in studying the moral development of children. Kohlberg interviewed children of various ages, presenting them with a series of dilemmas and asking questions designed to elicit their moral judgments and the supporting reasons. Analyzing their responses, Kohlberg concluded that there are six levels of moral development. Children begin with a self-centered view of "right" as whatever avoids punishment, and eventually they progress through six stages to the fully mature view of rightness as conformity to universal principles. (At least, the fortunate ones progress that far. Some people get stuck at lower levels.) Here are the six stages:

1. The earliest is the Stage of Punishment and Obedience, in which right is conceived as obeying authority and avoiding punishment.
2. Then the child moves on to the Stage of Individual Instrumental Purpose and Exchange—here, right is acting to meet one's own needs and allowing others to do the same, while making "fair deals" with others to further one's ends.
3. Next is the Stage of Mutual Interpersonal Expectations, Relationships, and Conformity. Right is defined in terms of the duties and responsibilities that go with

one's social roles and one's relationships with other people; a critical virtue is "keeping loyalty and trust with partners."

4. In the Stage of Social System and Conscience Maintenance, the idea of doing one's duty in society and maintaining the welfare of the group becomes paramount. (The demands of personal relationships are subordinated to following the rules of the social group.)

5. In the Stage of Prior Rights and Social Contract or Utility, right consists of upholding the basic rights, values, and legal arrangements of the society. (At this stage and at the next, personal relationships are subordinated to universal principles of justice.)

6. Finally, the most morally mature people reach the Stage of Universal Ethical Principles, in which full moral maturity is manifested through one's fidelity to abstract principles that all humanity should follow.

Heinz's dilemma was presented to an 11-year-old boy named Jake, who thought it was obvious that Heinz should steal the drug. Jake explained:

> For one thing, a human life is worth more than money, and if the druggist only makes $1,000, he is still going to live, but if Heinz doesn't steal the drug, his wife is going to die.
> *(Why is life worth more than money?)*
> Because the druggist can get a thousand dollars later from rich people with cancer, but Heinz can't get his wife again.
> *(Why not?)*
> Because people are all different and so you couldn't get Heinz's wife again.

But Amy, also 11, saw the matter differently. Should Heinz steal the drug? Compared to Jake's forthright statements, Amy seems hesitant and evasive:

> Well, I don't think so. I think there might be other ways besides stealing it, like if he could borrow the money or make a loan or something, but he really shouldn't steal the drug—but his wife shouldn't die either . . . If he stole the drug, he might save his wife then, but if he did, he might have to go to jail, and then his wife might get sicker again, and he couldn't get more of the drug, and it might not be

good. So, they should really just talk it out and find some other way to make the money.

The interviewer asks Amy further questions, making it clear that she is not being responsive—if Heinz does not steal the drug, his wife will die. But Amy will not budge; she refuses to accept the terms in which the problem is posed. Instead she recasts the issue as a conflict between Heinz and the druggist that must be resolved by further discussions.

In terms of Kohlberg's stages, Jake seems to have advanced one or two full levels beyond Amy. Amy's response is typical of people operating at Stage 3, where personal relationships are paramount—Heinz and the druggist must work things out between them. Jake, on the other hand, appeals to impersonal principles—"a human life is worth more than money." Jake appears to be operating at level 4 or 5.

**Gilligan's Objection.** Kohlberg began his studies of moral development in the 1950s, when psychology was dominated by behaviorism and the popular image of psychological research featured rats in mazes. His humanistic, cognitively oriented project showed a different way of pursuing psychological investigations. But there was a problem with Kohlberg's central idea. It is legitimate and interesting to study the different ways that people think at different ages—if children think differently at 5, 10, and 15, that is certainly worth knowing. It is also worthwhile to identify the best ways of thinking. But these are different projects. One involves observing how children in fact think. The other involves the assessment of ways of thinking as better or worse. Different kinds of evidence are relevant to each investigation, and there is no reason to assume in advance that the results will match. Contrary to the opinion of older people, it *could* turn out that age does not bring wisdom after all.

Kohlberg's theory has been a target of feminist thinkers, who have given this criticism a special twist. In 1982 Carol Gilligan, like Kohlberg a professor in Harvard's School of Education, published an influential book called *In a Different Voice: Psychological Theory and Women's Development,* in which she objects specifically to what Kohlberg says about Jake and Amy. The two children think differently, she says, but Amy's way of thinking is not inferior. When confronted with Heinz's Dilemma, Amy responds in a typically female fashion to the personal aspects of the situation, whereas Jake, thinking like a typical male, sees only "a conflict between life and property that can be resolved by a logical deduction."

Jake's response will be judged "at a higher level" only if one assumes, as Kohlberg does, that an ethic of principle is superior to an ethic that emphasizes intimacy, caring, and personal relationships. But why should we make any such assumption? Most moral philosophers have favored an ethic of principle, but that is only because most moral philosophers have been males.

The "male way of thinking"—the appeal to impersonal principles—abstracts away the details that give each situation its special flavor. Women, Gilligan says, find it harder to ignore these details. Amy worries that "If [Heinz] stole the drug, he might save his wife then, but if he did, he might have to go to jail, and then his wife might get sicker again, and he couldn't get more of the drug." Jake, who reduces the situation to "a human life is worth more than money," ignores all this.

Gilligan suggests that women's basic moral orientation is caring for others—"taking care" of others in a personal way, not just being concerned for humanity in general—and attending to their needs. This explains why Amy's response seems, at first, confused and uncertain. Sensitivity to the needs of others leads women to "attend to voices other than their own and to include in their judgment other points of view." Thus Amy could not simply reject the druggist's point of view; she could only insist upon further talking with him and trying somehow to accommodate him. "Women's moral weakness," says Gilligan, "manifest in an apparent diffusion and confusion of judgment, is thus inseparable from women's moral strength, an overriding concern with relationships and responsibilities."

Other feminist thinkers have taken up this theme and developed it into a distinctive view about the nature of ethics. In 1990 Virginia Held summed up the central feminist idea: "Caring, empathy, feeling with others, being sensitive to each other's feelings," she said, "all may be better guides to what morality requires in actual contexts than may abstract rules of reason, or rational calculation, or at least they may be necessary components of an adequate morality."

Before turning to the implications of this idea for ethics and ethical theory, we may pause to consider how "feminine" it really is. Is it true that women and men think differently about ethics? And if it is true, what accounts for the difference?

**Is It True That Women and Men Think Differently?** Since Gilligan's book was published, there has been a great deal of research on "women's voices," but it remains unclear whether women and men really think differently. One thing seems certain, however: Even if they do think differently, the differences cannot be very great. In the first place, they will be differences of emphasis rather than differences in fundamental values. It is not as though women make judgments that are incomprehensible to men, or vice versa. Men can understand the value of caring relationships, empathy, and sensitivity easily enough, even if they sometimes have to be reminded; and they can agree with Amy that the happiest solution to Heinz's Dilemma would be for the two men somehow to work it out. (Not even the most reprobate male thinks theft would be the *best* thing that could happen.) For their part, women will hardly disagree with such notions as human life being worth more than money. Plainly, the two sexes do not inhabit different moral universes.

Suppose we concede, however, that there is a difference in style between people who are more inclined to think in terms of principles and people who are more inclined to adopt a "caring perspective." Is the former style exclusively male and the latter exclusively female? Plainly not. There are women who are devoted to principles and men who care. So, even if there are different styles of moral thinking, there is no style that is exclusively male or female.

Still, we should not be too quick to dismiss the notion that there are typically male and female perspectives. There are plenty of general differences between men and women that don't apply to every individual. Women are typically smaller than men, but that doesn't mean that every woman is smaller than every man.

The difference in moral thinking could be like that: Women might typically be more attracted to a caring perspective, even though not every woman is more caring than every man. To many people, including a large number of feminist writers, this seems plausible. Its plausibility would be increased, however, if we could explain *why* there should be such a difference. Why should women be more caring?

**What Could Account for Such a Difference between the Sexes?** There seem to be two possibilities. One is that women think differently because of the social role to which they are assigned.

Women have traditionally been given responsibility for home and hearth; even if this is nothing but a sexist outrage, the fact remains that women have occupied this role. It is easy to see how being assigned to such duties and coming to understand this as "one's place" could induce one to adopt the values that go with it. Thus, the ethics of care could be just part of the psychological conditioning that girls routinely receive. (This theory could be tested by looking at girls raised in nontraditional homes. Would they still be natural caregivers? What about boys raised in nonstandard ways?)

The second possibility is that there is some sort of intrinsic connection between being female and having an ethic of caring. What could this connection be? Since the obvious natural difference between the sexes is that women are the childbearers, we might conjecture that women's nature as mothers somehow makes them natural caregivers. Even girls like Amy, who at age 11 has had no experience mothering, might come equipped by nature for the task, psychologically as well as physically.

The theory of evolutionary psychology might explain how nature works this trick. Evolutionary psychology, a controversial theory developed in the last third of the 20th century, interprets major features of human psychological life as the products of natural selection—people today have the emotions and behavioral tendencies that enabled their ancestors to survive and reproduce in the distant past. This could have produced different patterns of behavior and emotional response in men and women.

We may think of the Darwinian "struggle for survival" as a competition to reproduce in the next generation as many copies of one's genes as possible. Any traits that help one to do this will be preserved in future generations; while traits that put one at a disadvantage in this competition will tend to disappear.

From this point of view, the overwhelmingly important difference between males and females is that men can father hundreds of children during their reproductive lifetimes, while women can have only one baby each nine months. This means that the optimum reproductive strategies for males and females will be different. For males, the optimum strategy will be to impregnate as many females as possible, investing in each infant only whatever resources are necessary for the maximum number to survive. For females, the optimum strategy is to invest heavily in each child and to choose as partners males who are willing to stay around and make a similar investment. This obviously creates a tension between male and female interests, and that may explain why the sexes could have evolved different attitudes. It explains, notoriously, why men are more promiscuous than women; but at the same time it explains what we are interested in here, namely, why women are more attracted than men to the values of the nuclear family.

This kind of explanation is often misunderstood. The point is not that people consciously calculate how to propagate their genes; no one does that. Nor is the point that people *should* calculate in this way; from an ethical point of view, they should not. The point is just to explain, if we can, the phenomena we observe.

## 12.2. Implications for Moral Judgment

Not all women philosophers have been self-consciously feminist; nor have all feminists embraced the ethics of care. Nonetheless, this is the ethical view most closely identified with modern feminist philosophy. As Annette Baier put it, " 'Care' is the new buzzword."

One way of understanding and assessing an ethical view is to ask what difference it would make in one's moral judgments and whether that difference would be an improvement over the alternatives. So, suppose one adopts an ethic of care. Would this lead to different moral judgments than if one adopted a principled "male" approach? Here are three examples.

**Family and Friends.** Traditional theories of obligation are notoriously ill-suited to describing life among family and friends. Those theories take the notion of obligation as morally fundamental: They provide an account of what we *ought* to do. But, as Annette Baier observes, when we try to construe "being a loving parent" as a duty, we immediately encounter problems. A loving parent acts from motives other than duty. If you care for your children because you feel it is your duty, it will be a disaster. Your children will sense it and realize they are unloved. Parents who act from a sense of duty are bad parents.

Moreover, the ideas of equality and impartiality that pervade theories of obligation seem deeply antagonistic to the values of love and friendship. John Stuart Mill said that a moral agent must be "as strictly impartial as a disinterested and benevolent spectator." But that is not the standpoint of a parent or friend. We do not regard our family and friends merely as members of the great crowd of humanity. We think of them as special, and we treat them as special.

The ethics of care, on the other hand, is perfectly suited to describe such relations. The ethics of care does not take "obligation" as fundamental; nor does it require that we impartially promote the interests of everyone alike. Instead, it begins with a conception of moral life as a network of relationships with specific other people, and it sees "living well" as caring for those people, attending to their needs, and keeping faith with them.

These outlooks lead to different judgments about what we may do. May I devote my time and resources to caring for my own friends and family, even if this means ignoring the needs of other people whom I could also help? From an impartial point of view, our duty is to promote the interests of everyone alike. But few of us accept that view. The ethics of care confirms the priority that we naturally give to our family and friends, and so it seems a more plausible moral conception.

It is not surprising that the ethics of care appears to do a good job explaining the nature of our moral relations with friends and family. After all, those relationships are its primary inspiration.

**Disadvantaged Children.** Each year over 10 million children die from easily preventable causes—disease, malnutrition, and bad drinking water. Organizations such as UNICEF work to save these children, but they never have enough money. By contributing to their work, we could prevent at least some of these deaths. For $17, for example, UNICEF can vaccinate a third-world child against measles, polio, diphtheria, whooping cough, tetanus, and tuberculosis.

A traditional "ethics of principle," such as Utilitarianism, would conclude from this that we have a substantial duty to support UNICEF. The reasoning is straightforward: Almost all of us have resources that we waste on relatively trivial things—we buy fancy clothes, carpets, and television sets. None of these is as important as vaccinations for children. Therefore, we should give at least some of our resources to UNICEF. Of course, if we try to fill in all the details and answer all the objections, this simple reasoning can become complicated. But its basic idea is clear enough.

One might think that an ethic of care would reach a similar conclusion—after all, shouldn't we care for those disadvantaged children? But that misses the point. An ethic of care focuses on small-scale, personal relationships. If there is no such relationship, "caring" cannot take place. Nel Noddings, whose book *Caring: A Feminine Approach to Ethics and Moral Education* is one of the best-known works of feminist moral theory, explains that the caring relation can exist only if the "cared-for" can interact with the "one-caring," at a minimum by receiving and acknowledging the care in a personal, one-to-one encounter. Otherwise, on her view, there is no obligation: "We are not obliged to act as one-caring if there is no possibility of completion in the other." For this reason, Noddings concludes that we have no obligation to help "the needy in the far regions of the earth."

Even though it might come as a relief to learn that we are free to spend our money as we please, it is hard to avoid the feeling that something has gone wrong here. Making personal relationships the whole of ethics seems as wrong-headed as ignoring them altogether. A more sensible approach might be to say that the ethical life includes both caring personal relationships *and* a benevolent concern for people generally. The obligation to support UNICEF might then be seen as falling under the latter heading rather than the former. If we were to take this approach, we would interpret the ethics of care as a supplement to traditional theories of obligation rather than as a replacement for them. Annette Baier seems to have this in mind when she writes that, eventually, "women theorists will need to connect their ethics of love with what has been the men theorists' preoccupation, namely, obligation."

**Animals.** Do we have obligations to nonhuman animals? Should we, for example, be vegetarians? One argument from "rational principles" says that we should because the business of raising and slaughtering animals for food causes them great suffering, and by becoming vegetarians we could nourish ourselves without the cruelty. Since the modern animal rights movement began in the mid-1970s, this sort of argument has persuaded many people (probably more women than men) to stop eating meat.

Nel Noddings suggests that this is a good issue "to test the basic notions on which an ethic of caring rests." What are those basic notions? First, such an ethic appeals to intuition and feeling rather than to principle. This leads to a different conclusion, for most people do not feel that meat-eating is wrong or that the suffering of livestock is important. Noddings observes that because we are human, our emotional responses to other humans are different from our responses to nonhumans.

A second "basic notion on which an ethic of caring rests" is the idea of an individual relationship between the one who cares and the one who is cared for. As we have noted, the cared-for must be able to participate in the relationship at least by responding to the care. Noddings believes that people do have this sort of relationship with some animals, namely pets, and this can be the basis of an obligation:

> When one is familiar with a particular animal family, one comes to recognize its characteristic form of address. Cats, for example, lift their heads and stretch toward the one they are addressing. . . . When I enter my kitchen in the morning and my cat greets me from her favorite spot on the counter, I understand her request. This is the spot where she sits and "speaks" in her squeaky attempt to communicate her desire for a dish of milk.

A relationship is established, and the attitude of care must be summoned. But one has no such relationship with the cow in the slaughterhouse, and so, Noddings concludes, even though we might wish for a world in which animals did not suffer, we have no obligation to do anything for the cow's sake, not even to refrain from eating him.

What are we to make of this? If we use this issue "to test the basic notions on which an ethic of caring rests," does the ethic pass or fail the test? The opposing arguments are impressive. First, intuitions and feelings are not reliable guides—at one time, people's intuitions told them that slavery was acceptable and that the subordination of women was God's own plan. And second, whether the animal is in a position to respond "personally" to you may have a lot to do with the satisfaction you get from helping, but it has nothing to do with the animal's needs or the good that you could accomplish. (Much the same, of course, may be said of the distant child's inability to thank you personally for the vaccination.) These arguments, of course, appeal to principles that are said to be typical of male reasoning. Therefore, if the ethics of caring is taken to be the whole of morality, such arguments will be ignored. On the other hand, if caring is only one part of morality, the arguments from principle still have considerable force. Livestock animals might come within the sphere of moral concern, not because of our caring relation with them, but for other reasons.

## 12.3. Implications for Ethical Theory

It is easy to see the influence of men's experience in the ethical theories they have created. Men dominate public life, and in politics and business, one's relations with other people are typically impersonal and contractual. Often the relationship is adversarial—others have interests that conflict with our own. So we negotiate; we bargain and make deals. Moreover, in public life our decisions may affect large numbers of people we do not even know. So we may try to calculate, in an impersonal way, which decisions will have the best overall outcome for the most people. And what do men's moral theories emphasize? Impersonal duty, contracts, the harmonization of competing interests, and the calculation of costs and benefits.

Little wonder, then, that feminists believe modern moral philosophy incorporates a male bias. The concerns of private life—the realm in which women traditionally dominate—are almost wholly absent, and the "different voice" of which Gilligan speaks is silent. A moral theory that accounted for women's concerns would look very different. In the smaller-scale world of home and hearth, we deal with family and friends, with whom our relationships are personal and intimate. Bargaining and calculating play a much smaller role, while love and caring dominate. Once the point is made, there is no denying that this side of life must also have a place in our understanding of morality.

This side of life, however, is not easy to accommodate within the traditional theories. As we noted, "being a loving parent" is not a matter of calculating how one ought to behave. The same might be said about being a loyal friend or a dependable colleague. To be loving, loyal, and dependable is to be *a certain kind of person,* and neither as a parent nor as a friend is it the kind of person who impartially "does his duty."

The contrast between "being a certain kind of person" and "doing one's duty" is at the heart of a larger conflict between two kinds of ethical theory. Virtue Theory sees being a moral person as having certain traits of character: being kind, generous, courageous, just, prudent, and so on. Theories of obligation, on the other hand, emphasize impartial duty: They typically picture the moral agent as one who listens to reason, figures out the right thing to do, and does it. One of the chief arguments in favor of Virtue Theory is that it seems well suited to accommodate the values of both public and private life. The two spheres require different virtues. Public life requires justice and beneficence, while the virtues of private life include love and caring.

The ethics of care, therefore, turns out to be one part of the ethics of virtue. Most feminist philosophers view it in this light. Although Virtue Theory is not exclusively a feminist project, it is so closely tied to feminist ideas that Annette Baier dubs its male promoters "honorary women." The verdict on the ethics of care will depend, ultimately, on the viability of the ethics of virtue.